ROUTLEDGE LIBRARY EDITIONS:
TRANSPORT ECONOMICS

Volume 21

TRANSPORT ECONOMICS

TRANSPORT ECONOMICS

P.C. STUBBS, W.J. TYSON AND M.Q. DALVI

Routledge
Taylor & Francis Group
LONDON AND NEW YORK

First published in 1980 by George Allen & Unwin (Publishers) Ltd
Revised edition 1984

This edition first published in 2017
by Routledge
2 Park Square, Milton Park, Abingdon, Oxon OX14 4RN

and by Routledge
711 Third Avenue, New York, NY 10017

Routledge is an imprint of the Taylor & Francis Group, an informa business

British Library Cataloguing in Publication Data
A catalogue record for this book is available from the British Library

ISBN: 978-0-415-78484-9 (Set)
ISBN: 978-1-315-20175-7 (Set) (ebk)
ISBN: 978-1-138-70056-7 (Volume 21) (hbk)
ISBN: 978-1-138-70063-5 (Volume 21) (pbk)
ISBN: 978-1-315-20459-8 (Volume 21) (ebk)

Publisher's Note
The publisher has gone to great lengths to ensure the quality of this reprint but points out that some imperfections in the original copies may be apparent.

Disclaimer
The publisher has made every effort to trace copyright holders and would welcome correspondence from those they have been unable to trace.

Transport Economics

Revised Edition

P. C. STUBBS

W. J. TYSON

M. Q. DALVI

London
GEORGE ALLEN & UNWIN
Boston Sydney

**George Allen & Unwin (Publishers) Ltd,
40 Museum Street, London WC1A 1LU, UK**

George Allen & Unwin (Publishers) Ltd,
Park Lane, Hemel Hempstead, Herts HP2 4TE, UK

Allen & Unwin, Inc.,
9 Winchester Terrace, Winchester, Mass. 01890, USA

George Allen & Unwin Australia Pty Ltd,
8 Napier Street, North Sydney, NSW 2060, Australia

First published in 1980
Revised edition 1984
Second impression 1986

British Library Cataloguing in Publication Data

Stubbs, P.C.
Transport economics. – Rev. ed. – Studies in economics; 15)
1. Transportation
I. Title II. Tyson, W.J. III. Dalvi, M.Q. IV. Series
380.5'9 HE151

ISBN 0-04-338121-9

Library of Congress Cataloging in Publication Data

Stubbs, P. C. (Peter C.), 1937-
Transport economics.
(Studies in economics; 15)
Includes index.
Bibliography: p.
1. Transportation – Great Britain. I. Tyson, W. J. (William James), 1946- . II. Dalvi, M. Q. (M. Quasim) III. Title. Series: Studies in economics (London, England); 15.
HE243.S8 1984 380.5'0941 84-12278
ISBN 0-04-338121-9 (pbk.)

Set in 10 on 11 point Press Roman at the Alden Press, Oxford, London and Northampton and printed in Great Britain by Hollen Street Press Ltd at Slough, Berkshire

PREFACE

This book was conceived when the three authors jointly taught a course in transport economics at Manchester University. During its gestation other books on transport economics have appeared although none fulfils the role originally intended for this one. Our aim is to provide the student with the basis to appreciate the key issues that affect the economics of transport, and in this we assume no prior knowledge of transport.

In general we have tried to pitch the level of the book at second-year standard, assuming some acquaintance with statistical techniques such as regression analysis. However, in Chapter 3 on demand modelling and in Chapter 7 on spatial equilibrium we are consciously offering material at a higher level for the brighter or the third-year student. Thus, if transport economics is offered as a second-year course, these areas can be considered optional; but if it is offered at third-year level, we hope that these chapters plus more extensive reference to cited works will provide the student with something to bite on. In Chapters 9 and 10 we offer an introduction to international transport as this is all too often neglected in other texts; lack of space, however, precludes the treatment of investment in ports and airports.

We should like to thank numerous colleagues and an anonymous referee for their comments; we should also like to thank Margot Tyson, Helen Grindrod and Edith Gillett (together with members of her academy) for typing the manuscript, Marjorie Watts for assistance with the diagrams, and Patrick Hanlon and Patricia Boyce for help with data.

Since the original edition was published in 1980, we have taken the opportunity to incorporate a number of minor revisions, though it has not been possible to examine the major changes in transport policy which have been introduced, nor all the detailed changes such as the 1984 Budget, in which the structure of Vehicle Excise Duty was raised to reflect more accurately the relative costs imposed by different vehicle types.

P. C. Stubbs
W. J. Tyson
M. Q. Dalvi
1984

CONTENTS

CHAPTER 1

The Characteristics and Scope of Transport Economics

Transport is a keystone of civilisation. The spread of production, trade and ideas and the economic ascendancy of mankind all depend upon movement. Personal mobility is one of democracy's most valued freedoms, and a surprisingly high proportion of our income is devoted to our movement and to the movement of the goods that we buy. However, the systematic economic analysis of transport is relatively recent.

Transport economics is basically a branch of applied microeconomics. While it uses many standard techniques of economic analysis, it faces a number of special problems and characteristics that justify its consideration as a specific branch of the discipline. The demand for transport is a derived one, and each journey is unique in time and space; it cannot be stored or transferred – and from these seemingly simple statements follows a host of implications. The complexities of economic problems involving transport are illustrated by the controversies over supersonic aircraft, the Third London Airport and motorway construction and by the difficulties posed by road congestion, declining public transport, air traffic control and the vagaries of ocean freight rates. Technology, with all its expense and uncertainty, has played a critical role, and it will continue to do so as the depletion of oil necessitates a replacement for conventional motor cars.

The simple canons of market economics cannot be applied to transport for a variety of reasons. Since journeys are unique in space and time monopoly is likely to arise in varying degrees, especially when technological change offers an advantage to a particular mode or where economies of scale affect one mode more than another. The state has therefore intervened in transport; railways in Britain have been regulated since 1844 to prevent any repetition of the monopoly abuse evident among canal companies. Since then regulations and often state ownership have pervaded all sectors of transport (Gwilliam and Mackie, 1975, Chapter 3). The danger that a monopoly will restrict output and force up price is well known, although sometimes the only means to realise economies of scale is to accept monopoly but constrain its behaviour by statute. In the short run the degree of monopoly may be intense as the user has no alternative; but as the time span lengthens so does choice, and the user may seek alternative modes, routes and sources of supply of the goods that he seeks or even other destinations that will satisfy the purpose of his trip.

The external effects of transport also warrant intervention. Pollution and congestion are both real costs imposed on the community by the users of transport, but they are not reflected in the private costs met by the individual user. Social decisions should, however, make allowance for these costs, and they should also recognise the need to preserve certain public goods (e.g. visual amenity) that are not priced in the market but are accepted as legitimate concerns for community planning and decision. Intervention may also be important where the individual fails to perceive the full economic implication of his own defective decisions. One example of this is compulsory safety tests for cars; another is the legal obligation to wear car safety belts that applies in Australia.

Another important source of difficulty in transport economics is indivisibility. This problem impinges on both pricing and investment. Many investments in transport are large and infrequently made, and there are problems over how their costs should be allocated. For example, if passenger and freight trains use the same track, how should track costs be allocated between them? At the time of writing British Rail charges its track costs to passenger trains, but this clearly represents a cross-subsidisation of freight services. Peak traffic also poses problems over the allocation of costs; and so does journey length, for often the cost of a journey is not simply proportional to distance but includes an element of cost for loading or boarding the vehicle, implying that cost per mile diminishes with the length of journey. Indivisibilities render marginal cost pricing difficult, however. Consider the cost of a train journey: should the first entrant of the carriage pay his full marginal cost? Clearly not; some form of averaging is necessary here although the ideal might be, as Dupuit (1844) put it over a century and a quarter ago, that 'the best tariff would be one which makes all users of communication pay a toll proportionate to the utility they derive from the passage'.

All the complications mentioned above make pricing and investment appraisal in transport a difficult and even subtle business. Investment appraisal has made great strides in the past half-century as economists have refined cost–benefit analysis to take close cognisance of non-market items; but transport economists remain a long way from infallibility in either pricing or investment, and the ultimate decisions are frequently political ones.

However, the difficulties of economic decisions should not distract from their importance for transport is vitally important. The figures in Table 1.1, published by the United Nations, show the percentage of gross domestic product derived from the transport and communications sector. The figure for Norway is enlarged by the importance of its maritime industry. Communication by post and telephone represents only a small proportion of these figures but the real significance of transport is underplayed by considering the service sector alone since many elements of the manufacturing sector (e.g. the motor industry) are key contributors to transport. Thus in Britain in 1975, 12.4 per cent of consumers' expenditure went on travel (if car purchase is included), while in the United States it has been claimed that 18 per cent of gross national product relates to highway transportation alone (Motor Vehicles Manufacturers' Association, 1975).

Table 1.1 *Proportion of gross domestic product derived from transport and communications*

Country	*Year*	*%*
Australia	1980	7
Canada	1980	7
West Germany	1980	6
Japan	1979	7
Norway	1980	11
UK	1980	7
USA	1978	7
USSR	1979	6

Source: United Nations Statistical Yearbook, 1981.

The pattern of transport has changed across recent years. Table 1.2 gives some figures for recent British trends in passenger and freight transport, which are fairly typical of those in advanced market economies.

However, the figures in Table 1.2 treat passenger-kilometres (and tonne-kilometres) as homogeneous although in practice they may differ widely. A faster journey, by saving time, may be valued differently. It may be more difficult and therefore more valuable to provide freight services for awkward goods or on difficult modes of transport for these reflect more closely the valuation that society puts upon them, although it is difficult to assess the changing nature of user valuation over time because taxes and subsidies on different modes have altered. Table 1.3 shows how British users distributed their expenditure on transport in the period 1972–82.

Table 1.2 *Trends in British transport, 1954–82*

	1954		*1972*		*1982*	
Passenger traffic ('000 million passenger km)						
Bus and coach	81	(38)	51	(12)	40	(8)
Car and motor cycle	76	(35)	347	(79)	452	(85)
Pedal cycle	19	(9)	4	(1)	5	(1)
Road subtotal	176	(82)	402	(92)	497	(94)
Rail	39	(18)	35	(8)	31	(6)
Air	0.3	(0.1)	2.2	(0.5)	2.9	(0.5)
Total	21	(100.1)	439.7	(100.5)	530.9	(100.5)
Freight traffic ('000 million tonne-km)						
Road			87.5	(65)	100.0	(59)
Rail			21.0	(15)	15.9	(9)
Coastal ship / Waterway			22.5	(17)	44.4	(26)
Pipeline			3.5	(3)	9.3	(6)
Total			134.5	(100)	169.6	(100)

Source: Department of Transport (1983).
Notes: Figures in parenthesis are percentages of totals.

It is evident from Table 1.3 that road traffic has made great inroads into rail traffic. By comparing the physical outputs in Table 1.2 it becomes apparent that consumers are willing to pay a premium for movement by road. The road system is much bigger than the rail network, and as well as this spatial flexibility the relatively modest loads required to fill a lorry give it greater temporal flexibility, just as the private car driver enjoys freedom to establish his own timetable. The hopes of some protagonists of public transport that such trends can be completely reversed are probably more pious than realistic, and the depletion of oil resources may be mitigated by developments in batteries and the increasing expenditure on fuel cell technology. Yet, it must be acknowledged that road traffic brings hazards as well as benefits. Road vehicles, by their numbers or weight, impose fumes, noise, congestion and accidents upon society, which make it necessary to consider adjustments where social costs outstrip social benefits. These issues are legitimate interests for the transport economist; and even if he cannot solve all the problems, he may shed light on issues where others are apt merely to generate heat. However, the economists must be aware of the conflicts that may arise between efficiency and equity. It is often possible

Table 1.3 *User expenditure on surface transport in Great Britain, 1972–82:*
(£ millions)

	1972	*1982*	*% rise 1972–82*
Expenditure (£ millions)			
Total passenger of which:	5,816	26,665	358
Bus and coach	555	2,005	261
Private vehicles	4,811	22,981	378
Taxis and hire cars	94	460	389
Rail	356	1,219	242
Total freight of which:	5,563	19,151	244
Road	5,293	18,500	350
Rail	260	581	123
Inland waterway	10	70	600
Total passenger & freight of which:	11,379	45,816	303
Total road	10,753	43,946	307
Total rail	616	1,800	192
Consumer cost indexes (1972 = 100)			
Car purchase		385	
Car running costs		431	
Rail passenger		421	
Road public transport		470	
All goods and services		364	

Source: Department of Transport (1983).

to show that a total transport operation would be made more profitable by eliminating some of its less efficient parts or that there would be financial gain by eliminating cross-subsidisation. This last-named is the practice whereby high prices, relative to costs, are charged on one service and the surplus revenue thus generated is used to augment the revenues of another service where prices are low relative to costs. This practice restricts demand in the low cost area and promotes it in the high cost area, and it is clearly apt to produce inefficient results in the private, accounting, sense. However, there may be broader social reasons for sustaining apparent anomalies. Where the elimination of these practices could destroy or impoverish disadvantaged communities the economist must heed the politician. Perhaps his most valuable role is to clarify the issues, the costs and the benefits to both politicians and public alike, for such a role is no mean task as the following chapters will show.

CHAPTER 2

The Analysis of Demand

INTRODUCTION

In this chapter we shall examine the demand for transport and the factors that influence the traveller to choose one mode of transport rather than another. The importance of analysing demand hardly needs emphasising, for in such long-lived investments as motorways, airports, docks and railways the skilful and accurate analysis of demand is a vital element of efficient investment decisions. Overinvestment is clearly wasteful, but underinvestment can prove expensive to remedy; it is difficult to add an additional lane to an existing motorway, for example. At the moment the demand for motor cars and motor travel dominates the pattern of travel, and so we shall devote some attention to demand studies; but modelling the total demand for travel and the way in which it is split among different modes has grown in importance recently and is now a vital part of transport planning, and in Chapter 3 we shall discuss models of passenger traffic.

THE INFLUENCE OF INCOME ON THE DEMAND FOR TRANSPORT

Economic theory suggests that the demand for goods and services depends largely upon consumers' income and the price of the particular good or service relative to other prices. The demand for travel in general is clearly dependent on the income of the traveller, but income also affects the choice of mode. Thus the average citizen of the United States travels further each year than the average Australian or Briton, who travels further than the average Russian, who in turn travels further than the average Indian.

Table 2.1 shows some national differences. The aggregate figures are an indication of the size of respective national transport modes, while the percentage figures emphasise the American propensity to travel by car, such that air travel seems relatively low. About half of the American

Table 2.1 *Passenger transport by mode in selected countries.*

	Car	*Bus*	*Rail*	*Air*	*Total*	*Annual passenger-km per person*
Passenger-kilometres ('000 millions)						
UK (1975)	357	54	35	2	448	8,000
Oceania (1970)	127	16	9	11	163	8,425
USA (1969)	2,578	141	43	70	2,832	13,985
USSR (1970)	56	198	265	79	598	2,462
World (1970)	5,742	1,384	1,140	463	8,729	3,036
Percentages of total passenger-kilometres						
UK (1975)	79.7	12.0	7.8	0.4	99.9	
Oceania (1970)	77.9	9.8	5.5	6.7	99.9	
USA (1969)	91.0	5.0	1.5	2.5	100.0	
USSR (1970)	9.4	33.1	44.3	13.2	100.0	
World (1970)	65.7	15.9	13.1	5.3	100.0	

Sources: Tulpule (1974); Motor Vehicle Manufacturers' Association (1975).

figures for bus traffic represents school children. The high percentage figure for air travel in the USSR reflects deliberate government encouragement for the state airline Aeroflot, against a background of general lack of support for personal movements.

It is also possible to examine the relationship between personal income and travel at the national level, as in Table 2.2. These British data show clearly how travel expenditure rises with income level. To avoid the problems caused by the tendency for household income to increase with persons per household the table shows expenditure by a standardised household of a man, woman and two children in 1982. Expenditure on buying and running cars obviously rises with income, as does expenditure on rail travel, but buses and coaches are evidently less attractive as income rises.

Figures are not generally available for the breakdown between urban and non-urban travel – this latter, ugly, expression is preferred to 'rural' because it includes interurban travel – but there are some estimates for the British pattern, shown in Table 2.3. These show the high dependence of non-urban areas, which are often ill-served by public transport, upon the private car.

The growth of motor car registrations and the decline in passenger-mileage on trains and buses illustrate the impact of the car on public transport usage. More specific analysis of the decline in bus usage in a variety of British urban areas has revealed that the decline in the number of bus journeys per head of population through the 1960s was closely correlated with the increase in the number of cars per head in each of the urban areas concerned. In seven cities in northwestern England a simple regression model relating bus journeys to the level of car ownership has 'explained' 87–98 per cent of the observed variation in bus journeys per head. Fare increases seemed to be only weakly associated with the decline in bus travel. Fairhurst (1975) has shown that the availability of public transport was a significant factor in explaining public patronage, so that declining services hastened the demise of public transport.

The underlying explanation of this phenomenon, as we have stressed, is the effect of rising real income per head. The British trends mentioned above accord with the established pattern in the United States, where Meyer, Kain and Wohl (1965) have observed that the income elasticity of demand was substantially positive for transport by private car but inconsequential or even negative for public transport. Moreover, the price elasticity of demand and cross-elasticity between modes appeared to be relatively less important.

The reasons for the preference for the private car that manifested

Table 2.2 *Weekly expenditure on transport in the United Kingdom, 1982*

	Weekly income of household[d] (£)					
	Under 125	*125–174.99*	*175–224.99*	*225–274.99*	*Over 275*	*Average of all households*
Transport expenditure						
Purchase	2.94	5.24	7.08	10.27	14.90	8.02
Car running and maintenance	5.96	8.84	11.49	14.07	18.65	11.82
Purchase and maintenance of other vehicles and boats[a]	0.19[c]	0.85	0.88	n.a.[c]	0.86	0.92
Rail fares	n.a.[c]	0.22	0.38	1.11	1.83	0.71
Bus and coach fares	0.99	0.96	1.03	0.86	n.a.[c]	1.17
Other travel and transport[b]	0.26	0.87	n.a.[c]	1.35	1.56	1.39
Total transport expenditure	10.57	16.99	23.20	29.52	39.80	24.02
As % of total household expenditure	10.9	13.4	15.4	15.7	16.9	15.1
Percentage of total transport expenditure						
Purchases of vehicles, spares, etc.	27.8	30.9	30.5	34.8	37.4	33.4
Car running and maintenance	56.4	52.0	49.5	47.7	46.9	49.2
Purchase and maintenance of other vehicles and boats[a]	1.8	5.0	3.4	n.a.[c]	2.2	3.8
Rail fares	n.a.[c]	1.3	1.6	3.8	4.6	2.9
Bus and coach fares	9.4	5.7	4.4	2.9	n.a.[c]	4.9
Other travel and transport[b]	2.6	5.1	n.a.[c]	4.6	3.9	5.8
Total	100.0	100.0	100.0	100.0	100.0	100.0

Source: Department of Employment (1983).

Notes: Certain figures do not sum exactly to totals because of rounding. (a) Includes bicycles and prams. (b) Includes taxis, hire cars, air and water travel. (c) Subject to sampling difficulty. (d) Household comprises two adults and two children.

Table 2.3 *Surface passenger-mileage in Great Britain by area and mode, 1970.*

	Passenger-miles (millions)	*%*
Urban areas		
Rail	9,210	8.88
Bus	17,500	16.86
Total public transport	26,710	25.74
Car	77,047	74.26
Total	103,757	100.00
Other areas		
Rail	9,515	6.55
Bus	16,600	11.43
Total public transport	26,115	17.98
Car	119,153	82.02
Total	145,268	100.00
All areas		
Rail	18,725	7.52
Bus	34,100	13.69
Total public transport	52,825	21.21
Car	196,220	78.79
Total	249,045	100.00

Source: Stubbs and Tyson (1972).

itself so strongly during the third quarter of this century are quite plain. In most cases the car possesses great advantages, especially in its flexibility. By offering literally door-to-door transport with a virtually infinite frequency of service and minimal perceived motoring costs, it has a qualitative superiority that no competing mode can match. Also, the competition from these other modes has weakened, most notably in the United States, as their service frequency has diminished and relative cost has increased.

DEMAND STUDIES

Economists and econometricians have analysed the demand for transport in a variety of ways, reflecting their different purposes. Since the rise of the motor car has been a predominant factor in determining the pattern of transport services in advanced economies, it is appropriate that we consider some of the economic analyses of demand for cars that have been undertaken. In this case analysis dates back over several decades. An early study commissioned by General Motors Corporation in the late 1930s was concerned primarily with the relatively short run – the period over which the company was concerned with its marketing and investment decisions (Roos and von Szeliski, 1939). Other studies have taken a longer view, being less concerned with the annual sales of new cars and more directed towards estimating the total stock of cars when demand is said to be *saturated*. Saturation occurs when everybody who wants a car actually has one and the ratio of cars per person ceases to rise. The speed with which it is reached and the ultimate extent of car ownership are important factors when the investments associated with the private car are being considered – especially the construction of roads and motorways, which usually incorporate a significant excess capacity over present levels to cater for the growth expected in the future.

The sophistication of demand analysis varies. Some studies have considered the level of demand for a particular mode in isolation; but as we shall show in Chapter 3, techniques have been devised to model the demand for transport in systems as a whole where several transport modes are offered and there is an explicit measure of inter-relationship between the demand for different modes. We shall assume that the reader is acquainted with the statistical technique of regression analysis, which examines the extent and nature of systematic relationships between economic variables. Readers unfamiliar with the technique may refer to a wide variety of econometrics textbooks (e.g. Johnston, 1972; Stewart, 1976; Walters, 1970).

The prime purpose of demand analysis is to enable future patterns of demand to be predicted from the detailed analysis of past relationships. Regression analysis is basically a form of extrapolation, albeit a sophisticated and powerful one if it takes into account a wide variety of explanatory variables. Yet, it must always be borne in mind that extrapolation should be subject to constant scrutiny.

Few econometricians have been bold enough to attempt the analysis of the entire pattern of consumer demand. In the United States Houthakker and Taylor (1970) have examined the determinants of demand for a wide range of goods and services, including various items of transport. Laudable though their attempt was, the scope of the work, covering eighty-two categories of personal consumption expenditure across the period 1929–65, limited the elaboration of individual categories. Thus, expenditure on new cars and net purchases of used cars were largely explained ($R^2 = 0.957$) by four factors: the corresponding level of *per capita* real expenditure on cars in the previous year; the increase in total personal consumption expenditure *per capita* over the past year; the total level of personal consumption expenditure *per capita* in the previous year; and a dummy variable to separate pre-Second World War behaviour from postwar behaviour. The income elasticity of demand was positive and much more important than the price elasticity of demand. Other items investigated by Houthakker and Taylor included oil and petrol transport tolls, car insurance, local buses and trains, taxis, commuter railways, intercity railways, intercity buses and airline travel. In all cases there was a strong correlation between the prior-year and current-year expenditures, which might be taken to imply a high degree of habitual behaviour. Petrol purchases and airline travel were positively affected by income levels, but rising relative prices for taxis, railways and buses all contributed to declines in the real level of expenditure on them.

However, a finer degree of explanation than this is needed. We shall therefore examine some more specific studies of the demand for cars, for public transport and for intercity transport and finally look at attempts to model the demand for transport as a whole, involving more than one mode.

THE DEMAND FOR CARS

Studies of the demand for cars have employed both cross-section data and time series. The purpose and emphasis of studies have differed. Short run studies have usually sought to analyse the factors that cause deviations of car purchase from an expected pattern; they are typified by stock adjustment models and are of more direct interest to the business economist or economic policy maker, although their findings have a relevance for the transport economist. Long run models of total motor-car usage are a more specific focus of interest for transport economists. International comparisons can also provide useful insights into the nature of demand, as in the simple model constructed by Silberston (1970). In this model an international cross-section comparison is conducted to try to determine what factors influence the level of automobile usage in different nations.

The model is restricted in its scope by the scarcity of internationally comparable data, and the subject for analysis is the number of cars per head of population, although some consideration of vehicle-miles may be preferred in an ideal case. Many possible determinants may be selected. Most obviously, real income per head will be influential, but other plausible factors are: the availability of good roads; population density and the extent of urbanisation; the availability of alternative transport (e.g. bus and rail services); and the costs and ease of car ownership, including such elements as car prices, running costs and consumer credit facilities. Statistical scarcities limit the variables to three, measured in 1964 in thirty-eight free-market economies and eight socialist economies; these variables are income per head, population density and major railway-route mileage. The last two variables seem to have no simple theoretical basis, for two reasons: while car ownership is relatively low in some densely populated urban areas, rail or air travel may be preferred in areas where major cities are widely separated by sparsely populated areas; and railway route mileage, while providing a possible proxy for alternatives to car use, may merely reflect the geography of a country.

Variations in private consumption expenditure in the market economies accounted for nearly three-quarters of the variation in car ownership, but the inclusion of population density and railway route distance per head would only have raised the degree of explanation to 83.2 per cent, and the population density coefficient was statistically insignificant. The railway variable was positive, so that rail travel did not seem to be an alternative to car ownership; rather, both were strongly related to income or consumption expenditure per head. The equation for all forty-six economies (i.e. both market and socialist) is

$$Y_1 = -36.6 + 0.145X_2 + 24.4X_4 - 58.0X_5 \qquad \bar{R}^2 = 0.904$$

$$(8.47)\ (0.011) \qquad (5.79) \qquad (10.4)$$

where

Y_1 = the number of automobiles per head;
X_2 = private consumption per head in US dollars;
X_4 = kilometres of railway route length per 1,000 persons; and
X_5 = a dummy variable, with a value of zero for market economies and one for centrally planned economies.

The figures in parenthesis are standard errors of the variables. The X_5 term can be interpreted to suggest that, if in 1964 a socialist economy had similar income levels and rail facilities to a market economy, there would have been fifty-eight less cars per 1,000 population in the socialist economy.

Studies of the long run demand for cars are best conducted within rather than between countries. In Britain the Transport and Road Research Laboratory (TRRL) has for some years produced forecasts of

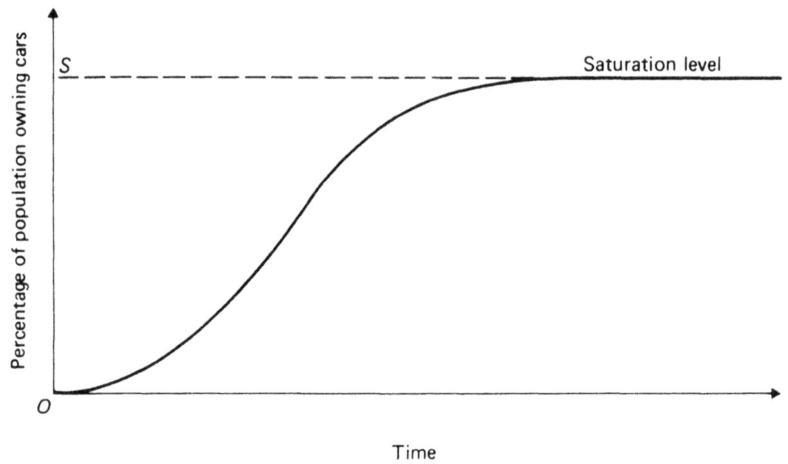

Figure 2.1 *The growth of car ownership*

vehicles and traffic with regular revisions. The basic method remains essentially the same as that used by Tanner in the early forecasts (Tanner, 1965). It assumes that there will be a continued increase in the number of cars per head in Britain, in a steady progression that seems to characterise the spread of ownership of many consumer durables in advanced economies. The growth of ownership, or *diffusion* as it is usually called, has been assumed (Tanner, 1974) to follow a logistic growth curve in which the upper and lower reaches of the curve are symmetrical. The upper limit, where the curve tends towards the horizontal, represents the eventual saturation of demand when, in effect, everybody who wants a car has one (Figure 2.1).

To predict the future number of vehicles it is necessary to know the specific form of the curve and the future growth of population, so that the number of vehicles per head can be converted to numbers of actual vehicles. Population projections are available from the Registrar-General in Britain and from various census bureaux in other countries, but estimating the nature of the diffusion curve is more problematic. Three constants are required: the current number of vehicles per head, its current rate of growth and the upper limit (i.e. saturation level). The saturation level is calculated after examining growth trends in both Britain and the United States. Data are available for the numbers of cars per head in British counties and American states and for the rates of growth of these numbers. Fitting a linear trend to the data suggests

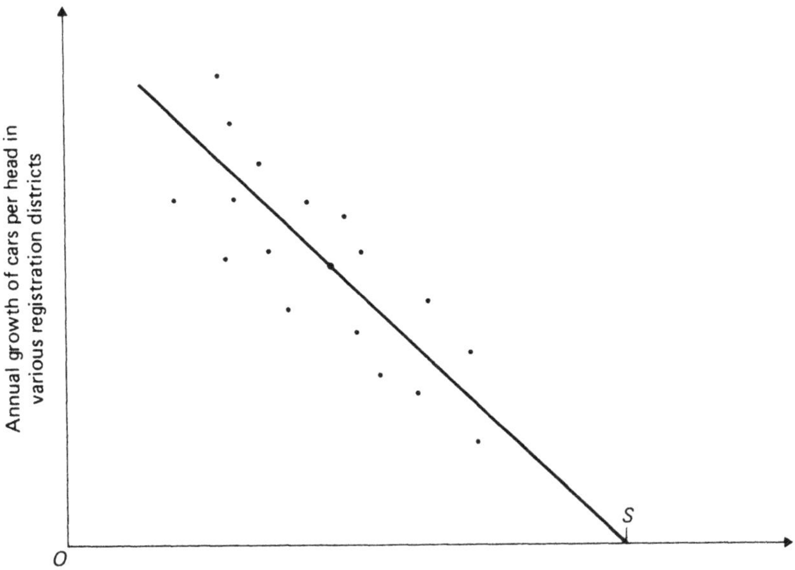

Figure 2.2 *The derivation of the saturation level*

that, ultimately, a level of car ownership should be reached at which there would be no growth in the number of cars per head.

Figure 2.2 shows that the method used by the TRRL to estimate the ultimate saturation level of car ownership. Unfortunately, it produces widely different estimates according to the period covered by the data, and figures mentioned range from 0.82 to 0.66 for Great Britain; the TRRL report of 1974 (Tanner, 1974) settles for a figure of 0.45, for example. However, it does seem a very tenuous and problematic form of extrapolation, although clearly the eventual figure adopted is crucial. Implicit in this approach to saturation is the expectation that factors applying in the past will apply broadly in the future; for example, the data for the postwar period reflect the falling real costs of cars and fuel and the extensive construction of motorways, which may not apply in future years. Hence, recent TRRL forecasts have employed a variety of assumptions about future rates of economic growth and future petrol prices to allow for uncertainty about them. These affect the speed of adjustment towards saturation although not the saturation level itself, and they produce high, medium and low forecasts for five-year intervals until 2010. Alternative real growth rates of 2, 3 and 4 per cent a year are specified, as are alternative time paths for petrol prices, giving three outcomes by the year 2000: 50p, 77p or 131p a gallon *at 1973 prices.* The assumptions of low growth rate and high petrol price produce a car population of 23.1 million by 2000 and 25 million by 2010, and corresponding figures for total vehicles of 27 and 29.2 million respectively.

This method of forecasting has been criticised for oversimplification, both in the past decade (Mogridge, 1967) and more recently (British Railways Board, 1976; Department of Transport, 1977c). Each of these critics has sought a more explicitly behavioural model based upon contemporary household expenditure patterns. Cross-section analysis from Family Expenditure Surveys has shown that households spend different amounts on motoring and other forms of transport according to their income level. Mogridge has assumed a growth rate of income and suggested that, as income levels grow towards the end of the century, so will expenditure on motoring. His model faces problems in converting his extrapolations of expenditure into physical vehicle stock, necessitating complex assumptions about car prices and depreciation. It also requires an estimate to be made of the saturation level, which he has estimated as 0.66 on the basis of one car for virtually every person eligible to hold a driving licence (i.e. about 60 per cent of the total population) plus an allowance for the fact that businesses in the 1960s owned about 10 per cent of the total stock of cars. In many respects this model relies upon extrapolation no less dangerously than the TRRL models, and its forecast car population of 42.2 million by 2010 now seems a fanciful reminder of the heyday of cheap oil.

The British Rail forecast has been made as a rejoinder to the Department of the Environment's 1976 Green Paper *Transport Policy: A Consultation Document* for the latter has broadly adopted the TRRL forecasts. British Rail has analysed travel patterns according to the purpose of journeys: journeys to and from work, journeys in the course of work, and leisure trips. An increase in real personal disposable income of 67 per cent between 1972 and 2000, implying a 2.5 per cent annual rise in gross domestic product, is expected; and when applied to a forecast income distribution for 2000 this increase suggests an increase of 65 per cent in the number of cars, compared with the TRRL and Department of the Environment's low forecast of 86 per cent. The gap between the two forecasts widens when expected distances covered are included. The TRRL forecasts assume that annual mileage per car will rise by 8 per cent between 1972 and 2000, on the basis of past correlations between rising income and rising mileage; whereas the British Rail forecast assumes that mileage per car will drop by 13 per cent, on the grounds that there will be a considerable reduction of in-work travel, and a slight reduction of travel to and from work, neither of which falls will be wholly offset by a predicted increase in leisure travel. Finally, British Rail has suggested that changes in the quality of different modes of transport will reduce car mileage by a further 18 per cent. These changes will include restrictions on the urban use of cars, forecast improvements in public transport, and increases in costs to car users between 1972 and 2000. The mileage elasticity of demand for petrol is estimated at 0.3 compared with 0.1 in the TRRL study, but the British Rail report fails to disentangle income effects on car mileage.

The outcome of the two forecasts is that British Rail expects only a 17 per cent rise in car mileage between 1972 and 2000, whereas the Department of the Environment low forecast is 84 per cent and the medium one 100 per cent. Both forecasts are open to criticism. The TRRL model has been challenged by British Rail for being too rigid and insensitive to variations in national income and petrol prices, while the British Rail model seems to be remarkably conservative about car usage. While the TRRL model does rest heavily upon its rather questionable approach to saturation levels, the British Rail economists have displayed a subconscious presupposition that factors will in future favour public transport and have made their estimates of the price elasticity of demand for petrol on short term data. Both forecasts accept that there is much uncertainty and scope for improvement in both methods and data. In the long run the private use of cars may be affected by factors that do not readily lend themselves to analysis at present. For instance, physical shortages of oil may bring greater price changes than have been foreseen and put such strains upon international payments that private motoring may be much restricted by deliberate government policy; technical progress may yield unforeseen fuel economies or new power sources although this may take decades rather than years; telecommunications technology may also facilitate the decentralisation of certain professional functions that currently necessitate travel. These possibilities could affect any forecast, but they emphasise the problems of predicting a quarter of a century forward.

Tanner (1977) has recently revised his earlier forecasts (Tanner, 1965, 1974) and taken account of some of the criticisms of the use of logistic curve. The data are not consistent with a symmetrical logistic curve, and the observed statistics suggest that the second upper part of the diffusion process is slower than the first lower part. Accordingly, Tanner has used a power growth function of which the logistic curve is merely a special restricted case. The power growth curve is more flexible in its approach than the logistic since it has one more parameter, but in practice Tanner's approach still requires a saturation level to be specified.

A choice of three saturation levels is offered (i.e. 0.4, 0.5 and 0.6); but since none corresponds to the 0.45 figure employed in the 1974 forecasts, comparison can only be approximate and suggests a slight reduction from the earlier estimates; for example, a car population of 23.1 million by 2000 in the 1977 estimates will require an ultimate saturation level of 0.5 rather than 0.45. Although the Advisory Committee on Trunk Road Assessment (Department of Transport, 1977c) has recommended the use of an ownership-forecasting model based more on behavioural principles (e.g. like that used by the Regional Highway Traffic Model), the government has affirmed its intention to employ Department of Transport forecasts based upon Tanner's findings (Department of Transport, 1978).

Long run models are concerned with trends but not with short run variations about the trend. Moreover, they emphasise the stock of cars, whereas short run models are often constructed to explain annual changes in the demand for cars including the replacement of scrapped vehicles. Short run models abound (e.g. Stubbs, 1972, p. 251), and they frequently become quite complex although econometrically they are more straightforward and satisfactory. It is possible to learn from these models, however, as they offer insights into which factors influence long run demand, and they may be useful should it ever become necessary to restrict private motoring sharply. A study of the demand for new cars by Armstrong (1974) has subdivided demand into *normal* (i.e. long run trend) and *abnormal demand* and also into three further elements: the demand for cars to replace formerly new cars, the demand for cars to replace second-hand cars and the demand by first-time buyers. In Armstrong's model there are four statistically significant determinants of normal demand. Personal disposable income is, predictably, important. Changes in indirect taxes (e.g. VAT) are also significant and are preferred to prices because of the problems of allowing for changes in the quality of cars, although indexes for this have been published. The two other factors are the price of new cars relative to used ones and a cyclical factor that encourages decisions to buy when the economy is in an upswing. All four factors are thus basically related to income and price. Items proving insignificant in the study included car-operating costs, supply shortages, which were made good by imports, and any trends towards smaller and cheaper cars.

Abnormal demand factors causing movements from the normal pattern merely advance or retard the diffusion process discussed earlier. The dominant influence here is a cyclical variable, namely, the rate of change of gross domestic product over the previous four quarters. Cyclical variations in total running costs, including depreciation, were found to be marginally significant. Hire-purchase variables were analysed separately, with variations in the minimum deposit ratio proving more significant than the maximum repayment period, the level of monthly payments or the level of hire-purchase debt outstanding. These abnormal factors were insignificant in the ultimate saturation level of ownership.

Thus, if policy required severe cuts in private car purchasing, the government would have to raise car prices sharply since it would not be practical to act on income levels or to alter conditions not considered in the National Economic Development Office (NEDO) model (e.g. statutory prohibition from selected areas, petrol price adjustments, improvements to competing modes). Armstrong's model was constructed before the big rise in fuel prices under the Organisation of Petroleum Exporting Countries (OPEC), but it does suggest that variations in running costs have little effect on car purchase.

We have seen that forecasting the demand for cars and car travel is in the long run a hazardous affair, that different authorities may reach widely different conclusions and that even individual authorities have to hedge against unpredictable future developments by offering a range of forecasts. Yet, the uncertainty surrounding car demand forecasts must inevitably make it difficult to forecast demand for travel by competing modes. In Chapter 3 we shall examine several modelling techniques devised to analyse the demand for simultaneously offered modes.

THE DEMAND FOR PUBLIC TRANSPORT

Numerous analyses of the demand for public transport, particularly suburban bus travel, have been conducted. Their significance is readily apparent. Operators and transport authorities need to know the pattern of demand in order to organise their short-run operational planning and also for longer run staffing and investment policies. A knowledge of demand is also vital for effective financial forecasting by the operator, who may seek to break even financially by altering the levels of fares or by adjusting the provision of services. It is also essential for the establishment of transport policy in general, in that the sensitivity of users to increases in the frequency and reliability of services may be influential in decisions such as whether to introduce bus lanes.

There are several elements of demand analysis that interest the transport economist or planner, of which we shall consider four: income elasticity; price elasticity; cross-elasticity and elasticity with respect to service characteristics. The income elasticity of demand for bus travel is negative, as we have seen, whereas that for travel by private car is positive. Since income growth is a factor beyond the operational influence of transport authorities they have spent less time in analysing it than they have devoted to price elasticity, and in several studies of the demand for public transport time trends have been used as proxies for the rising level of income. Cross-elasticities are usually examined in modal split models, which will be examined later in Chapter 3; so here we shall concentrate on price and service elasticities.

The price elasticity of demand is usually a straightforward concept expressed as

$$\frac{\text{the proportionate change in demand}}{\text{the proportionate change in price}}$$

or

$$\frac{dQ/Q}{dP/P} = \frac{dQ}{dP} \cdot \frac{P}{Q}$$

Three broad qualifications should be acknowledged before we consider the results of empirical studies.

The first is the distinction between *point* and *arc elasticity*, mentioned in basic textbooks. Point elasticity yields a unique estimate for a infinitesimally small segment of a demand curve; but it can seldom be applied to urban-bus demand analysis because fare changes usually involve sizable steps along the demand curve, which involves measuring arc elasticity, or rather the elasticity between two separate points on the demand curve. Commonly, constant elasticity is assumed between the points, and the elasticity thus measured is similar to that found by the arc elasticity approach. However, constant elasticity cannot be assumed along extended lengths of a demand curve; and care would be necessary if, for example, the transport authorities wished to go beyond modest fare changes and to estimate potential demand if public transport were made free. Moreover, where fares are very high they represent a bigger claim on income and may play a major part in the decisions to travel, and fare elasticity will tend to be high; whereas where fares are low they have little impact on the passenger, and fare elasticity will be low.

The second consideration is the relationship between the money price of a journey and the real cost of the journey to the traveller as revealed by his behavioural choices. Travellers are influenced in their choice of transport by more than money cost alone. Other things being equal they will prefer the faster mode to the slower and the more reliable to the less. Thus, a journey represents an 'expenditure' of time as well as of money; the sum of all such 'expenditure' may be called the *generalised cost*, and it is virtually certain to exceed the money cost alone. Consequently, the impact on demand of a change in fares will be limited if the fare forms only a small proportion of the total generalised cost of the journey. The fact that transport is a derived demand is also important here. Transport is only a means to an end; and if the cost of the trip is only a small item when compared with the utility yielded by the trip (e.g. the purchase of a remarkable bargain, attendance at a workplace), the user may appear relatively insensitive to changes in travel costs. In particular the characteristics of journeys just mentioned are likely to restrict sensitivity to price changes.

The third consideration is important in practice; and although it need not involve the student directly some awareness of it is essential. It is the practical difficulty of attempting the empirical analysis of demand, involving issues both of measurement and of interpretation. Any analysis of the price elasticity of demand should relate to changes in real fares after making allowance for inflation. In practice inflation is more-or-less continuous whereas fare changes are spasmodic. Consequently, real fares increase sharply in real terms at a time of fare increases, but they drift downwards during the intervening periods of fare stability when other prices are rising. The effects of this leapfrog tendency must be allowed for in demand analysis. It raises the issue of what time period should be considered, which involves the calculation not only of real price changes but also of the public response to fare changes. For example, fare increases may in the short run provoke users to cut their patronage of buses, perhaps by drop-back or stage shedding, which mean boarding later or alighting earlier along a route, thus reducing the cost of travel by a modest amount of walking; but in the long run resolution may soften, and users may revert to their earlier behaviour after a certain time.

Problems also arise if other factors change during the period in which the effect of changing fares is being examined. Consider a rise in bus fares, which diminishes demand and results in a reduction in the provision of buses; the abandonment of services or a reduction in frequency is a reduction in overall service quality, which will further depress demand. On the other hand, a reduction in fares may generate increased demand and the provision of extra buses, which in turn will increase demand by improving the quality of service since extra buses represent higher frequencies and shorter waiting times. In both these cases price and qualitative improvement have to be disentangled to assess the price (i.e. fare) elasticity of demand. Other factors that may alter ridership by passengers include: changes in the size and age structure of the population; general fluctuations in the economy affecting unemployment, which reduces travel; and the growth of car ownership, which reflects rising real income. During the survey period the motivation for trips may vary, in as much as the demand for transport is a derived one. In the long run there may be shifts from spectator to participant sports or vice versa, television may supplant much theatre or cinema going and the length of the workweek may alter. The relative price and quality of the different modes of transport can change and result in changes in consumer preference; for example, the relative price of private and public transport may alter independently of the retail price index, which is commonly used to deflate money prices.

Finally, there is the choice of data. It may be obtained in several ways, as Collings, Rigby and Welsby (1976) have pointed out. Patronage may be compared before and after fare changes, although this approach is apt to involve many of the problems touched upon in the previous paragraph. Likewise, fare experiments may be employed to generate data; but the same problems arise, plus the likelihood that the public may respond only half-heartedly, believing the experiment to be merely a temporary aberration. Cross-section studies that compare demand, fares and service characteristics simultaneously in different areas may be useful in providing data not normally found in time series, and they avoid the problem of temporal shifts in the demand curve. They can take several forms: comparisons of different groups of travellers; disaggregated models employing data for each individual separately, which are often used to evaluate customers' choice of transport mode (i.e. modal split) and their valuation of travel time; transportation study models, which will be discussed in Chapter 3; and analyses of specific groups of travellers. However, cross-section studies can only infer the effect of fare differences on ridership since they compare different groups of people. By contrast time series can measure the effect of actual fare changes on a known population. If time series data exist for an area or undertaking for a considerable period of time, it may be possible to estimate demand curves provided that care is taken to allow for as many as possible of the variables other than price that affect the curve, including many of those described in the previous paragraph and others (e.g. seasonal variations if quarterly data are used). In practice the number of variables for which data are available is likely to be limited.

A typical model employing time series might regress the number of journeys made against fare levels, vehicle distance (as an indicator of the availability of supply) and a time trend (which would catch rising income levels and private car ownership and use). The results for such a model, applied to data for British municipal undertakings, have been reported by Smith and McIntosh (1974). Real fare elasticities ranged from –0.21 to –0.61, generally lying between –0.2 and –0.4, and vehicle mileage elasticities varied from 0.4 to 1.12, averaging 0.71. The time trend in all municipalities was negative, as expected, and varied from less than 1 per cent to over 3 per cent. In another model Collings, Rigby and Welsby (1976) have added variables for seasonality and unemployment in an analysis of forty-six British bus undertakings between 1973 and 1975. Passenger, or journey, elasticity averaged –0.28 while revenue elasticity averaged 0.595. Hence, an increase of 1 per cent in fares was associated with a 0.28 per cent fall in passenger journeys, but revenues would rise by 0.595 per cent. *Ceteris paribus*, their model should have yielded a revenue elasticity equal to (1 minus passenger elasticity), but stage shedding and changes in concessionary fares negated this.

Elasticities have occasionally been studied at a more detailed level. Bly (1976) has outlined a number of elasticity characteristics. Demand for the journey to work is less elastic than that for other journeys, and this is reflected in various empirical findings that peak demand is less elastic than off-peak. Figures for Stevenage in 1971/72 were –0.27 and –0.64 respectively, and a study in Cumbria in 1976 has revealed a peak elasticity of –0.3 (Tebb, 1978). Data for large cities such as London, New York and Los Angeles, although limited, have confirmed that off-peak travel is sensitive to changes in fares. London Transport has estimated the fares elasticity of demand as –0.2 in the peak and –0.4 in the off-peak. The demand for season tickets, which are usually associated with the journey to work, is also relatively inelastic, but it is sensitive to the differential between daily fares and season ticket charges. Journeys of over 1 mile (1.6 km) apparently display lower elasticity than short journeys, perhaps because on short journeys walking is a readier alternative and also because on short trips the existence of a minimum fare sometimes represents a higher fare per unit of distance travelled. Access to alternative modes of transport, notably through the ownership of a car, has been observed to increase the elasticity of demand, and so does the possibility of drop-back or stage shedding, noted earlier, with the result that passenger trips diminish less than passenger-mileage after an increase in fares. The demand for urban rail travel appears to be less elastic than that for bus travel.

These findings have clear operational implications. Over 65 per cent of the cost of bus services in Great Britain is accounted for by labour costs, and against a background of a steady fall in patronage there is recurrent pressure to pass on cost increases as higher fares. The elasticities discussed above show that a typical increase in fares reduces the number of passengers but increases the total revenue earned; for example, given an elasticity of –0.3 and a fare increase of 10 per cent the number of passengers would drop to 97 per cent, but revenue would rise to 106.7 per cent. By concentrating fare increases on the less elastic segment of the market (e.g. peak period travellers) the loss of ridership may be minimised.

To some eyes such a policy is myopic and ultimately doomed to failure since it will tend to result in reduced services, further reductions in patronage and so on in a continuous downward spiral in the provision of public transport. To them the answer is radical: free public transport supported by municipal or national government finance. Normal price-elasticity calculations cannot be used as a guide in this area since the price change term in the simple elasticity calculation would be minus infinity; but in terms of generalised cost the shift of patronage to public transport would clearly be much less than total.

In fact a good deal of data about the effect of zero-fare policies is available from both theoretical studies and practical experiments. Kemp (1974) has reported a number of these. A study in Boston, Massachusetts, in 1967 has extrapolated from observed behavioural data to estimate that free urban transit would add \$8.4 million to the existing \$70.4 million operating costs of the Massachusetts Bay Transportation Authority but would save \$3.5 million in collection costs. The benefits were tentatively assessed to include: improved access to jobs for ghetto residents; increased shopping trips to the declining city-centre shopping area; a reduction in vehicle emissions of not more than 4 per cent; and a reduction in the need for parking spaces by a 9 per cent cut in morning rush-hour traffic and a 6 per cent cut in evening rush-hour traffic. However, the study has concluded that many of the benefits could be achieved more economically by other means. Quarmby (1967), in his study of Leeds in 1966, has used discriminant analysis to show that a zero public-transport fare would divert 17 per cent of car users on to public transport.

Experiments with zero fares have the advantage that they avoid the risky extrapolation of demand models based upon small segments of the demand curve, but they have the limitation that they lack credibility and thus have limited effects on consumer behaviour. The biggest city to apply zero fares has been Rome, where for a nine day period (mostly unrepresentative) in 1971–72 and also for two months beginning in May 1972 fares were not collected on peak hour buses and trams. The results in the first experimental period were varied, but there was little diversion from private motoring in peak periods. During the second period ridership was 11 per cent higher than in the previous May; but a reserved bus lane on one particular route appeared to be much more effective, increasing bus speeds by 10 per cent and ridership by 26 per cent. The effect of zero fares has been investigated in Britain by Daly and Zachary (1977) who have examined the behaviour in seven cities of public transport employees who were enjoying free travel concessions and compared it with the behaviour of a control group of normal fare-paying travellers. They have concluded that 22 per cent of car owners who did not need cars for their job would divert to public transport if it were free; that 10 per cent of those workers who had a car available for the journey to work would lose the choice, presumably to other members of the household, and would travel by public transport; but that car ownership would fall by only 3 per cent.

Some US cities have introduced permanent and major fare reductions. Most notable is Atlanta, Georgia, where in 1972 fares were cut by about 62 per cent and service provision was increased on several routes by an amount equivalent to an increase of 30 per cent in vehicle-mileage. Whereas fare elasticity in relation to fare increases in 1971 had been around –0.6, the elasticity associated with the fare reductions of 1972 was only between –0.15 and –0.2. Ridership increased by 19 per cent, and the net financial effect was an annual reduction in revenue of about $10 million. Demand elasticity in respect of vehicle miles was about +0.3. Similar policies in San Diego and Cincinatti increased ridership but diminished total revenue.

We may conclude then that major fare reductions in public transport fares or even free public transport is not a unique panacea for the problems of urban congestion. They could certainly diminish private car usage, the rising trend of which might in a few years restore congestion to its former level. A concerted effort to reverse this trend would require an array of policies, which would be likely to include service improvements in public transport and positive discrimination against private motorists.

CHAPTER 3

Models of Passenger Traffic

THE DECISION-MAKING FRAMEWORK

Two principal limitations affect an individual's travel behaviour. First, travel demand, unlike the demand for other commodities, is a 'derived demand'; travel is normally demanded not for its own sake but as a means of consuming some other good or service. A trip may be made because a household member wishes to buy commodities or service or to obtain other satisfactions (e.g. to purchase food, to visit friends, to earn income). Second, in the short run the travel decisions of the individual are subject to his residential location, workplace, car ownership or availability, and the availability of various modes at his residential location. However, in the long run factors such as location and car ownership are also decision variables. Furthermore, the attributes of the transport system may influence these decisions. Conventional demand modelling has treated travel demand and locational decisions as independent phenomena, at least in the sense that there is no feedback from one to the other. Consequently, it has been impossible to provide reliable forecasts of the effects of changes in transport system attributes on travel demand, without taking into account at the same time the effects of changing location.

In principle there is no barrier to incorporating individual decisions on residence, work location and car ownership as integral parts of inter-related trip decisions within a single decision framework. Indeed, as we shall see later, several attempts have been made to develop models of residential location that take into account transport system attributes. However, in practice it is difficult to obtain data that are adequate for estimating a simultaneous model of the travel and location decisions. Consequently, it is customary in trip generation submodels either to assume away locational changes by taking trip lengths as fixed or to allow them indirectly as measures of the relative attractiveness of destination zones.

The traveller must decide whether to make a trip, where and when to make it, which route to take and which mode to select. He bases these decisions on such factors as his needs, income, circumstances, occupation and car ownership and also on the terms upon which the different travel choices are offered to him: the travel times, costs and service levels of the competing alternatives. These alternatives can be different modes, different times of day or different destinations. The alternatives also include the option of travelling less frequently; for example, if the time or cost of travelling increases, the household may find it necessary to plan its shopping trips more carefully and to make fewer trips as a result.

One of the essential requirements of a travel demand model is that the model be *behavioural*. A behavioural model seeks to describe the causal relationships between socioeconomic and transport system attributes on the one hand and trip making on the other. The objective of such models is to explain why travel decisions vary as conditions change; otherwise, it is not possible to predict how the traveller will behave if his individual circumstances change or the terms upon which the competing alternatives are offered to him change. In short, only by explaining the causal relationships can the model be used to forecast the effects of future changes in the performance of the transport system.

The conventional models of travel demand separate the demand function into trip generation and attraction, trip distribution, modal split and route assignment. Observations are zonally aggregated, and parameters of the demand functions are usually estimated by using single equation estimation methods; origins or flows of travel demands have been determined by relating output to price, income and other variables. In practice the single equation approach tends to conceal many of the important aspects of the tripmaker's behaviour; for example, the feedback referred to above, between the individual's land use and locational decisions on the one hand and his travel decisions on the other, is not accounted for in the single equation methods. For this reason a simultaneous or multiequation approach to demand modelling has recently been proposed, which purports to portray the underlying travel-demand structure more accurately. We shall describe this approach briefly in a later section.

The remainder of this chapter will discuss passenger demand models under three main headings: urban passenger travel, intercity passenger travel, and modal split and the prediction of modal choice.

Much of the recent work in passenger traffic modelling has focused on the estimation of urban passenger demand. Consequently, we shall describe the basic structure of passenger demand models in relation to the urban travel demand. However, the models developed at the urban level are also applicable to the estimation of intercity travel demand.

While we shall abstract from model description at the intercity level, some degree of repetition is nevertheless unavoidable in presenting the results of intercity-travel demand studies. As far as possible our presentation will avoid mathematical or statistical details and deal only with the main features of these models. For a comprehensive summary of the urban-travel demand models the reader is referred to Domencich and McFadden (1975) and Williams (1977). The intercity-passenger demand models have been discussed by Meyer and Straszheim (1971) and Quandt (1970), who have also provided a good discussion of modal split studies. Following the conventional treatment of transport economics we shall abstract from a detailed description of trip distribution models, as these are essentially mechanical allocation devices that are devoid of any behavioural content. Interested readers may, however, refer to Wilson (1970) for an authoritative treatment.

MODELS OF URBAN PASSENGER TRAVEL

In this section we shall describe the models developed to estimate urban travel demand. We shall discuss procedures used to estimate single-equation demand models and then describe the multiequation approach to travel demand modelling. The single equation models follow a sequential process in which the trip decision is broken down into a set of separate, but ordered, decisions relating to:

(1) trip generation and attraction;
(2) trip distribution;
(3) modal split;
(4) route assignment.

The basic structure of these models is set out below to highlight the fundamental properties of such systems.

In conventional modelling attention is focused primarily on the calibration of trip distribution, followed by modal split and route assignment to the relative neglect of the trip generation stage. Indeed, trip generation is treated perfunctorily by applying growth factor methods to forecast trip ends. This is rather unfortunate as the trip generation model, from the point of view of consumer demand analysis, is basic in understanding the motivations that prompt people to travel in the first place. For this reason we shall first review the basic model structure summarily and then deal with trip generation models in greater detail in order to focus on some important aspects of this model.

THE BASIC MODEL STRUCTURE

Trip Generation. The basic model structure conventionally used to forecast urban passenger demand follows a sequential process in which trip ends (i.e. the number of trips that are likely to originate or terminate in each of the traffic zones) are calculated first. In most transportation studies trip ends have been forecast by modelling for trip origins only, but in others trip destinations have been calculated separately in order to cross-check the estimates of trip generation models.

Both types of trip ends have usually been estimated by means of regression analysis; however, as we shall observe later, category analysis (Wootton and Pick, 1967) has recently been used, particularly in the United Kingdom, to estimate trip origins. Typically, the most important independent variables used to explain trip behaviour in trip generation models relate to some socioeconomic characteristics of the zone (e.g. population, population density, car ownership, family incomes, the number of employed residents). Trip attractions are estimated more or less in a similar way, the main difference being that some additional variables indicating the land use characteristics of the zone are also included in the model.

The most serious shortcoming of the generation or attraction models is that they do not incorporate an explicit supply variable, so that by assumption the models assert that trip frequency is independent of any physical transport constraints or of the price of transport. In an attempt to rectify this deficiency and in particular to introduce elasticity considerations into travel generation, some recent studies have included accessibility variables in the trip generation models (for a review see Dalvi, 1977), but these attempts have not proved fully satisfactory.

Trip Distribution. This model, which is usually carried out by means of a constrained gravity model or an opportunity model, distributes the predicted number of trips between each origin zone i and each destination zone j. The gravity model in its most general form can be written as

$$T_{ij} = kO_iD_jf(C_{ij})$$

where

T_{ij} = the number of trips between origin i and destination j;
O_i = the number of origins (i.e. the number of demand requirements) generated at origin i;
D_j = the number of destinations (i.e. the number of opportunities) that are available at zone j;
$f(C_{ij})$ = the cost of travelling between i and j; and
k = a constant of proportionality.

This is the unconstrained version of the gravity model. To use it for the purposes of travel demand forecasting the following constraint equations on T_{ij} should always be satisfied:

$$\sum_j T_{ij} = O_i$$

$$\sum_i T_{ij} = D_j$$

That is, the row and column sums of the trip matrix should be the number of trips generated in each zone and the number of trips attracted, respectively. These constraints equations can be satisfied if K is replaced by the product

$$K = A_i B_j$$

where

$$A_i = \left[\sum_j B_j D_j f(C_{ij}) \right]^{-1}$$

and

$$B_j = \left[\sum_i A_i O_i f(C_{ij}) \right]^{-1}$$

The constraints A_i and B_j are also called *balancing factors*. Their values are determined by solving the constraint equations iteratively. The modified gravity model is then

$$T_{ij} = A_i B_j O_i D_j f(C_{ij})$$

In transport-planning studies the O_i trip ends are usually defined and known as *productions* (i.e. the home end of home-based trips or the origin of non-home-based trips) and the D_j trip ends as *attractions* (i.e. the non-home end of home-based trips or the destination end of non-home-based trips). Hence, it is customary to describe the modified gravity model as the production–attraction, constrained or doubly constrained, trip-distribution model, as T_{ij} is constrained to add up to an independently given number of productions and attractions.

The impedance function, $f(C_{ij})$, is defined as the generalised cost of travel, which in principle must include all the relevant elements as its argument, including the travel time, cost, comfort and convenience of the mode concerned. In practice, however, the impedance function usually includes car travel time only, so that changes in other service variables or in the characteristics of the public transport system frequently have no influence on predicted trip distribution.

The intervening opportunities model is based on a single notion that the number of trips from an origin zone to a destination zone is proportional to the number of opportunities at the destination zone and inversely proportional to the number of intervening opportunities. The underlying assumptions of the model are that the traveller considers each opportunity as being reached in turn and that every destination point has a stated probability of being accepted if it is considered. The probability of a destination point being accepted, if it is considered, is a constant that is independent of the order in which the destination points are considered; that is,

$$dP = L[1 - P(V)]dV$$

where

dP = The probability that a trip will terminate when dV possible destinations are being considered;
$p(V)$ = the probability that a trip will terminate by the time V possible destinations have been considered;
V = the number of possible destinations already considered; and
L = a constant representing the chance of a possible destination being accepted.

The integral of the above expression is

$$P(V) = [1 - K\exp(-LV)]$$

where K is the constant of integration. Now, the expected trip interchange from zone i to zone j, T_{ij}, is equal to the number of origins at i, O_i, multiplied by the probability of a trip terminating at j; that is,

$$T_{ij} = O_i[P(V_j + 1) - P(V_j)]$$

where $(V_j + 1)$ is the number of opportunities between i and j, nearest to i, and V_j is the number of opportunities between i and j but excluding j. The Vs thus represent the sum of all the possible opportunities considered before reaching a given zone, so that all destination zones have to be ordered in terms of their travel time from the origin. The usual statement of the intervening opportunities model takes the form

$$T_{ij} = K_i O_i[\exp(-LV_j) - \exp(-LV_j + 1)]$$

The value of K_i can be chosen so that the resulting matrix T_{ij} satisfies the constraint equation

$$\sum_j T_{ij} = K_i O_i [1 - \exp(-V_j N)] = O_i$$

where N is the total number of zones.

Modal Split. The modal split model varies more widely in practice than the previous elements of the urban-travel demand model. Some of these model formulations will be described in detail in a later section. In the urban transportation studies it is customary to estimate modal split after trip distribution has been estimated. The model most commonly used is based on a generalised distribution model developed by Wilson (1970), which takes the form

$$P_{ij}^k = \frac{T_{ij}^k}{T_{ij}} = \frac{\exp(-BC_{ij}^k)}{\sum_k \exp(-BC_{ij}^k)}$$

where

P_{ij}^k = The proportion of travellers using mode k between zones i and j;
T_{ij}^k = the number of trips between i and j by mode k;
T_{ij} = the total number of trips between i and j;
C_{ij}^k = the generalised cost of travel between i and j by mode k; and
B = a constraint measuring the disutility of travel felt by people from travelling by different modes.

In the two-mode model the expression reduces to

$$P_{ij}^1 = \frac{1}{1 + \exp[-B(c_{ij}^2 - C_{ij}^1)]}$$

This is the only model that is fundamentally behavioural and policy oriented, but because it is tacked on the end of the planning process the policy variables are only able to change the split between modes. The total number of trips and the distribution between zones have already been predetermined, largely without regard to the transport system attributes.

Route Assignment. The final step is route assignment. The model assigns trips to the transport network by selecting routes that minimise travel time for a predetermined number of journeys. The route assignment model in effect generates an impedance measure T_{ij} for the given mode of transport for each given set of trips, which could be fed back into the trip distribution and/or modal split models, thereby introducing an element of equilibrium into the process. In practice, however, this is usually not done. The feedback effect on trip generation cannot be estimated even in principle for models in which system attributes are not included in trip generation.

TRIP GENERATION MODELS

The earliest transportation studies used growth factor methods to forecast trip ends for the target year. The mechanical nature of these forecasts was readily recognised, but at the same time little effort was devoted to constructing behavioural models of trip generation because of the need to deal with data representing zonal aggregates of trips and socioeconomic variables. In the United States, for example, earliest attempts to develop regression models of trip generation failed because of the bias introduced by zonally aggregated data. To obviate this problem Wootton and Pick (1967) have introduced category analysis to predict trip ends. The category model breaks down households into a selected number of categories on the basis of factors like family income, the level of car ownership and the number of persons employed. It then assigns trip rates to each category as observed in the base year. Trip rates are predicted for the final year by assuming that the base-year trip rates will remain unchanged over the planning horizon. The model lacks any goodness-of-fit test to judge the stability of trip rates and hence to assess the statistical accuracy of trip forecasts. More significantly, however, like the conventional trip-generation models this model too is not policy oriented, as it does not account for the effects on trip rates of changes in accessibility factors. There is essentially no interaction between system performance and the decision on trip frequency.

These deficiencies of category analysis have recently led to a revival of interest in regression analysis for estimating trip generation. The new regression models are generally characterised by two fundamental features.

(1) The selection of explanatory variables is invariably guided by policy considerations instead of by forecasting convenience as was previously the case.
(2) The behavioural unit is either the individual himself or his household, not a collection of areally aggregated units that usually have no common behavioural links.

In what follows we shall first discuss some of these issues briefly and then present an illustrative trip demand model in order to show how to make the entire travel demand analysis behavioural and policy-responsive.

The Behavioural Unit. The usual unit of analysis in trip generation models is data aggregated to some areal unit, to meet the requirements of the trip distribution and assignment models as evolved in the urban-transport planning process. However, the trips attracted to or generated by any parcel of land must have been initiated by the decisions of individual travellers. Since in a demand model the aim is to know and to be able to model the real decisions faced by an individual in his travel behaviour and the factors influencing those decisions, the most pertinent behavioural unit is the individual or his household.

Effects of Areal Aggregation. Apart from developing a behavioural model of travel demand there are other very important reasons for treating individuals or their households as behavioural units of trip generation. These reasons concern the composition and ultimately the size of the data sample base used to calibrate the model. In developing a regression model of trip generation the analyst is attempting to explain the differences in observed travel behaviour. The more differences that he is able to examine and explain, the more confidence he can have in his results; thus, large samples are preferred. However, when household observations are aggregated into origin zones, as is customary in the urban-transport planning process, the number of observations that are available to be analysed and the variability within the sample are seriously reduced.

Research by members of the Federal Highway Administration in the United States has shown that in one instance approximately 80 per cent of the variability in socioeconomic variables of household occurred within traffic zones and that only 20 per cent occurred between zones (Fleet and Robertson, 1968). Hence, by aggregating households into zones much of the information in the sample is lost. At the same time, aggregation to zones may cause the number of observations that are available for analysis to drop from many thousand to a few hundred, not because there are only a few zonal pairs but because no trips are exchanged between the bulk of the possible pairs. This is particularly true for public transport trips because the system may provide only limited coverage for the urban area. Thus, aggregation obscures much of the large sample. It is important to recognise that the analysis depends on the number of different observations that are available for analysis, not merely on the number of people interviewed. The sample response rate is meaningless when the observations are aggregated into a small number of zones.

It would therefore be useful to design an urban trip-generation model based on disaggregated household or individual observations instead of on zonal aggregates as is the customary process. If zonal estimates are required for trip distribution or assignment, it will still be more sensible to calibrate behavioural trip-generation relationships at the household level and then to forecast trip level demand at the zonal level by directly aggregating over the values of the explanatory variables for a representative sample. Such attempts have recently been made for calibrating travel demand for the inner London area (Dalvi and Martin, 1976). Alternatively, statistical procedures are available that allow the aggregation process to be carried out algebraically or by numerical analysis (McFadden and Reid, 1974).

Determinants of Trip Generation. Explanatory variables included in the trip generation models fall into three main categories:

(1) those relating to the socioeconomic background of travellers;
(2) those pertaining to the transport system performance; and
(3) those relating to the land use or economic characteristics of the origin or destination zones between which trips are measured.

Among these variables, those in the first and third categories have traditionally been included in conventional travel-demand analysis, particularly in studies based on zonally aggregated data. It is only in recent years, and particularly with the shift of interest towards policy-oriented and behavioural trip-generation models, that transport system variables have been introduced in trip demand models.

In trip generation studies it has been customary to hypothesise person or vehicle trips per household to be a function of:

(1) *Under socioeconomic characteristics of the household:*
car ownership,
household size,
household income,
the type of dwelling unit,
the number of employed persons,
the residential consumption of the household; and

(2) *Under transport-system performance characteristics:*
door-to-door travel time,
travel cost,
the comfort and convenience of the journey (measured by some proxies),
distance from the central business district (CBD).

The theoretical reasons for including these variables have been extensively discussed in the literature. Generally, socioeconomic variables, particularly income, car ownership and employed persons, have been found to be the main factors affecting travel demand. The transport-system performance attributes have customarily been included in the form of a general accessibility variable; but as this variable measures the general accessibility of the given zone to every other zone in the area, rather than the accessibility of the destinations that are relevant for the particular zone, it has not been found to be a particularly significant determinant of trip generation. It must, however, be emphasised that the regression models of trip generation, based on disaggregated data, have been developed only recently; hence, the findings of the studies are still tentative. By contrast category analysis of trip demand, customarily used in the British transportation studies, has not been designed to explain trip behaviour. It is merely a trip-forecasting device. Furthermore, there is the more basic limitation from which all conventional trip-generation models suffer, namely, that these models use a single equation approach to explain what is otherwise essentially an interactive decision process. This means that the trip generation process is subject to what is known in econometrics as a *simultaneous equation bias*. We shall return to this point later.

AN ILLUSTRATIVE TRIP-DEMAND MODEL

In this section we shall construct an illustrative trip-demand model incorporating the elements described so far, to show how a potential traveller's decision can be handled simultaneously without resorting to distinction between trip generation, attraction, distribution, route assignment and modal split. The approach is nevertheless single equation in orientation.

For the purposes of estimation trips are generally disaggregated by purpose, since each trip purpose has a different valuation in the consumer's preference scale. For our present purpose trips will be classified not only by purpose but also by mode and the time of day during which trips are made. Hence, with m purposes, n modes and r time periods there are mnr separate demand equations. However, our illustrative model will concentrate on only one trip purpose, namely, the demand for shopping trips from zone i to some other zone j. Let us hypothesise that the demand for these trips is related to the three categories of factors described in the previous section. First, factors relating to the transport system performance have to be considered. These factors are mode as well as time specific; that is, it is plausible to hypothesise that the tripmaker is likely to be influenced by all the travel time components and the user travel prices for each mode or modal combination and for each hour of the day. Thus, with n modes and r daily time periods a total of nr sets of time components or user prices will be required for each demand equation. A vector notation is therefore needed to represent such multiplicity of variables. Second, factors relating to the tripmaker's socioeconomic situations must be considered. Some of these factors have been enumerated above, and the list can be extended to include many others depending on the level of specification desired. Thus, household structure, for example, can be differentiated in terms of its employment or age composition if such differentiation is expected to improve estimation. Third, the characteristics of the shopping destination under consideration (i.e. zone j) must be considered with respect to the desirability of that zone as a place to shop. The latter may be characterised, for example, by the shopfloor area devoted to retail activity, the number of retail employees and the number of stores in the zone.

To simplify presentation further our model will assume a two-mode transport system and describe demand characteristics in terms of two daily time periods only. A typical equation for the travel demand by an individual located in zone i to drive to zone j for a shopping purpose during the first period of the day then has the following functional form:

$$q(ij/A, S, H_1) = \phi \begin{bmatrix} t(ij/A, S, H_1), & t(ij/A, S, H_2), \\ t(ij/R, S, H_1), & t(ij/R, S, H_2), \\ p(ij/A, S, H_1), & p(ij/A, S, H_2), \\ p(ij/R, S, H_1), & p(ij/A, S, H_2), \\ s(A, S), & l(j/A, S), \ u \end{bmatrix}$$

where

$q(ij/A, S, H_1)$ = The quantity of round trips to zone j demanded by an individual at zone i using mode A for purpose S at time period of the day H_1;

$t(ij/M, P, H_x)$ = a vector of travel time components associated with trips made by the individual to zone j using mode M (where $M = A$ or R) for purpose P (where $P = i \ldots s \ldots M$) at time period H_x (where $H_x = H_1$ or H_2);

$p(ij/M, P, H_x)$ = a similar vector for the user travel-price components;

$s(M, P)$ = a vector of the tripmaker's socioeconomic characteristics that may be associated with the mode and purpose of travel; and

u = an error term.

The hypothetical demand equation shown above has been formulated in terms of an individual. In trip demand studies, however, it often becomes necessary to aggregate or deal with groups of individuals. No particular problems will be posed if aggregation to the household level is desired. The socioeconomic and land-use characteristics vectors remain more-or-less unchanged, and the system performance vector can be readily adjusted in order to make the various demands representative of the mean values of the household as a whole. The difficult problem arises when, through data limitation, the demand equation has to be modelled only for zonal aggregates. In this case care must be exercised to ensure that the vectors of the explanatory variables are so grouped as to be representative of the mean values of the parameters concerned. We have said that the best approach is to develop a demand model on the basis of individual or household observations and then to aggregate the values of the explanatory variables to the areal aggregation needed, in order to forecast total tripmaking in respect of trips demanded from, say, origin zone i to destination zone j.

It must be realised that, as the number of travel time, price and socioeconomic components increases, the number of variables in the demand equation becomes enormous. This may create difficulties for the use of statistical estimation techniques, particularly if zonal aggregates are used for estimation. Since there must always be sufficient degrees of freedom for an efficient estimation it is preferable, if not necessary, to reduce the number of variables substantially, even at the risk of some mis-specification of the model.

THE MULTIEQUATION TRIP-DEMAND MODEL

A simultaneous or multiequation approach to travel demand modelling arises from a simultaneous decision-making process in which it is assumed that an individual's travel decision follows a number of interrelated decisions. For example, an individual's choice of a particular destination to make his shopping trip may be conditioned by his choice of mode. Although in theory each decision is related to the rest, in practice only the decisions directly involved in carrying out a particular activity, in terms either of their substitutability or of their complementarity, are considered. In general an individual's travel decision is conditioned by the following related decisions:

(1) the choice of locations (i.e. employment location or residential location or both);
(2) housing consumption;
(3) car ownership;
(4) frequency (for non-work trips);
(5) modal choice, if feasible alternatives exist;
(6) destination (for non-work trips, feasible alternatives); and
(7) route choice, if applicable.

Not all these decisions may be directly relevant to making a particular trip decision at any moment of time. For example, the choice of residential location in general affects an individual's choice of destination for non-work trips; however, in choosing a particular destination at any given time the fact that he owns a car, rather than his residential location, may be a dominant factor in his decision. Indeed, whether a particular decision-making structure is sequential or simultaneous depends essentially upon the choice of time horizon. Over a longer horizon all related decisions may appear to be simultaneous, involving behavioural feedbacks. Over a shorter horizon, however, some decisions may still be made simultaneously while for others a sequential structure appears to be more appropriate. In a recent paper Ben-Akiva *et al.* (1976) have split travel decisions into two sets of choices: the long-run *mobility* decisions of location, housing, car ownership and mode to work; and the short-run *travel* choices of frequency, mode, destination, route, and time of day for non-work trips. Ben-Akiva *et al.* have assumed a sequential or recursive structure for the two sets of decision; that is, the long-run mobility choices are made first, with travel choices indeterminate, and the travel choices are made subsequently, conditioned upon the outcome of the mobility decisions. However, within each group of choices decisions are assumed to be made simultaneously by a joint process in which the full range of possible trade-offs is considered by the household.

The use of the hierarchical choice structure permits the development of two different models: one for mobility and one for travel choices. These models are termed *block-conditional,* where the blocks of mobility and travel choices as single units have a conditional structure, while each block by itself has a joint structure and hence must be modelled simultaneously (Ben-Akiva *et al*, 1976).

However, it must be emphasised that although this block conditional approach is conceptually appealing there is no *a priori* ground why this particular causal ordering should be more realistic than others. In fact this structuring is as restrictive as the original structure formulated by Kain (1964) in which the following sequence is assumed:

residential space consumption ⟶ car ownership ⟶ modal choice ⟶ trip length (via residential location)

Both structures postulate only one-way feedback: the block-conditional structure assumes feedback from mobility choices to travel choices, although within each block simultaneous interactive feedbacks are permitted; while Kain's structure allows unidirectional interactions between each individual mobility and travel decisions. Such unidirectional decision structure, although Kain has modelled it by using a simultaneous equation approach, fails to yield unbiased parameter estimates.

If it is true that the interdependences of travel decisions are inherent in the behavioural mechanism that generates them, the best approach is to treat them simultaneously in a complete demand model that embraces all the relevant feedbacks within a single framework. One such system is an interactive causal relationship as depicted in Figure 3.1.

In this structure each decision is approximated by defining a separate but appropriate endogenous variable for it. It is customary to distinguish between *structural equations* and *reduced form equations*. In the structural equations there are as many equations as there are endogenous variables, each representing a single behavioural relationship to be identified. However, as these relationships are formed on the basis either of theory or of *a priori* knowledge derived from experience, their specification may entail including more than one endogenous variable in a given equation. In that case the structural equation cannot be solved.

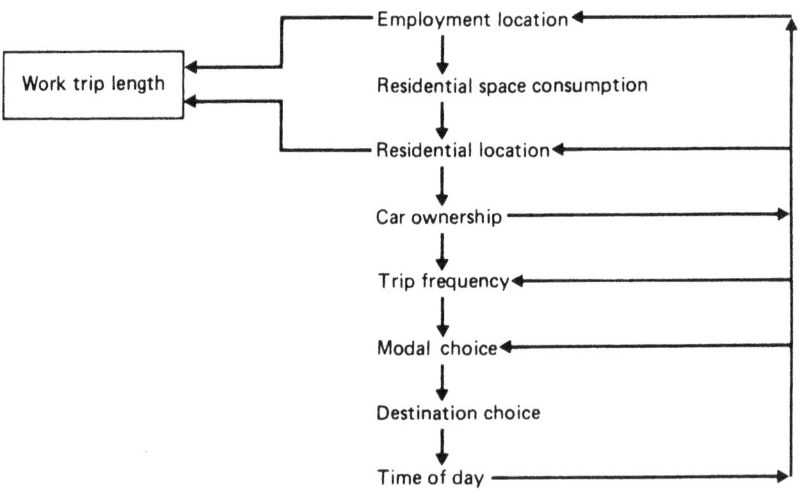

Figure 3.1 *The transport modelling sequence*

From a purely econometric point of view the two or more endogenous variables appearing in the single structural equation are jointly determined by the same generating function, so that their values are correlated with the error term. Consequently, the application of ordinary least squares fails to yield unbiased parameter estimates. The bias persists even for infinitely large samples.

One way of dealing with this situation is to convert the structural system, developed on theoretical grounds, into its reduced form by a mathematical transformation process such that each reduced-form equation contains only one endogenous variable. It is then possible to apply ordinary regression to obtain consistent parameter estimates. The reduced form coefficients are, however, generally a complicated function of the structural coefficients, and so their interpretation becomes difficult. Alternative estimation techniques are available and are being increasingly applied to estimate multiequation systems in the transport area. We shall not go into these complications here. Interested readers may refer to one of the references cited above for detailed discussion.

MODELS OF INTER-CITY PASSENGER DEMAND

Interest in intercity passenger-demand studies is relatively recent and has centred mainly on the estimation of a single linear forecasting equation for a particular mode. Early efforts were usually built on a simple gravity-model formulation, but lately the models have been extended to incorporate price, income and similar effects that economists consider to be paramount when estimating demand relationships. Some of the most advanced techniques of econometric estimation have been applied in this area (e.g. constrained regression, Bayesian estimation, iterative techniques for fitting non-linear functions), but on the whole the results of these have been less fruitful here than in urban travel studies. In this section we shall review the application of gravity models to the analysis of intercity passenger demand and then describe the abstract mode formulation of intercity passenger-demand models.

Of the numerous applications of gravity models for estimating intercity passenger demand in recent years, probably the most elaborate application has been in respect of the Northeast Corridor of the United States (Systems Analysis and Research Corporation, 1963; Meyer and Straszheim, 1971). The model consists of eight equations: the four major intercity travel modes serving corridor cities, each stratified by business and personal travel. Logarithmic demand equations are used.

In notation the complete model for business travel is

$$\log D_{ij}^{mp} \equiv \log K_{mp} + e_m \log (E_i E_j) + \sum_{q=1}^{4} p_{mp}^{q} \log p_{ij}^{qp}$$

$$+ \sum_{q=1}^{4} t_{mp}^{q} \log T_{ij}^{qp} + Y_{mp} \log Y_i + a_{mp} \log A_j$$

where

D_{ij}^{mp} = the number of round trips originating at city i going to city j via mode m for purpose p;

K_{mp} = a constant for the demand model for mode m for purpose p;

e_m = the elasticity of demand for trips by mode m for business with respect to the weighted employment product;

E_i, E_j = the employment in cities i and j respectively, weighted by trips per employee;

p_{mp}^{q} = the elasticity of demand for trips by mode m for purpose p; with respect to the price of trips by mode q for purpose p;

p_{ij}^{qp} = the one-way cost of travel between cities i and j via mode q for purpose p;

t_{mp}^{q} = a similar elasticity coefficient with respect to travel time;

T_{ij}^{qp} = the one-way travel time between cities i and j by mode q for purpose p;

Y_{mp} = the elasticity of demand for trips by mode m for purpose p with respect to *per capita* personal income;

Y_i = *per capita* personal income in city i;

a_{mp} = a similar elasticity coefficient with respect to destination city attractiveness; and

A_j = the attractiveness of city j.

A number of interesting features of the model may be observed. As attraction factors in business travel the explanatory variables are: the logarithms of the product of employment at origin and destination; incomes; and a measure of attractiveness at the destination city. Price and travel time variables for the given mode and for competing modes are included as impedance factors. Travel time is measured from door to door, to include walking and waiting time and also time spent in the collection or distribution phases (i.e. time spent travelling from the line-haul vehicle to the origin or destination). However, no effort has been made to estimate the parameters of each individual component of travel time in this study.

The large number of variables in the model causes problems of multicollinearity to arise. Accordingly, the study has attempted to use a constrained regression model, in which additional information is employed in the form of linear constraints on the range of values that the estimates of the regression coefficients can assume. Thus, each demand elasticity is constrained to have correct sign, and a maximum value is specified for each elasticity; for example, all own elasticities are constrained to lie between –5 and 0 (for a detailed discussion of constrained regression techniques, see Systems Analysis and Research Corporation, 1963).

The elasticities estimated in the Northeast Corridor study seem to accord with *a priori* expectations fairly well. For example, the business travel equation for rail yielded the following elasticities: an employment product elasticity of 0.9; a rail cost elasticity of –0.35; a cross-elasticity for bus cost of 2.3, indicating that rail and bus travel were highly competitive in terms of price; a rail time elasticity of –4.4, suggesting that the demand for rail travel was strongly sensitive to improvements in travel time; and a cross-elasticity for air travel time of 0.36. Other findings suggest that the demand for business trips for all modes was inelastic with respect to own price, with air travel exhibiting the highest price elasticity of demand. Personal travel demand appears to have been more elastic with respect to own price than businesss travel for all modes except bus transport. Another interesting point is that intercity passenger travel was more sensitive to changes in travel time than changes in travel cost, for both business and personal trips and for all modes. The estimates of the time elasticities for both personal and business travel were very high, the demand for business trips being more time sensitive than the demand for personal trips.

In the United Kingdom British Rail has developed a relatively simple gravity model to analyse the demand for intercity travel, under the acronym MONICA (Model for Optimising the Network of Inter-City Activities). It seeks to explain the volume of passenger journeys by rail as a function of several variables characterising the environment in which the travel takes place. Its most general form can be written

$$J_{ij} = f(P, D, S, C, E)$$

where

J_{ij} = rail journeys from city i to city j;
P = population;
D = an impedance function, distance;
S = the supply of a given quality of service by rail;

C = the availability of competing modes; and
E = the effect of socioeconomic features on demand.

The application of the model meets difficulties in identifying trip ends, in so far as some rail journeys are merely elements in a longer total trip; railheads are assessed as catchment areas, weighting local populations according to their distance from the appropriate station. The model covers sixty-four town pairs, and six socioeconomic factors pertaining to them have been selected from many tried, as reducing the error of the model by modifying the P term. The six socioeconomic variables are:

(1) the percentage of 'non-family households' (i.e. those comprising either one person or two or more unrelated or distantly related people), such households being more likely to travel and, in doing so, to use rail;
(2) the percentage of retired people, which yields a negative coefficient and, although correlated with (1), interacts beneficially;
(3) the number of hotel beds per 1,000 local residents, which is a proxy for commercial and recreational attractiveness;
(4) the percentage of people engaged in posts and telecommunications, which is a significant term that probably captures the regional importance of certain towns;
(5) the percentage employed in rail transport, which allows for abnormal propensities to travel by rail because of such factors as concessions to workers' families; and
(6) the percentage employed in air and sea transport, which only marginally improves the equation but seems to reflect the influence of sea ports on travel.

However, it is recognised in the MONICA model that the use of the six variables is tentative and that they cannot be used immediately for predictive purposes. Whereas population, price, rail speed and road speed, the latter pair entering the S and C variables, account for 78 per cent of variance, the six socioeconomic terms account for only 13 per cent of variance, but they do improve the standard errors of the price and quality variables.

The impedance term, D, can be envisaged either as distance or as a generalised cost function incorporating some combination of fare and journey time; but because of problems fare (i.e. price) alone has been selected. Some account of journey time is taken in the quality term, S, which is a combination of the speed and frequency of service.

The model has been designed primarily as an aid to managerial decision making, without the need for extensive data collection or for estimates of modal split. It has been used to simulate the effects of introducing new high-speed trains on selected routes where there is potential conflict between speed, reflecting the number of stops that are operationally feasible for very fast trains, and the loss of traffic if certain intermediate stations are no longer served. By fitting different values to the MONICA equation is has been possible to estimate the net generation of revenue. Gravity models can thus be useful for the prediction of intercity travel by a variety of modes, and in the future their numbers and sophistication are likely to grow.

ABSTRACT MODE MODELS

One of the interesting developments in consumer choice theory is the idea that goods are not the direct objects of utility; they possess characteristics and these characteristics give rise to utility (Lancaster, 1966; Ironmonger, 1972). In general a good possesses more than one characteristic, and many characteristics are shared by more than one good. A consumer spending his income in a free market in fact collects a bundle of characteristics with reference to which his utility is maximised. So long as certain convexity properties of the utility function are preserved, the model based on the selection of characteristics leads to as determinate a solution of the consumer choice problem as the conventional approach that only takes account of the consumption of goods *per se*.

The 'abstract mode models' of intercity travel demand are essentially based on these ideas, although their original formulation by Quandt and Baumol (1966) was independent of the writings of consumer demand theorists. Thus, transport demand in this approach is not formulated in terms of the demand for travel by such conventional modes of transport as trains, aircraft or cars; it utilises instead a number of abstract modal types, none of which may correspond entirely to any specific present or future mode of transport. Each abstract mode is characterised by several independent variables describing its supply characteristics (e.g. speed, frequency of service, comfort, cost). When a consumer chooses one mode in preference to another he is assumed to prefer one set of characteristics over another. The abstract mode theory therefore presupposes 'modal neutrality' on the part of individuals; that is, modes are chosen purely on the basis of their characteristics and not on the basis of what they are called.

The actual specification of the demand model is, however, conceived as a combination of a gravity model – representing the interactions between points and hence determining trips generated and their destinations – and a modal choice formulation based on performance characteristics of alternative modes. The performance characteristics are defined relative to the level of that characteristic attained by the best mode between the city pair in question. Thus, the decision by an individual to undertake travel between a city pair and the choice of his mode depends on:

(1) the usual exogenous motivations for travel (i.e. the various gravity-type attraction factors);
(2) the absolute performance level of the 'best' mode on each criterion; and
(3) the performance level of each mode on each criterion 'relative' to the best mode.

On the basis of these assumptions a typical formulation of the model is

$$T_{ij}^{k} = \alpha_0 \; (P_i)^{\alpha 1} \; (P_j)^{\alpha 2} \; (C_{ij}^{b})^{\alpha 3} \; (C_{ij}^{r}k)^{\alpha 4} \; (H_{ij}^{b})^{\alpha 5} \; (H_{ij}^{r}k)^{\alpha 6} \; (D_{ij}^{r}k)^{\alpha 7} \; (Y_{ij})^{\alpha 8}$$

where

T_{ij}^{k} = the number of trips between cities i and j by mode k;
P_i, P_j = the populations at cities i and j respectively;
Y_{ij} = the weighted average of *per capita* income at cities i and j;
H_{ij}^{b} = the least travel time between cities i and j;
$H_{ij}^{r}k$ = the travel time by the kth mode divided by the least travel time between cities i and j;
C_{ij}^{b} = the least travel cost between cities i and j;
$C_{ij}^{r}k$ = the travel cost of the kth mode divided by the least travel cost between cities i and j; and
$D_{ij}^{r}k$ = the departure frequency for the kth mode divided by the highest departure frequency.

The following points about the model are noteworthy.

(1) This is basically a linear demand model, with an estimating equation linear in the logarithms of the variables.
(2) One of the important advantages of the model is the economy that it makes in the use of data for estimation. If the number of city pairs is m and the number of existing modes is n, the number of observations will be of the order mn, which is substantially more than the number of observations, m, that would be available for estimating an abstract mode equation.

(3) It is not required that an exhaustive set of data be available. If the relevant observations on the variables relating to some city pairs and modes are not available, the model and its coefficients can still be estimated (Quandt and Young, 1969).

Despite these advantages the empirical results of the abstract mode model have not been very encouraging. The first empirical test of the model by Quandt and Baumol (1966) used sixteen city pairs in California for air, bus and car journeys. Most of the elasticity coefficients had expected signs and were statistically significant. However, the limited tests so far made have failed to establish whether the travel demand for all modes can be estimated as a single equation by pooling data across modes. The car journey data have proved difficult to pool with the data for the other modes. The income elasticity estimated from the abstract mode formulation appears to conceal considerable differences in income elasticity among the users of different modes, especially car users. In addition the abstract mode formulation has yielded parameter estimates with higher variances than models individually specified for each mode.

In view of these limitations attempts have been made to improve the original formulation of the abstract mode model by providing for different income elasticities for the different modes and routes and also by imposing various types of *a priori* restrictions on the estimation of parameter values (Quandt and Young, 1969). However, this sort of accounting for differences across modes makes the abstract mode model less abstract. Besides, neither the individual modal models nor the abstract mode model is well grounded in the theory of consumer behaviour. The decision-making unit is not specified, in contrast with most aggregated models, so that no account is taken of the differences in the tripmaker's utility functions or income levels in estimating demand parameters. However, Blackburn (1970) has attempted to construct a travel demand model based on the individual's utility differences that also takes into account differences in income levels.

MODAL CHOICE MODELS

As mentioned earlier, modal choice models represent attempts to develop relationships that determine what share of total traffic will use each mode, with attention usually centred on the split between car and public transport. While modal split models have figured in both urban and interurban demand studies, they have been more sophisticated, in both the choice of variables included and the estimation techniques used, in urban transport studies. Accordingly, our comments will chiefly be concerned with the procedures applied in urban modal-split studies.

These studies can be classified in three ways. First, there is the type of study that relates the use of public transport in an urban area both to city characteristics (e.g. size, density, age) and to population characteristics (e.g. income, car ownership) (Beesley and Kain, 1965). Second, there are models of modal choice developed as part of a comprehensive transport-forecasting process; typically, the aim of such models is to predict public transport and private car usage for all trips made between any pair of the zones into which the urban area is divided, so that factors such as relative travel times, costs and service differentials have usually been emphasised. Third, some researchers have developed models to explain and predict individual choices of mode, taking account only of individual mode and household characteristics.

Studies of the first type are of little use for policy decisions (e.g. for encouraging the patronage of public transport or for restraining the use of private cars). As mentioned earlier, empirical relationships incorporating size, density, urban land area and other city characteristics as independent variables embody no *a priori* causal hypotheses about people's travel choices. True, long term increases in such factors as city density and car ownership and the accompanying suburbanisation of the population have traditionally exerted a powerful influence on the growth in car ownership; but these factors are of little use in predicting how people will react in the short term or even in the medium term, when confronted with new modal situations.

By contrast the modal choice models developed as an integral part of transport-planning models have laid emphasis on policy-oriented variables such as income and relative times and costs, which economists have always considered crucial in determining modal choice. However, it has always been a matter of dispute exactly where in the planning process modal split should be introduced (i.e. whether the sequence of trip generation, distribution, modal split and assignment is really meaningful in describing trip decision process). The issue once again depends on the validity of single-equation demand-model studies, including modal split, as the estimation of modal choice is determined on the assumption that the trip itself, its purpose and its destination have already been established.

Almost all the elaborate attempts made so far to model modal choices within a comprehensive transport-planning framework have been carried out in North America. As an illustration we shall describe the model developed for Washington, DC, on behalf of the National Capital

Transit Authority (Dean *et al.*, 1963). In this study modal split followed the trip distribution stage, and zonal interchange data were first stratified by trip purpose (i.e. work and non-work) and then by the ratio of car trip costs to transit trip costs, by the ratio of transit service to automobile service and by the median income in residence zone. This stratification defined 160 subclasses. Diversion curves relating the percentage of public transport usage to the ratio of car travel time to public-transport travel time were then obtained for each subclass. This produced a reasonably close fit of actual modal choice for the sample data, especially for work trips to the CBD. Public transport journeys not oriented to the CBD were not accurately forecast. Travel time ratios for non-work journeys were taken from off-peak periods and had to be applied to both peak and off-peak periods, which probably accounts for the less satisfactory predictions of non-work trips.

As regards the estimation of the individual choice of mode, the model originally developed by Warner (1962) is probably the most comprehensive to date. He has used a discriminant analysis to predict the probability that an individual traveller with certain characteristics will choose a particular mode for his trip. The model takes the following form.

A linear discriminant function is defined as

$$Z_{ij} = \sum A_p X_{pij}$$

where

Z_{ij} = the relative disutility of the jth person (where $j = 1$ to n_{ij}) in the ith mode (where $i = 1, 2$);

X_{pij} = a factor value coefficient for the pth factor (where $p = 1$ to k) of the jth person in the ith mode; and

A_p = a weighting coefficient for the pth factor.

The task of discriminant analysis is then to find the best values of A_p to explain the observed choices of a sample of travellers.

It has been shown that under certain assumptions it is possible to estimate the coefficient of the discriminant function by ordinary least-squares procedures (Quarmby, 1967). The dependent variable is then converted into a dummy variable Y_{ij}, where Y_{ij} takes the value of one or zero depending upon whether $i = 1$ or 2 respectively (i.e. whether the jth person observed takes mode 1 or mode 2). The estimation model assumes the form

$$Y_{ij} = \alpha_0 + \alpha_p X_{pij} + U_j$$

where

X_{pij} = a factor value coefficient as above;

α_p = the regression coefficient of the pth explanatory variable; and

U_j = the jth error term.

Once the parameters of the discriminant function are computed the next step is to calculate the probability of choosing the given mode in question rather than the other, where this probability takes a value depending on the value of the discriminant function. The modal probabilities so calculated are then used for modal prediction (e.g. for evaluating the effectiveness of schemes such as improvements in public transport systems).

Warner (1962) has used data gathered by the Cook County Highway Department from interviews taken in a suburban area of Chicago for trips to the Loop – Chicago's CBD. By directly using individual travel and household data he has avoided the zonal aggregation inherent in procedures used by most other studies. Apart from its statistical sophistication, Warner's method is particularly attractive because it explains modal choice in terms of variables that are as direct as any in their presumed influence. Consequently, more confidence is attached to predictions from this model than to predictions from many other modal-split models. Warner has not bothered to develop his model beyond predictions based on individual observations; he has not, for instance, suggested a way of modal choice on area or corridor basis. These sophistications, including further improvements in the specification of the model, have occurred in later applications of this approach (e.g. Quarmby, 1967; Lisco, 1967).

Despite the variety of models and applications the results obtained from modal split studies are similar in important aspects. Thus, Meyer and Straszheim (1971), surveying the results of eight modal-diversion curves obtained for some American cities, have observed remarkable uniformity in preference patterns in urban modal choices. For example, all their diversion curves indicate that public transport usage drops quickly when and if any disadvantage appears in the time required for transit trips. The only notable difference in the results appears to be the level of the captive public-transport market in each city, represented by the existence or non-existence of a right hand tail on the diversion curves. This difference is, however, attributed to differences in the demographic, social, income and density characteristics of the different cities.

Essentially the same pattern of preference in modal choice seems to prevail in other countries (Quarmby, 1967; Donnea, 1971). In general it has been found that commuters with the car as an alternative mode of travel are highly sensitive to savings in travel time and will quickly shift from public to private transport whenever public transport suffers from any perceptible disadvantage in the time required for competing journeys. The effect of cost differences on modal split is also similar to the American experience, especially in most European cities. Differences, if they do appear, seem mainly due to high American income-levels, which permit more people to own private cars, although over time the differences in this regard seem to be disappearing. Government pricing and restraint policies also tend to make the use of the private car less feasible in many parts of the world. For example, fuel taxes are quite high and account for a major proportion of general taxation revenue in the United Kingdom; whereas in the United States fuel taxation rates are very low, and the proceeds are usually earmarked for highway development. The pattern varies widely, however, because fuel taxes in parts of Latin America, Africa and Asia are practically non-existent. However, even with due allowance for these institutional differences the most common result to emerge from the modal split studies is that the private car is on the whole a superior mode among all the modes of transport that are available, particularly in low-density urban areas.

CHAPTER 4

The Analysis of Supply

INTRODUCTION

The aim of this chapter is to consider factors affecting the supply of transport services. Most introductory textbooks advance the hypothesis that the supply of a commodity is a function of its price, the prices of other goods and services, the prices of factors of production, the state of technology and the objectives of the firm. The analysis then proceeds to postulate an upward-sloping function relating the price of the commodity to quantity supplied on the basis of certain *ceteris paribus* assumptions. A more advanced analysis can then be pursued, part of which incorporates the theory of costs. Transport economics represents a somewhat specialised application of cost theory, and it is therefore in this area that attention will be concentrated.

Costs are incurred in purchasing factors of production for use as inputs in the production process. The cost of producing any particular output depends on two factors: the technical relationships between the quantities of inputs and outputs (the production function), and the economic relationships between the quantities of inputs and their prices. Thus, the two sets of relationships combine to give one relationship between the quantity of output and the cost of producing it, which comprises the firm's supply function. However, because the first set of relationships (between quantity of inputs and quantity of outputs) varies from industry to industry (and for that matter among product groups within an industry) it is not possible to have a universal 'theory of costs' that is applicable to all industries. Largely as a result of the characteristics of its production functions the transport industry represents a special application of the theory of supply.

Before proceeding, three preliminary points will be set out: the definition of costs, the main areas of analysis of transport costs and the plan of this chapter.

When analysing costs the first important distinction to make is between total, average and marginal costs. These concepts should already be familiar, but they are of such importance as to merit repetition.

Total cost represents the sum of money payments incurred in the production of a given quantity of a good or service, and total cost divided by the number of units produced is the *average cost* per unit. *Marginal cost* is the addition to total cost incurred by increasing the production of the commodity by a small amount – usually one unit. The relationship between average and marginal costs is essentially mathematical rather than economic. What is most relevant to remember for this analysis are the conclusions that when average cost is rising marginal cost must be above average cost and that when average cost is falling marginal cost must be below it. The proof of this point can be derived intuitively from a consideration of the definitions themselves, and a more formal and rigorous exposition can be found in any microeconomics text (e.g. Baumol, 1965).

Of equal importance is the definition of the term 'cost', as economics is concerned with resource allocation the economist uses the concept of *resource cost* or *opportunity cost*, which is an attempt to reflect the value of resources used in producing a particular output. As such it may differ from the money or accounting cost of producing the same output. The opportunity cost of utilising a resource in a given way is the value of the output that it could produce if it were put to its next most remunerative use. In the case of factors purchased in the market the opportunity cost to the firm is the price that it has to pay in the market (i.e. the benefit that it could derive from spending the money concerned elsewhere). In the case of factors owned by the firm the opportunity cost may have to be imputed as it may not appear automatically in the firm's accounts, and this is a frequent source of divergence between accounting and opportunity costs. One way of calculating the opportunity cost of a particular output is to consider the net cost savings that would accrue if its production were discontinued – a method that has been widely used in transport economics.

The second preliminary is to delineate the main problems incurred in transport costs, which will be discussed in this chapter (making no attempt, however, to be fully comprehensive). The first problem is the identification of costs of individual traffics. This arises in policy problems, such as whether a particular railway line or bus service is unremunerative, whether the price charged to a particular consignment is equal to the opportunity cost of carrying it, and whether there is justification on cost grounds for the higher train fares charged at peak times. The second problem is the identification of cost functions. This can help to answer the question of whether and to what extent economies of scale exist in the transport industry. It is of particular relevance for policy both in the United Kingdom and abroad where the transport sector is often the subject of reorganisation. Since 1947 there have been four distinct 'reorganisations' of the transport sector in the United Kingdom, instituted by the Transport Acts of 1947, 1953, 1962 and 1968 on the grounds that efficiency would be increased by larger or smaller undertakings. As an example, the 1966 government stated in a White Paper that 'the efficiency of bus operation is hampered by the small size of the undertakings' (Ministry of Transport, 1966, paragraph 56), apparently without producing any evidence to support the statement! In this context, therefore, it is clearly important to know what the shape of the cost function is, whether economies of scale can be achieved and, if so, at what size of undertaking they will be maximised.

The rest of the chapter is devoted to these problems, starting with a consideration of the relevant economic theory and then discussing the methodology and results of empirical work, dealing with each problem in turn. As a rule detailed discussion of the policy implications of such work is reserved for later chapters. Finally, one aspect of cost not discussed in this chapter is the distinction between private and social cost, since we feel that at this stage its inclusion would only serve to complicate the issues involved. It can be dealt with more appropriately in the chapters on pricing and investment, where the necessary theoretical background can be introduced as an integral part of the argument. The analysis in this chapter is therefore in terms of private costs (incurred by transport operators and users) rather than social costs (incurred by the community as a whole).

THE IDENTIFICATION OF THE COSTS OF INDIVIDUAL TRAFFICS

THEORETICAL CONSIDERATIONS

A prerequisite for cost identification, indeed for any form of costing, is a clear specification of the unit of output to be costed. In industries producing a single identifiable homogeneous product no problems arise, but unfortunately the transport industry does not come into this category. By their very nature as providers of services to different individuals transport undertakings are multiproduct enterprises in which the product is heterogeneous. The service offered to one person at one time will be no substitute for that offered to another at another time, on the grounds that the cross-elasticity of demand will be close to or actually zero. (Cross-elasticity of demand, or elasticity of substitution, is defined as the percentage change in the quantity of good A demand divided by the percentage change in the price of good B. As such it measures the responsiveness of the demand for one good to the price of another, i.e. the ease with which they can be substituted.) A change in the fare for passenger X's journey is therefore unlikely, *ceteris paribus*, to influence passenger Y's demand. Furthermore, in many branches of the transport sector the industry operates a 'public' service in the sense that its facilities are used jointly by a number of individuals (e.g. the passengers on a bus or train, the consignees of the packages carried on a freight service). Only comparatively rarely does one individual make exclusive use of transport facilities (e.g. taxis, wagonload consignments of road freight, trainload consignments on railways), and even then facilities are available for other people to charter at different times. For these reasons a transport undertaking should be thought of as producing a number of products that may be physically homogeneous as output units (e.g. passenger-miles) but heterogeneous on grounds of substitutability.

One result is that costs must be calculated for several output levels, each representing a different degree of disaggregation of the total output of an undertaking At one extreme is the individual passenger journey or freight consignment, comprising an individual or an object transported over a given distance. The most common output definition to arise from this is the passenger-mile or the ton-mile, although in some cases the distance element is ignored altogether. Bus undertakings, for instance, often measure the demand for their services in terms of passenger numbers rather than passenger-mileage, and most estimates of the decline in bus transport are based on this statistic alone. At the next level is the bus or train journey; and in some cases (e.g. taxis) the journey is also the demand unit. Above that for public transport is the route, comprising all the bus or train journeys operated between two points. Beyond this the bus company or railway as a whole is a further unit for analysis. In addition there is the time dimension of transport services, which will be discussed more fully below when the problem of peak costing is considered.

Because of the nature of the production function in transport and the existence of costs that are joint to several outputs the selection of the unit of output to be costed is very important. However, at the same time there is no 'correct' unit of output that can be selected for all purposes and used universally; the selection of an output unit depends on the purpose that the costing is to serve.

The main reason for this, which is the source of the first major difficulty in transport costing, is that the unit of supply is often larger than the unit of demand. As an example, it has been pointed out above that the unit of demand measurement for bus services is the passenger-mile. However, the minimum unit on which supply can be varied is the bus-mile, and a bus typically carries upwards of forty passengers. In this case, given that the service is to operate at all (notionally for the 'first passenger') the opportunity cost of carrying further passengers on a trip is almost zero. In other words, as very few costs would be avoided if one fewer passenger travelled almost all the costs of running the service are joint costs of all passengers using it. This problem is less severe in freight transport, where wagonload consignments are more common. However, in some branches (e.g. parcels carriage) the above point holds, as it does in railway freight operation, where consignments of less than a trainload are still accepted. Indeed, British Rail is presently actively attracting some wagonload traffic on its Speedlink network of express freight trains.

Joint costs are very important, although the difficulties that they raise may have been overstated. In fact the principal distinguishing features of transport are that for many reasons joint costs exist and hence that the marginal cost (i.e. avoidable or opportunity costs) of any unit of output is less than the average cost of producing it. Before drawing any general conclusions on the problems raised and ways of overcoming them, however, the reasons for the existence of joint costs in transport will be discussed.

The first reason is that the provision of one service often necessitates the provision of another. Most often this is so when an operator has a unidirectional demand to operate from A to B and therefore must operate in the opposite direction (i.e. from B to A) so as to recommence work from A. Effectively, the cost of operating in the reverse direction is a necessary part of the operation from A to B, and thus the service from B to A can be provided at zero marginal cost. Peak bus and train services and many railway-freight flows exhibit this trait. If demand in both directions is evenly balanced, this argument can be applied to the service in either direction. Clearly, the costs of operating in any direction are joint costs with the costs of running in the other direction, and only the avoidable costs of operating a round trip can be identified. In both cases joint costs have arisen through indivisibilities in the size of one of the assets used in the provision of the service – the vehicle itself.

Joint costs also arise with other assets (e.g. stations, bridges, railway track, signalling systems), which, once purchased, are capable of providing service up to the limit of their capacity for the rest of their lives at low opportunity cost. The reason is that maintenance and operation costs are often a small proportion of total cost, which includes initial capital expenditure. Furthermore, many are specific to their present use (e.g. a railway track) and so have a low or zero value in an alternative use.

In this case it may be argued that such costs are joint to all traffics using them, as in fact the Beeching Report does in respect of British Rail's track costs:

> Railways are distinguished by the provision and maintenance of a specialised route system for their own exclusive use. This gives rise to high fixed costs ... The total cost of providing the route system ... amounts to nearly a quarter of the railways' total revenue. This is a fixed cost, in the full sense of the term (British Railways Board, 1963, pp. 4 and 9).

There is, however, a danger that the apparent existence of joint costs will be taken as sufficient reason for not considering the problem in more detail. In this particular case it has been argued that track costs are not fixed to the same extent as the Beeching Report implies. The argument has been put by Joy (1964) that different types of track (e.g. single, double or triple track) can be provided on any route and that track can also be maintained to different standards according to the characteristics of the traffic using it. At the time British Rail had five maintenance categories, the highest of which was for track carrying frequent high-speed passenger trains. There were considerable differences in the costs of maintaining a mile of track to each standard, the limits being £2,000 and £15,000 per year in 1961, and therefore Joy has argued that any maintenance above the minimum standard was avoidable if certain identifiable traffics did not run. It thus followed that only the costs of providing this minimum standard of track were truly fixed costs of railway track and therefore joint costs of all traffics. The remaining costs, although possibly joint to more than one unit of traffic, could specifically be allocated to certain groups. This argument resulted in an estimate of £35.6 million for fixed track costs as opposed to Beeching's £125 million.

Although Joy's argument applies specifically to track costs it can obviously apply to other assets sharing the characteristic of railway tracks that their scale can be varied (e.g. stations, marshalling yards, signalling systems). In the case of track costs Joy has argued that the necessary adjustment in scale can be made relatively quickly:

> The number of tracks on each route can easily be adjusted downward to match a fall in traffic density ... a double track may have its capacity reduced in line with traffic requirements by reducing it to single track. This requires only the isolation of the second track.

In the case of other assets, however, adjustments in scale may not be possible in such short time periods, which raises the question of the existence of joint costs as a result of time. Many assets discussed in the preceding paragraphs (e.g. buildings, permanent ways, tunnels, bridges) have a long life with a low opportunity cost during their life but a high replacement cost at the end of it. Thus, the capital cost of providing the asset is a joint cost of all traffics using it during its lifetime.

Time can also influence the level of joint costs in another way where factors such as labour have to be hired for minimum periods of time – in the case of labour a 40-hour week, usually comprising five 8-hour days. Once a train driver is employed for this period no costs are avoidable until it ends, and the costs of employing him are the joint costs of all outputs provided in that period. As a high proportion of costs in the transport industry are of this nature the potential severity of costing individual traffics becomes apparent.

From the above analysis the main conclusion is that the avoidable cost (i.e. opportunity cost) of a particular output depends on the proportion of total costs forming joint costs: the higher the proportion of joint costs, the lower the avoidable cost as a proportion of total cost. The factors affecting the proportion of joint costs are:

(1) the size of the output unit being costed;
(2) the time period for which the costing is to be carried out; and
(3) the nature of the assets involved, especially where indivisibilities occur.

Examples of all three points can be found above.

The questions arising from this are the choice of output unit and the time period for costing. Although what follows is not meant to be the 'last word' on these issues it represents our views on the problems.

It is apparent from the foregoing that, the larger the unit of output being costed in relation to the size of the undertaking as a whole, the smaller will be the proportion of joint costs and therefore the closer will avoidable costs be to the total costs of providing the output. Variations of this kind range from an individual passenger journey to all services operated by, say, British Rail. Clearly, however, both examples are extreme, and the former at least is hardly likely to be required for policy purposes. It may therefore be concluded that the most appropriate and meaningful unit of output for costing will depend on the objective being achieved by the costing exercise. If, for instance, it is to determine whether a particular trip by a train is remunerative or not, the avoidable costs of operating that trip will be relevant. Similarly, if the aim is to determine whether passenger trains on a line or the line itself is remunerative, different units will be appropriate. The general conclusion, however, must be that the unit of output to be costed needs careful and precise definition but must include a degree of flexibility to meet different circumstances.

As far as time period is concerned, the above discussion should be enough to allow the conclusion that the proportion of joint costs will fall as the time period considered increases. Again, extremes (e.g. one day, 100 years) are of little practical use, and the choice of time period for analysis should be flexible, depend on the purpose of costing and be specified very clearly.

Given these conclusions, unless one is prepared to take an extreme position some allocation of joint costs among traffics is an essential feature of public transport. Very few consumers derive sufficient benefit from a trip to afford to be the 'first' passenger on that journey let alone on, say, the railway in question. It is only by effectively averaging joint costs among passengers that a public transport undertaking, and possibly any transport undertaking, can operate at all. The important points are as follows. First, joint costs should be accurately identified, and this can be achieved by clear statements of the unit of output being costed and the time period under consideration. Second, the principle on which the allocation is to be made should be stated explicitly. In doing so, however, it should be recognised that the resulting cost estimate is not the avoidable (or marginal) cost of producing the output concerned.

The discussion above is particularly relevant to two policy problems: the peak and the withdrawal of unremunerative services. Both have been the subject of empirical studies and can best be analysed through discussion of the methodology and results of these studies.

EMPIRICAL ANALYSIS – PEAK COSTING

Costing would not be so complex if demand for transport were evenly spread over time, but unfortunately this is not the case with many transport services. For example, the demand for bus travel is greater at certain times of the day than at others largely because most trips to and from work and school are made between 0700 and 0900 hours and 1600 and 1800 hours. Table 4.1 shows the distribution of weekday passengers carried by an urban bus operator over the day. It can be seen that almost 40 per cent of passengers are carried in the four busiest hours (0700 – 0900 and 1600 – 1800) and over 54 per cent in the six busiest (0700 – 1000 and 1500 – 1800). Demand in the peak hour is over twice the level between the peaks. A similar pattern can be seen for many train services, particularly in urban areas, while demand for railway freight services is often concentrated into night hours. Another peak is seasonal demand for some coach, train and airline services,

Table 4.1 *Percentage distribution of bus passengers throughout the day and number of buses in service – weekdays.*

Hour	*% of passengers*	*Buses in service*
Pre 0600	0.4	185
0600–0700	1.8	689
0700–0800	7.6	1,096
0800–0900	11.6	1,119
0900–1000	6.1	1,055
1000–1100	5.7	568
1100–1200	5.6	490
1200–1300	5.4	490
1300–1400	5.9	490
1400–1500	5.5	515
1500–1600	8.3	854
1600–1700	12.2	1,079
1700–1800	8.4	1,079
1800–1900	3.5	779
1900–2000	3.2	492
2000–2100	3.1	458
2100–2200	2.7	442
2200–2300	2.3	435
2300–2400	0.7	435
All day	100.00	

services, concentrated in the summer months because of the pattern of holiday traffic. Hibbs (1971b) has discussed its impact on the coach industry.

Peaks in demand are not peculiar to transport. For instance, the daily demand for coal is higher in winter than in summer; but whereas the coal industry can produce coal at much the same rate all year, storing any surplus in summer when supply exceeds demand and selling from stock in winter when demand exceeds supply, transport cannot be stored. So if peak demands are to be met, enough capacity (i.e. buses, trains, railway track) must be installed to meet the maximum level of demand.

Table 4.1 also shows for the same operator the pattern of buses in service during weekdays. Although about 500 buses are enough to meet off-peak demands, an extra 600 or so are needed solely for peaks and only operate for 4 hours a day while the rest of the fleet operates for about 16 hours a day.

As there are no grounds for believing that the annual cost of providing a bus varies with the time it is in service – for example, licence fees, basic maintenance to ensure roadworthiness and capital costs are all largely invariant with output – costs per unit of production (i.e. vehicle-hour or vehicle-mile) will be higher for the 600 peak buses than for the 500 buses running throughout the day.

While at first sight it might be thought that labour costs per vehicle-hour will be the same for all buses, the indivisibilities mentioned above mean that this is not so in practice. A bus driver must be employed for a minimum of 40 hours a week, usually divided into five 8-hour days. Thus, if he drives a bus for only 4 hours a day, labour costs per vehicle-hour will be higher than those of a man driving for 7 hours a day on an all-day bus. In fact peak bus drivers have to be paid more than the minimum 8 hours' daily pay to compensate for the inconvenience of having their working day split into two periods, one to cover each peak with a spell off duty in between. So labour cost too is higher per unit of output for peak-only buses.

The theoretical implications of the peak problem in transport have been recognised for some time (e.g. Ponsonby, 1958), but only relatively recently has any attempt been made to quantify it. Empirical work by Tyson (1971, 1972a) is among the earliest in this field in the United Kingdom.

To estimate peak costs accurately requires two stages. First, it is necessary to identify the costs of the vehicles used only at peaks. This is fairly straightforward in principle because avoidable costs can be measured, but in practice there are various complications, discussed in more detail by Tyson (1972a). For the same operator as in Table 4.1, Table 4.2 sets out the costs of the 600 peak-only buses in 1971. Although the figures are out of date the relative levels of costs are important and have probably not changed much. These 600 buses contributed 22 per cent of output (measured by bus-miles) but accounted for 34 per cent of total costs, thus confirming that their cost per unit of output was in excess of that of all-day vehicles. Costed as a group on a marginal basis it is highly unlikely these vehicles' marginal revenue would exceed their marginal costs. Tyson (1972a) gives actual calculations.

Table 4.2 *Costs of peak-only buses per year, 1971*

Cost group	*Amount (£'000)*
Running cost: 8.81 million miles @ 5.973p	526.2
Vehicle cost: 600 buses @ £3,803	2,281.8
Crew costs (includes extra time for split shifts)	1,793.0
Total	4,601.0

In attempting to estimate the total costs of peak operation account must therefore be taken of the higher unit costs of the peak-only buses. Allocation of the joint costs of buses running in the peaks and in the off-peaks is also needed. Before doing this, however, it is important to ensure, following Joy's (1964) point, that these costs really are joint costs.

Applying the avoidable cost approach to each of the three components of cost in Table 4.2 gives the following results. First, running costs vary directly with mileage and can therefore be allocated on an avoidable cost basis to peak and off-peak. Second, some crew costs will be avoidable if off-peak services are withdrawn and are thus solely off-peak costs. This applies to costs incurred at weekends, in the evenings and to some extent between peaks. Vehicle costs and the proportion of crew costs incurred during and immediately around the peaks, however, are potential joint costs. If, however, it can be argued that the operator basically exists to provide peak services and would continue to do so even if off-peak demand were negligible, these costs will clearly be opportunity costs of the peaks only and not joint costs; off-peak operation can be costed on a marginal basis. On the other hand, if it is argued that the operator will only provide the services concerned if both a peak and an off-peak demand for them exists, there will be a joint cost element. Given that many urban bus and rail operations are so highly peaked at present, the former hypothesis may be nearer the truth.

The effects on costing can be seen from Table 4.3, where the costs of peak and off-peak services are estimated on the assumptions that off-peak services are costed marginally and that joint costs are for convenience allocated between peak and off-peak operation in proportion to the time spent operating in each time period. In both cases peaks are defined as 0700–0900 and 1600–1800 hours. This table shows quite clearly that on the first basis peak services cost considerably more than they generate in revenue and that there might, for example, be a case for a price increase. It is interesting to note that, if joint costs are allocated among peak and off-peak traffics, peak services will still show a significant deficit. The most important effect, however, is on Sunday services, which break even on the first basis but show a loss of over 18 per cent on the second. This shows that determining the basis for costing has considerable significance especially when these cost and revenue comparisons could affect prices. The decision on which basis to adopt is one to be made by the operator rather than the economist, however.

General conclusions are that, no matter what costing basis is adopted, peak services are unremunerative while off-peak ones generate a significant surplus of revenue over costs. Perhaps most important of all is that

Table 4.3 *Peak and off-peak costs and revenues on two bases.*

Period	*Cost, C (£'000)*	*Revenue, R (£'000)*	*R – C (£'000)*	*R – C as % of C*
Basis A: off-peak operation costed marginally				
Weekday peak	8,121	5,774	– 2,347	28.90
Weekday off-peak	3,081	4,285	+ 1,204	39.08
Saturday	1,196	1,832	+ 636	53.18
Sunday	988	1,020	+ 32	3.24
Total	13,386	12,911	– 475	3.55
Basis B: joint costs allocated between peak and off-peak				
Weekday peak	6,601	5,774	– 827	12.53
Weekday off-peak	4,083	4,285	+ 202	4.95
Saturday	1,455	1,832	+ 377	25.91
Sunday	1,247	1,020	– 227	18.20
Total	13,386	12,911	– 475	3.55

costing on the basis of a uniform cost per mile or per hour, which does not take the peak into account, can be totally misleading and give rise to erroneous policy conclusions.

In brief, the policy conclusion that follows from the above results is that a differential between peak and off-peak bus fares may be justified on cost grounds or that some reduction in the level of peak bus services is required. This and other issues concerned with peak pricing will be discussed in Chapter 5. As far as costing is concerned, a clear understanding of the joint cost problem is needed to identify correctly the costs of peak and off-peak traffics.

EMPIRICAL ANALYSIS – THE WITHDRAWAL OF SERVICES

Another important application of cost identification concerns the withdrawal of public transport services. During the 1960s in particular many railway services were withdrawn; and while rail closures have continued on a smaller scale, since 1970 the withdrawal of bus services, especially in rural areas, has become the more important policy issue. In deciding whether to close a service a comparison must be made between costs and revenues. What is important, however, is to ensure that costs and revenues are properly defined. Costs that will be avoided and revenue that will be lost if the service is withdrawn are the relevant criteria. The problem again is correctly to identify avoidable costs, and in particular account must be taken of joint costs and indivisibilities over time. If, for example, local passenger services are to be withdrawn from a railway while freight and possibly express passenger services are to continue, most track and signalling costs will not be avoided because they will have to be incurred for the remaining services. In the accounts, however, a proportion of these costs may be allocated to the local passenger services. Similarly, the railway or bus company may be paying interest on capital expenditure incurred in the past in purchasing assets with no alternative uses (e.g. depots, bridges, tunnels). This expenditure is unaffected by the closure, assuming now that complete closure of the line is contemplated, and it is therefore irrelevant to the question of whether or not to keep the services. Other assets will have an opportunity cost because they can be put to alternative uses (e.g. buses, locomotives, carriages, stations). However, their value in this alternative use may be less than the costs of interest and depreciation allocated to them in the accounts. While accounting depreciation is usually calculated at $1/n$th of the capital cost of the asset each year, where n is the number of years over which it is being depreciated – twelve years is common for a bus – and capital cost is usually historic cost, the decline in opportunity cost over time may be at a different rate, or the assets may depreciate as a function of use rather than of time. Complications of this nature mean that accounting costs may be a very poor guide to opportunity costs and thus need to be interpreted very carefully. Howe and Mills (1960) have discussed this problem in more detail with respect to railways, and Tyson (1972b) has analysed its significance for bus services.

This type of problem with railway costs became particularly acute after 1969 when a way of allocating joint costs among services was agreed by the British Railways Board and the Department of the Environment as a basis for calculating grants on unremunerative services. Full details of the allocations were never published officially, but an outline of the problem and the system can be found in the 1967 White Paper on *Railway Policy* (Ministry of Transport, 1967). However, dramatic differences between avoidable and allocated costs came to light in several closure notices. For instance, in one service in Greater Manchester allocated costs were over £200,000 a year while avoidable costs in the first year after closure would have been £20,000, rising to about £50,000 after five years.

The increase in avoidable costs over time reveals another problem of estimating opportunity costs: the time period to be considered. If an asset such as a garage or bridge will need heavy maintenance work in, say, four years' time and revenue will be insufficient to justify the costs, avoidable cost will exceed revenue from that year onwards. In the meantime, however, so long as revenue covers avoidable cost in the three intervening years the line should stay open. Howe and Mills have pointed out that for a time British Rail was making decisions based on average avoidable costs over a five-year period rather than on the costs in each year, although this practice was subsequently changed. In any case the relevant question when the work is due is whether revenues over the next period of years will justify the expenditure.

Problems of this kind are not so severe with bus services because indivisibilities are not so great. However, a similar difficulty arises when a service operates for only part of the day. Many rural bus operations are off-peak, and because buses and crews are still needed for peak services the avoidable cost of the off-peak service is often very low indeed. It is possible that some such services could be operated literally for the costs of fuel and tyres. These problems came to light after 1970 when a number of applications for grants towards the operating losses of rural services, made under section 34 of the Transport Act 1968, were based on average and not marginal costs. Again, this has to some extent been remedied. Tyson (1972b) has discussed this issue in more detail, citing an example of a service with an allocated cost of 23.5p per mile and an opportunity cost of 4.65p.

Although not strictly the subject matter of this chapter it is interesting to conclude by mentioning that estimating the revenue that is likely to be lost by the withdrawal of a service gives rise to a similar set of problems. In particular the revenue actually collected on the service gives a poor guide because some of it may be transferred to other services; on the other hand revenue may be lost on other services also because some passengers can no longer reach them. In the long term this may hasten still further loss of revenue if a car has to be purchased, which can then be used for all trips made by bus or train and not just trips on the service withdrawn. Howe and Mills (1960) have discussed this, and White and Heels (1976) have given an interesting empirical example of a rail branch line that generates revenue for other services that is far in excess of its own operating loss.

CONCLUSIONS

The main danger is that incorrect decisions on closures will be taken and resources allocated to other services when the benefit from their continued use on the service in question exceeds avoidable costs. Considerable attention was given to these problems in rail closure cases in the 1960s, and learning from this experience decisions on rural bus service withdrawals have generally been based on better, although not ideal, estimates of avoidable costs. There is still some evidence, however, that the impact of the peak on both bus and train costs has not been fully recognised (see Transport and Road Research Laboratory, 1974).

COST FUNCTIONS

A further part of costing in transport is the identification of the relationship between cost and output, termed the cost function. This relationship can be expressed in terms of either total or average cost and, of course, the marginal cost function can be derived from it. Given the significance of costs in determining the supply of transport, this is an important area of analysis. The resumé of elementary theory in the opening paragraphs of this chapter, however, points to a major difficulty, namely, that output is only one factor affecting costs, others being the costs of inputs, the efficiency of the firm and its objectives. A simple analysis is therefore likely to be misleading. Fortunately, using the statistical tool of multiple regression analysis it is possible to deal with this difficulty and to identify separately the effects on costs of each factor. Yeomans (1968) has discussed the technique in more detail. At the policy level cost functions can help to answer questions on scale economies. If the cost function exhibits economies of scale (costs per unit of output decline as output rises), up to a certain output level there may be a case for forming larger undertakings. If at the same time the cost function is U-shaped and diseconomies of scale exist beyond a certain level of output, it will be important to identify this point and to pursue a much more cautious policy on undertaking size. This has been a particularly critical question in UK transport policy, which, as already outlined, ever since the Railways Act 1921 has tended to create larger transport undertakings by statute.

Two approaches may be made to the problem of estimating the cost–output relationship in practice: time series and cross-section. The time series approach involves taking observations of the cost and output of one undertaking over a long time period, often several years, to establish the relationship between the two. Several difficulties can arise. First, prices may change over time, and this needs to be corrected by expressing costs at constant prices. Second, production techniques can change; examples in transport have been the changes from petrol to diesel buses and from steam to diesel and electric trains. Third, output variations may be so small relative to total output that a satisfactory statistical relationship cannot be established.

In response to the latter problem in particular the cross-section approach is often adopted. This takes observations at one time period of a large number of operators with different output levels. Again there are difficulties, the most important being that factors other than size may vary among operators and lead to cost variations as well. These problems can usually be solved, using multiple regression analysis, by taking these other variations (e.g. factor prices) into account.

These studies have been made in many branches of the transport industry. Lee and Steedman (1970) carried out an analysis of forty-four municipal bus operators in the United Kingdom to see if economies of scale existed. This comprises an examination of factors affecting each component of total costs per vehicle-mile operated: power costs, repair and maintenance costs, traffic operation costs and management costs. Their main conclusion is that no evidence of economies or diseconomies of scale existed except for repair and maintenance costs, which statistically gave the poorest results anyway; here they found that the curve was an inverted U-shape, being lowest for very small and very large undertakings. Of the many factors that did affect the variation in costs among operators, most (e.g. average speeds, fuel consumption, labour prices) were beyond the immediate control of the operators themselves. Indeed, the only significant factor affecting costs that operators could influence themselves was the proportion of one-man operation. However, Lee and Steedman have added a significant rider to the policy implications of their analysis. This is that their results only held within the range of operator size of their sample (i.e. about 30–1,600 buses). Since their work was carried out much larger undertakings have been formed, some, for example, with up to 3,000 buses in their fleets. The existence of economies or diseconomies of scale in such large concerns at this range has not yet been investigated empirically. For a great range of outputs, however, the cost function shows constant returns to scale.

Studies of the bus industry in India and the United States by Koshal (1970, 1972) conclude that there are constant returns to scale in both cases once exogenous factors of the type discussed above have been removed. Evidence on cost functions in road haulage in the United Kingdom is somewhat conflicting. Harrison (1963) has given the best summary, while the Department of the Environment (1972) has presented the results of another study, which found that smaller operators appeared to have some cost advantages over larger firms but that these might have been because the owner's own time spent running the business was not fully costed. In India Koshal (1972) found that there was evidence of economies of scale, provided that operation was restricted to distances below 600 miles, and that benefits might be obtained from merger into larger undertakings.

CONCLUSIONS

The costing of transport services needs to be analysed at two levels: the undertaking as a whole, and the individual traffics that it provides. At the former level most studies have found constant returns to scale in bus operation and hence constant average and marginal costs. In road haulage Indian experience indicates economies of scale, but studies in the United Kingdom have been less conclusive. However, there is no evidence that considerable scale economies exist in the United Kingdom.

At the level of individual traffics the behaviour of costs is much more complex. Largely because of the numerous indivisibilities discussed earlier marginal costs and average costs diverge. In some cases it is possible to provide extra output at fairly low marginal cost (e.g. off-peak bus and train services), while in others marginal costs are very high and in excess of average costs because of poor capacity utilisation (e.g. peak services). In public transport at least it is usually possible to accommodate extra demand without increasing output. For these reasons costing needs to be carried out on a specific basis, which must take into account the policy decisions being based on it. No simple functions that characterise the elementary expositions of supply theory exist, and transport costing at this level is a complex issue.

It is clear, however, that the analysis of transport costs at both levels can help the policy problems posed at the start of the chapter. Empirical studies discussed in the chapter have shown that a case for higher peak than off-peak bus and rail fares can be made on cost grounds, that costs saved by bus and railway service closures can easily be wrongly estimated, particularly in the short run, and that little case can be made for reducing costs by creating larger bus and road haulage concerns.

CHAPTER 5

Pricing Policies in Transport

INTRODUCTION

Prices play a key role in resource allocation. They are particularly important in transport because it is an intermediate good used in the production of almost every other commodity in the economy. The subject will be treated in this chapter as follows. First, pricing principles will be discussed; then current pricing policies in the transport sector will be analysed, making a distinction between the pricing of road space and public transport pricing. With each, current practice will be compared with the principles, and the implications of some suggested modifications will be examined. Finally, some of the more complex problems of finding the best relationship between the prices of public and private transport will be analysed. Attention will be concentrated throughout on matters affecting economic efficiency, and in consequence aspects such as the effects of alternative pricing policies on income distribution will be given only passing mention.

PRICING PRINCIPLES

THE RELATIONSHIP BETWEEN PRICES AND OBJECTIVES

Pricing is a means to an end and must be related to an objective. In the elementary theory of the firm a pricing rule is derived from the profit maximisation objective. However, as relatively little transport is provided by private enterprise, with the exception of some road haulage, this aim will not suffice for the transport sector; and because in addition governments play a considerable role in providing transport (discussed in Chapter 8), a more appropriate objective is one based on the aim of efficient resource allocation, which will be taken as maximising the benefit to the community derived from the goods and services that transport resources produce. In effect this means choosing to produce a particular set of commodities, and in this process pricing has a vital role.

DERIVING THE PRICING RULE

Only a simple account will be given of the derivation of a pricing rule from this economic efficiency objective (for further analysis see Millward, 1971). In Figure 5.1 *CD* is a demand curve, which can be interpreted as showing how much consumers are willing to pay for each unit of the commodity. If consumers are assumed to be rational, willingness to pay must equal the benefit derived from each unit; so total benefit is given by area *OCD*. *EF* is the marginal cost curve, the area under which represents total costs. If output is set at *OA* units, total benefit minus total cost will be maximised, and this output could be brought about in the market by setting price equal to *OB* (i.e. equal to marginal cost). The pricing principle is therefore that price should equal marginal cost if the efficiency objective is to be attained.

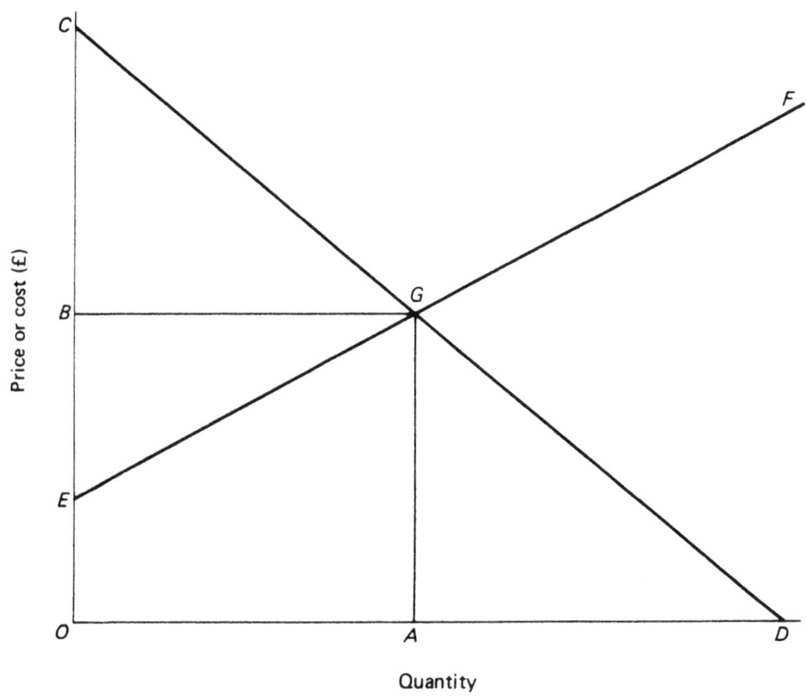

Figure 5.1 *The determination of price*

IMPLICIT ASSUMPTIONS AND SOME COMPLICATIONS

The marginal-cost pricing principle, however, rests on several assumptions, not all of which are explicit. Because of its importance in the transport sector it is necessary briefly to set these out although they cannot be discussed at length. A much more thorough treatment of this material can be found in Millward (1971).

The first implicit assumption is that the only costs and benefits involved are those borne by producers and consumers (i.e. those contained in the demand and marginal cost curves). In transport, however, this is frequently untrue because transport services impose costs and confer benefits to a significant extent on 'third parties'. For example, aircraft impose noise costs on non-users, particularly people living near airports; and commuter railways confer benefits on road users by taking some traffic from roads and thus relieving congestion. As costs and benefits to the whole community are the basis of the pricing principle such third-party costs and benefits (called *externalities* in technical terms) must be included. This is achieved by the principle that price should equal marginal social cost, social costs being defined as including externalities.

A second problem concerns income distribution and arises particularly if one pricing policy is being changed for another – a proposal found frequently in transport where existing pricing policies do not accord with the principle. If individuals each consume differing amounts of the service whose price is changed, their real incomes will be affected differently, and the distribution of real income among them will change. Such a change in income distribution may conflict with the community's objectives for income distribution even though resources will be allocated more efficiently. This had led to suggestions that prices in the transport sector should not equal marginal social costs. An alternative view, held by us, is that adverse effects on income distribution should be corrected by other and more efficient means (e.g. taxation policy). This issue has been discussed extensively in the 1976 Consultative Document (Department of the Environment, 1976).

Third is the problem of what pricing rules to follow in transport if marginal social-cost pricing is not applied in other sectors of the economy. In principle marginal social-cost pricing will only achieve the objective if applied everywhere; and if this is not the case, it will not necessarily be correct to apply it only to transport. This is a very complex issue and has been discussed more fully by Millward (1971 chapter 4). Our intuitive judgement is that the benefits within the transport sector of introducing the principle outweigh potential losses in other sectors.

Next is the problem of long-run and short-run marginal costs, first met in Chapter 4 when discussing the effect of time on avoidable costs. Which should be used as the basis for prices in circumstances where there will be a large difference between them? This has been debated at great length by economists without a unique solution emerging (see Turvey, 1968, Chapters 1 and 2). In general long-run marginal costs seem more appropriate as a basis for transport prices, because in this way it can be ensured that consumer benefits from expensive long-life assets equal or exceed the value of the resources used in providing them. This is especially relevant when the replacement of an asset or an expansion of the transport network is being considered. On the other hand there are very important exceptions to this rule, which will be discussed below.

Finally, the pricing principle is complicated by the fact that transport is supplied in larger units than those in which it is demanded. The strict application of the rule would mean that the first passenger on a train or bus would pay the whole costs of running the vehicle while everyone else would pay only the costs of printing his own ticket. Some modification of this is needed in public transport at least.

A MODIFIED PRINCIPLE

Taking this into account a modified pricing principle for the transport sector could be that prices should be set so that the beneficiaries from a service pay the long-run marginal social costs of providing it and the structure of prices reflects the structure of costs. The first part of this takes into account externalities and the indivisibility problem discussed above. The second part needs clarification but means, for example, that, if costs are related to the distance over which a service operates, fares should also be distance based. The application of the principle therefore means that the long-run marginal costs should be compared with some measure of benefit. This could in the first instance be marginal revenue from the users of the service, or it could be an assessment of social benefits. It should be appreciated that the application of the principle relies heavily on the choice of an appropriate output unit to which to apply it. Following the discussion in Chapter 4 care should be taken to avoid aggregation that results in two distinct products being considered together.

There are exceptions. For example, if revenues or benefits fail to cover long-run marginal costs, the service should be discontinued. In this case the appropriate question will be: 'Do benefits cover the costs that could be avoided in the short run if the service were withdrawn?'

If benefit does exceed short-run marginal cost, the best pricing policy will clearly be one based on recovering short-run marginal costs, for in this way no one will be prevented from using the service who obtains from it a benefit that is greater than avoidable costs. Long-run marginal costs are relevant to the question of whether to disinvest in the service. Similarly, if demand exceeds supply, charging more than a policy based on long-run marginal cost will be appropriate. In this situation price is being used primarily as a rationing device, but the benefit/revenue and long-run marginal cost comparison is being used to determine whether capacity expansion is justified. Despite these necessary complications, however, the principle does give a guide against which pricing policies in the transport sector can be evaluated, and it is to this task that most of the rest of the chapter will be devoted.

THE PRICING OF ROAD SPACE

INTRODUCTION

In 1982 roads carried 94 per cent of passenger-miles and 59 per cent of freight ton-miles in Great Britain (Department of Transport, 1983). The price of road space is a significant proportion of the costs of road traffic. For private cars the only other costs are the direct ones of providing and operating the cars. Thus, discussing the pricing of road space automatically involves analysing much of the price of transport by private cars, which alone accounted for 80 per cent of passenger-miles in 1975.

THE EXISTING PRICING SYSTEM

Strictly speaking there is no pricing system for road use in the United Kingdom. Instead, road users pay taxes as a condition of using roads, and the roads themselves are provided and maintained by central and local government funds. The rates of tax are not set with any pricing principle in mind, nor is the expenditure on roads related to income from road user taxation. In 1982/83 road user taxation accounted for 11 per cent of government tax revenue while expenditure on roads comprised 6.5 per cent of public expenditure. However, these taxes can be regarded as a surrogate pricing system, and as any modification is likely to be based on them or compared with them they merit examination in this context.

Road user taxes fall into four groups – fuel taxes, vehicle taxes, expenditure taxes and miscellaneous charges – and each will be discussed in turn.

Fuel taxes. These comprise excise duty of 74p per gallon and value-added tax (VAT) at 15 per cent: 24p per gallon. The only exception concerns fuel used by bus operators, who obtain a rebate for most of their operations.

Tax paid is a function of mileage travelled and fuel consumption, which in turn depends on average speeds, type of vehicle, etc. For illustrative purposes Table 5.1 shows tax paid per mile by vehicles of different engine sizes. These figures are averages based on a range of operating conditions, and in general the lower the speed the higher the fuel consumption and hence the higher fuel tax per mile. Receipts from fuel duty were £4,881 million in 1982.

Table 5.1 *Fuel tax paid per mile by various vehicles.*

Vehicle type	*Tax (p per mile)*
1,000-cc car	4.04
1,500-cc car	4.73
2,000-cc car	5.34
3-ton lorry	4.81
5-ton van	6.46
22-ton lorry	14.77

Vehicle excise duty. This must be paid before a vehicle can be used on the roads. Although licences are issued for four or twelve months the effective minimum period is one month because refunds are given if a licence is surrendered. Rates of duty in 1984 are given in Table 5.2. From this it can be seen that, while the duty paid by a private car is invariant with its size, other vehicles (e.g. lorries, buses) are taxed according to size rather than at a flat rate. Total receipts in 1982 were £1800 million.

Expenditure taxes. These comprise VAT and car tax, which replaced purchase tax in April 1973. They apply to new cars, and in addition VAT is charged on dealers' margins on second-hand cars and on car servicing etc. Rates in 1984 were 10 per cent for car tax and 15 per cent for VAT. Receipts from car tax totalled £570 million in 1982 while VAT receipts totalled £2445 million, including the tax levied on petrol and diesel fuel (already discussed under fuel taxes). Import duties are payable on imported vehicles and yielded £87 million in 1982.

Table 5.2 *Vehicle excise duties, May 1984*

Vehicle type		*Duty p.a. (£)*	
Private cars		90	
Goods vehicles		*Without trailer*	*With trailer*
General haulage vehicle up to	16 cwt unladen	90	90
	2 tons unladen	171	171
	6 tons unladen	445	445
	10 tons unladen	951	951
Probable goods vehicle of	15,000 kg gross		
	2 axle rigid	850	970
	3 axle rigid	340	460
	4 axle rigid	340	460
	2 axle articulated	590	n/a
	3 axle articulated	440	n/a
36,000 kg	2 axle articulated	3,100	n/a
Buses and taxis			
Seating capacity: up to	20	45	
	30	54	
	40	63	
	50	72	
	60	81	
	70	90	
	80	99	

Other charges. Specific charges are made for services such as driving tests, statutory vehicle examinations and the issue of driving licences. Compared with other sources their contribution to the total is negligible and they will not be considered further as part of the charging system for road use because their levels are meant to be set so as to offset the costs of the services concerned.

Summary. In the analysis of road user taxes and road pricing it is usual to regard only fuel taxes and vehicle excise duties as relevant. VAT and car tax are omitted because it has been argued that, as they are only paid when a vehicle is purchased, they have little or no effect on the use made of it (Ministry of Transport, 1968). Furthermore, as Prest (1963) has argued, motorists as a group must expect to pay some tax *per se* in the same way as other groups of consumers. To the extent that this is so these taxes can be considered to be this 'pure' tax element.

What remains as a surrogate or potential road charge is a two-part tariff comprising fixed and variable charges. The fixed charge (i.e. excise duty) is a payment for admission to the road system and is determined by vehicle size and type, while the variable charge (i.e. fuel taxes) a payment for the use of that system. To see how closely this corresponds to the pricing principles that users should cover long-run marginal costs and that the structure of prices should reflect the structure of costs it is necessary to consider the structure of the costs of providing and using the road system.

THE STRUCTURE OF COSTS

While the principles of road pricing have been discussed for many years and the present system has been criticised, little attention was given to costs until the mid-1960s. The best summary is the work published by the Ministry of Transport (1968) and updated by the Department of the Environment (1976), in which costs have been classified into three groups as follows:

(1) User costs. These comprise vehicle-operating costs and are almost wholly private costs although they are affected by congestion, which will be discussed below. With this exception it can be assumed that, so long as they are perceived correctly, journeys will only be undertaken if benefits exceed user costs.
(2) Public costs. These are the costs of providing the road system.
(3) Community costs. These in effect are externalities, i.e. costs imposed by road users on non-users (e.g. noise, pollution and accident costs).

Public costs and community costs. In this analysis, which is concerned with all the costs of road use, it is the latter two categories that are of particular interest, together with any elements of user costs that are imposed by one group of road users on others and that do not enter the cost function of those imposing the costs. Table 5.3 gives estimates of public costs for 1975/76.

In addition to these costs are externalities such as accident, noise and pollution costs. Estimates of their magnitude are difficult to obtain although the Department of Transport has estimated that the total cost of road accidents in 1975 was at least £816 million. A proportion of this was borne by road users themselves through insurance premiums and personal losses. However, there is a substantial element of externality involved. Problems of valuing road accident costs (Dawson, 1971) are much less severe than those of valuing pollution and noise costs, for

Table 5.3 *Public road costs at 1975/76 price levels.*

Cost	*£ million*[a]
Capital: new construction and improvement[b]	1,120
Maintenance and cleansing	525
Lighting	70
Police and courts	80
Total	1,785

Source: Department of the Environment (1976, Volume II, p. 108).

Notes:

(a) Costs are averages of expenditures between 1973/74 and 1975/76 at 1975/76 price levels.

(b) Capital costs are actual capital expenditures rather than a capital charge based on the value of the road system.

which only approximate estimates have ever been produced. These have been discussed in Watkins (1972).

Having classified costs the next stage is to try to determine how they vary so that a comparison can be made between the structure of costs and that of charges. This subject has been treated extensively by the Ministry of Transport (1968). In broad principle the Ministry decided to allocate costs on the basis of cost responsibility, which meant that, if specific elements of any cost category were incurred for a particular vehicle class, those costs would be allocated to that class alone while the remaining costs would be shared among all vehicles according to road use. This is effectively the approach taken to the joint cost issue in the case of road track costs.

In detail, the summary of the conclusions of the 1968 study, updated by subsequent research on cost responsibility, is as follows:

Capital costs. Once incurred these costs are no longer avoidable and are not strictly relevant to pricing, but when a new road is being planned they are relevant. It is thought that 17.5–20 per cent of capital costs are incurred solely because of large vehicles (i.e. lorries over 3.5 tons laden weight and buses) as such vehicles require roads and bridges to be built to higher standards than would otherwise be necessary. The rest of capital costs are a function of expected traffic flows and are usually allocated among vehicle classes on the basis of mileage run weighted by the amount of road space occupied per vehicle. (This is measured in *passenger car units* (p.c.u.), which are meant to express the contribution of vehicles to traffic flow on a standard basis. For example, a bus is regarded as the equivalent of three cars.)

Maintenance costs. These depend on three characteristics of traffic using the road: vehicle mileage, total weight of vehicles and the fourth power of their axle weights (Department of the Environment, 1976).

Lighting costs. These are difficult to allocate because lighting benefits both road users and non-users, and it is impossible to exclude non-users from using it. Lighting is therefore a 'public good' (see Millward, 1971, for a general discussion of public goods), and its costs are not relevant to pricing policy.

Police costs. Again these are difficult to allocate on a cost responsibility basis although in the Ministry of Transport (1968) study it was thought that most police costs were incurred in respect of light vehicles. Table 5.4 gives a breakdown of a cost responsibility allocation for 1975/76.

Accident costs. These vary with the severity of the accident, but accident rates for each vehicle type appear to be a function of vehicle-mileage and the location of the journey.

The implications of the above analysis for road pricing can be summarised as follows if the principle set out at the beginning of the chapter is accepted. Costs that vary directly with road use by individual vehicles and that could therefore be avoided if a journey were not made could be recovered most efficiently by a charge directly related to road use. As such costs *also* vary with vehicle type, maintenance costs being the best example, the charge should vary in this way too. Fuel duty seems to be a somewhat crude method of raising these charges. The amount paid for a vehicle's journey, as already discussed, varies with vehicle size, engine efficiency and traffic conditions and is unlikely to equal marginal cost. Even before the question of congestion and other externalities is raised there are already grounds for criticising fuel duties as a pricing mechanism.

Given the different rates of involvement in accidents among vehicle types, which are reflected, for example, in differences in insurance premiums, any charges for the externality element of accident costs would also vary with vehicle type and distance, but rates should vary from place to place. Research discussed in Watkins (1972) has also indicated that charges for noise costs would vary with mileage, vehicle type and location, which is important because the numbers affected by a given noise level depend on the density of development and physical topography, which vary from place to place.

Costs not varying directly with vehicle use, because they are a function either of vehicle numbers or of the joint costs of all vehicles or

Table 5.4 *Department of Transport allocation of public road costs, 1975/76.*

Category		*Amount (£ million)*	%
Capital expenditures		1,120	100
New construction:	15% to vehicles over 3.5 tons	160	14
	85% to all vehicles on p.c.u. basis	920	82
Car parks:	100% to cars	40	4
Current expenditures		665	100
Maintenance and police:	89% to all vehicles	590	
	of which:		
	21% on mileage basis	125	19
	36% on p.c.u. basis	210	32
	10% on weight basis	60	9
	33% on axle weight basis	195	29
	11% to pedestrians	75	11

Source: Department of the Environment (1976, Volume II, p. 111).

particular groups of vehicles, also need to be covered by the pricing system since they are part of the long-run marginal costs of providing the road system. If these costs are quantitatively significant, they can probably be recovered by a fixed charge per vehicle, varying if necessary with vehicle type, payable on a periodic basis. Thus, the existing principle of a two-part tariff is compatible with a system based on long-run marginal costs. However, much work would be needed to determine whether the amounts collected in the two elements were correct and whether variations among vehicle types were correct and a crude analysis suggests they are not.

The treatment of capital costs raises a number of problems, which have been discussed extensively in the official literature on road pricing (Ministry of Transport, 1968; Department of the Environment, 1976). The conclusion from this is, quite correctly, that capital expenditure in previous years should not be recovered as it cannot be avoided once incurred. Future capital costs are an avoidable cost of expanding the system and should be included as part of the long-run marginal cost. Ideally, they should be recovered only from vehicles benefiting from the improved sections of road as it is to accommodate these vehicles that they are incurred. In practice pricing will be more complex than this, because the level of the capital costs of many improvements or new roads is likely to be determined by the peak rate of traffic flow, and it is the vehicles comprising this flow that will benefit from the improvement. A further complication is that benefits from a road improvement are not necessarily confined to the traffic using it; traffic on other roads that lose traffic because of the improvement may also benefit. In principle such charges could be recovered as part of the variable charge, but this would necessitate a complex charging system. In practice, although not ideal in principle, capital costs might have to be recovered as part of the fixed charge, and this area is one needing much more analysis.

User costs. User costs are borne directly by users as part of their private cost functions, with one important exception: the costs caused by the delays that road users impose on one another. Although these are externalities as far as other road users are concerned, they are not externalities imposed by road users as a group on the community as a whole except perhaps in an indirect way through the prices of final goods.

Congestion costs arise from the nature of the speed–flow relationship on roads and the speed–cost relationship for vehicles. In brief, once a given level of traffic flow is exceeded the average speed of traffic

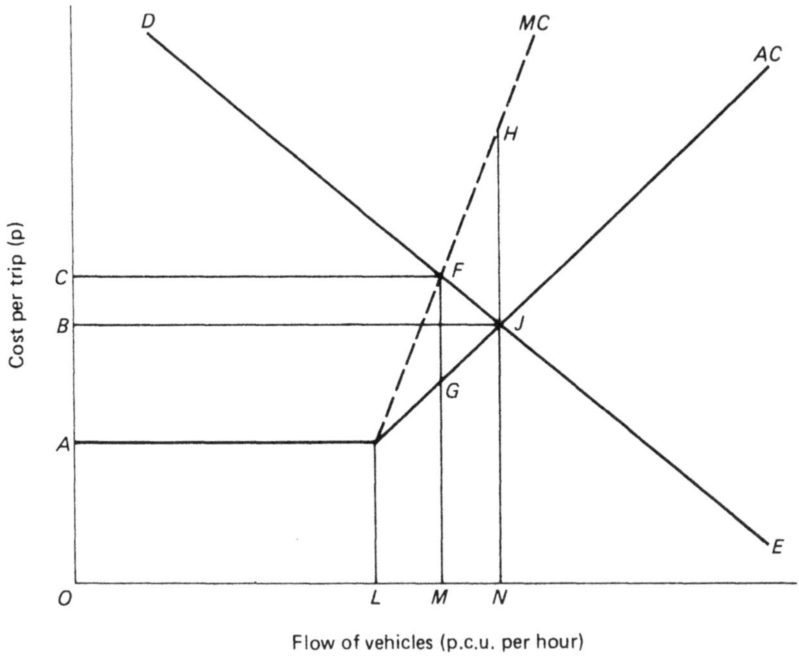

Figure 5.2 *The estimation of congestion prices*

on a road will fall. The point at which this begins and the rate of fall of speed with flow both depend on the characteristics of the road itself (e.g. its effective width). As speed falls the operating cost per mile of vehicles rises (Everall, 1968) in the range 0–45 miles per hour, and the time taken to travel a given distance also increases. Given that time has an opportunity cost and a value (see Chapter 6), two elements of the total cost of making a trip rise as speeds fall with increased traffic flows. Hence, it is possible to draw a rising average cost curve as in Figure 5.2, which must have a marginal cost curve lying above it. Figure 5.2 depicts the situation on a road of given length assuming that the vehicles using it are homogeneous, although this is merely a simplifying assumption. *DE* is the demand curve. At traffic flows up to *OL* p.c.u. per hour the cost per trip is *OA*, comprising time and operating expenses. Beyond this flow speed falls, and thus the average user cost per trip rises. In the absence of any special congestion charge flow will settle at *ON* vehicles per hour (i.e. where the demand and average user cost curves interesect) at a cost of *OB* pence per journey. However, beyond a flow of *OM* the value of the trip to the consumer, shown by the height of the demand curve, is less than marginal cost, shown by the height of the marginal cost curve.

What is happening is that at traffic flows above *OL* vehicles per hour each extra vehicle is slowing down the whole traffic flow and raising the operating costs of all the other vehicles in the flow. It is this effect on the other vehicles' costs that creates the externality. Because this does not enter the operating cost functions of the vehicles concerned it is ignored in the decision to make a trip, for which the criterion is a comparison of average costs and benefits – hence the actual flow of *ON* vehicles.

To accord with the pricing principle, price should equal marginal cost to give a flow of *OM* vehicles, at which point the marginal cost to all traffic from the last trip just equals the benefit to which it gives rise. This could be achieved by imposing an extra 'tax' of *GF* pence, thus raising the average cost curve sufficiently to achieve the optimal traffic flow. The benefit from the reduced traffic flow is the reduction in the operating cost of all the remaining vehicles, while the loss is the loss in benefit from the *MN* journeys that cannot now be undertaken. This can be measured by the difference between the areas under the marginal cost and demand curves, i.e. *MFHN* (cost reduction) minus *MFJN* (benefit loss), which equals *FHJ*.

The inclusion of congestion cost therefore means that the price charged for road space must include it in addition to covering the public costs and community costs associated with each trip. The extent of the benefits from reduced congestion depends on the shape of the demand and cost curves and the traffic flow in relation to the characteristics of the road. As the latter element will vary from time to time during the day and year as well as with location, this introduces another element into the charging system.

ALTERNATIVES TO THE PRESENT PRICING SYSTEM

In the light of the above analysis of the structure of costs it can be concluded that, if prices were to equal marginal social cost, they would vary with:

(1) vehicle type;
(2) mileage travelled;
(3) location; and
(4) the time of day and/or year.

Because of the nature of public costs in particular a two-part tariff would be justified with a charge per vehicle per time period and a charge per mile. Both elements could vary on the above bases. The existing taxation system is a two-part tariff, but it suffers from the drawback that fuel taxes in particular do not vary sufficiently on these bases to make the charge equal to the marginal social cost of any trip.

As a result several alternatives were considered by the Smeed Committee (Ministry of Transport, 1964), which was responsible for the conclusion in the above paragraph on the suitability of existing taxes. After rejecting simple solutions based on modifications to existing taxes (e.g. higher fuel taxes in urban areas) the Committee considered two supplements to it (i.e. parking charges and supplementary licences) and one alternative (i.e. direct charging).

Parking charges. In principle it would be possible to impose an extra parking charge in congested areas, but this would not correspond to marginal social-cost pricing for several reasons. First, the charge would not vary with the distance travelled on congested roads. The car travelling 2 miles would be charged the same as that travelling 10 miles. Second, traffic not parking (e.g. through traffic and delivery vehicles) would escape altogether. Third, it could encourage the practice of cruising around rather than parking, thus adding to congestion. Finally, there would be problems of applying the tax to parking facilities that are not open to public use. However, the possibility of extending local authority control of parking supply to privately owned car-parking facilities, other than those associated with residences, has been raised in the 1976 Consultation Document on transport policy (Department of the Environment, 1976) and is likely to merit further attention in future as part of an alternative means of traffic restraint. A consultation document on this was issued in 1977. The Smeed Committee estimated that a parking charge would only give about 40 per cent of the net benefits of a full road-pricing system.

Supplementary licences. This is a system whereby an extra licence is purchased on a daily basis in order to permit entry to specific areas. Through traffic is therefore included in the scheme. It still fails to vary the charge in accordance with distance travelled in the area concerned, unless a very complex zonal system is used. At this point, however, administrative costs start to eat into the benefits from the scheme.

Thomson (1967) has discussed the feasibility of parking charges and daily licences in central London and estimated the charges necessary for both schemes, suggesting a supplementary parking charge of about 4p per hour or a daily licence fee of 30p per day as optimal for central London at 1964 price levels. The latter, however, would provide over twice the net benefit of the former, even if it could be applied to all parking spaces including privately owned ones.

Direct charging. Two methods of direct charging for road use have been proposed. In both the charge varies directly with distance travelled, and rates could be made to vary with time, place and vehicle type. The first comprises a meter mechanism in the vehicle, not unlike a taxi-meter, which would count the number of 'units' consumed in an area. Each 'unit' would be either a journey over a specific length of road or a period spent stationary. The price would vary with time and place by altering the length of road or period allowed per unit. The meter would either work on a prepayment system or be read periodically like gas and electricity meters with accounts sent in arrears. Its main disadvantage would be the possibility of fraud, given that the meter is in the vehicle and would require manual activation.

The second system comprises an electronic identification disc attached to each vehicle and a series of receptor loops placed under the roadway. The distance between loops could vary from road to road, and at uncongested times some of them could be switched off thus allowing price to vary with location and time. Each time a loop was passed the identification signal from the car would be stored in a computer, and the charge would be based on the number of loops crossed. In many ways this is akin to the present system used for charging for telephone services. Although such a system would be costly to introduce throughout Great Britain's 211,000 miles of road, most of the benefits would be derived from its application to a comparatively small proportion of these in urban areas. The Transport and Road Research Laboratory has worked on both the technical and economic problems of direct charging. A summary of its work and of alternatives to the present pricing system can be found in Maycock (1972).

With direct charging, therefore, prices could be set equal to marginal social costs for all trips in urban areas. Although the costs of introduction would be considerable so too would be the benefits, particularly when extra road capacity was either an unfeasible or a prohibitively expensive alternative to traffic congestion.

SUMMARY AND FUTURE PROSPECTS

The main conclusions of the discussion of road pricing are:

(1) The present system of vehicle and fuel taxes does not ensure that the price paid equals the marginal social cost of individual trips. It

may be argued that it was never intended to do this, but it even has serious shortcomings as a way of recovering the costs of providing the road system if allocated on a cost responsibility basis. In the 1976 Consultation Document the Department of the Environment has shown that in 1975/76 the ratio of revenues from taxes, excluding car tax, to public costs varied from 2:1 for private cars used for non-business purposes to 0.8:1 for buses and goods vehicles weighing over 30 cwt unladen (Department of the Environment, 1976, Volume II, p. 112). For heavy goods vehicles over 30 tons in weight the ratio drops to 0.6:1. While it is not suggested that the ratios should be equal among all classes of traffic or equal to unity, the disparity does indicate that even at this broad level the cost–revenue relationship varies. If costs have been identified accurately, the implication is that the prices determining revenue (i.e. the tax rates) merit examination and adjustment.

(2) Of the alternatives the most promising (i.e. direct charging) is technically the most complex and politically the most sensitive.

Official interest in road pricing appears to be waning. The House of Commons Expenditure Committee reporting on urban transport in 1973 was not very enthusiastic about direct charging (House of Commons, 1972, Volume I). In the 1976 Consultation Document the Department of the Environment has recognised the case in principle, but in practice it has considered that changes in the existing taxation system should be used to help to equalise the ratios of revenue to the cost of road provision, that charges on heavy goods vehicles should be increased to cover environmental costs and that traffic congestion should be dealt with not by pricing but by direct restraint using (e.g. bus priorities, control of parking provision, banning cars from central areas). These schemes suffer from many of the criticisms of parking charges and supplementary licences, but they might at least offer improvement on the present situation in the short term when 'road pricing and supplementary licensing are too complex and too expensive to be justifiable for most cities, at least in the next decade' (Department of the Environment, 1976, Volume I, p. 42).

PUBLIC TRANSPORT FARES

In the United Kingdom buses are more important than railways as a means of public transport. Their respective shares of passenger-mileage in 1975 were 12 and 8 per cent, and in urban areas except London this difference is more marked. In Greater Manchester, for example, passenger-mileage in 1982/83 was 913 million while by rail it was only 150 million. Bus fares, however, have received less attention in the literature than rail fares, and to correct this imbalance most space in this section will be devoted to them.

PRESENT FARES POLICIES

To understand fully the rationale of present pricing systems it is necessary to appreciate the history of and the institutional constraints surrounding the bus industry, a full account of which can be found in Hibbs (1975). It will suffice for present purposes to know that bus fares are controlled by statute (discussed briefly in Chapter 8) and that both operators and the authorities controlling fares favour a single set of fares throughout a bus operator's area or, at most, two or three scales. This, coupled with the fact that such control has prevented bus operators from maximising profits, has meant that they have pursued a form of average cost pricing.

As discussed above, the strict application of the marginal social-cost pricing principle is not possible because of imbalances between the units of supply and demand. Any charge must include some degree of averaging, and the question to be debated is how much. The answer favoured by current practice is to have a single scale of fares chosen in such a way as to ensure that the total revenue for the whole undertaking equals the total accounting costs. Fares charged for individual passengers vary with distance although this relationship is not direct, fare per mile falling as distance travelled increases. It is unusual for different fares scales to be applied on different routes or at different times of day by an operator, and where they are the differences are unrelated to cost.

ALTERNATIVES

Research by Tyson and others has shown that this fares policy fails to meet the first part of the pricing principle: that benefits to the users of each product, measured by revenue, should cover long-run marginal cost. In practice the users of peak services do not meet the costs of providing them while the users of off-peak services more than do so. This situation also applies to individual routes (see Tyson, 1972b). The surplus from one route or time period is used to finance the loss on others – a practice known as cross-subsidisation.

From a resource allocation standpoint cross-subsidisation is inefficient. Passengers in the off-peak period, for example, are being denied services that would yield benefits that were greater than their resource costs, while in the peak services are being provided whose benefits are less than their resource costs. Hence, some improvement in the ratio of benefits to costs would be achieved if resources were switched from peak to off-peak. Cross-subsidisation has also been criticised on other grounds by, among others, Hibbs (1971a) and Ponsonby (1969). They have argued, for instance, that it is undemocratic in that those who cross-subsidise are neither consulted nor represented, and it can also be argued that it diverts managements' attention from the individual parts of their undertakings. This is reflected in the fact that the costing of individual bus routes has only been developed since 1970.

To eliminate cross-subsidies a different approach to pricing should be adopted by the bus industry. Differential fares for peak and off-peak operation would be needed and probably route differentials as well. Some experiments by, for example, Greater Manchester Transport and London Transport have shown that at least peak and off-peak differentials are feasible.

The relationship between peak and off-peak fares would depend, first, on the marginal costs of peak and off-peak services and on price elasticities of demand. The price elasticity of demand for bus services has received some attention in the last five years, and recent work has been summarised by Bly (1976). Research by Tyson (1975a) in Greater Manchester has revealed that, in response to differential peak and off-peak fares, peak demand is relatively insensitive to price; also, from observing the reaction of total revenue to reduced off-peak fares he found that the price elasticity of demand of off-peak traffic was almost unity. Thus, a deficit on peak operations could be eliminated by a fares increase while a surplus in the off-peak could probably be eliminated by a fares reduction. Tyson's original study of peak costs (1971) concludes that an increase of 20 per cent in peak fares, with constant off-peak fares, would be needed to eliminate the cross-subsidisation and to meet the first part of the pricing principle. In Greater Manchester in 1971 an increase of about 35 per cent on top of the existing differentials of 16–25 per cent would have been necessary, and the figure for many urban operators is probably similar.

The second part of the pricing principle concerns the relationship between the structure of prices and the structure of costs. In this respect the bus industry's policy is much closer to the principle. Although fares are distance related the indirect nature of the relationship means that fares scales can be represented by a fare per trip and a fare per mile travelled – a two-part tariff in fact. Thus, in 1983 fares in Greater Manchester could be represented by the relationship:

$$\text{fare} = 21.4 \text{ per trip} + 5.8 \text{ per mile}$$

This gives a predicted fare of 44 for a 4-mile trip compared with an actual fare of 46, showing that actual fares are not always exactly on the scale. This reflects the structure of the costs of carrying individual passengers because some costs vary directly with route lengths (i.e. are related to passenger journey lengths) and others are invariant with passengers carried or vary more with passenger numbers. Fare collection costs enter the latter group. Whether the balance between the two elements is the right one, however, is open to doubt. Research in Dublin (National Prices Commission, 1973) has indicated that the fare per mile was likely to be too low to allow the marginal costs of route extensions to be covered. In this case relatively minor alterations to the existing system would have been needed to conform to the principle.

Finally, there is the suggestion that price should equal the short-run marginal costs of individual passengers' journeys (Turvey and Mohring, 1975), comprising the costs of the ticket and of stopping the bus to allow passengers to get on and off. Even if, as Turvey and Mohring have suggested, delays imposed by such stops on passengers already on the bus were also included – they are a form of congestion cost – fares would be very low indeed. While this would optimise the use of existing resources, one feature of the bus industry is that in a relatively short time (i.e. less than a year) long run adjustments in output can be made by varying the levels of all factor inputs. Given this, the Turvey–Mohring principle offers little practical guidance on service levels justified in the long run, although the authors have considered this question in their paper.

To summarise the bus industry's position, the existing pricing policy is not in accord with the principle adopted for this analysis. Nor, incidentally, is it consistent with profit maximisation. To bring it closer to the principle would involve a more complex pricing system that would differentiate fares according to the costs of providing the services concerned.

As far as railways are concerned, their principal problems are joint costs and indivisibilities, which mean that long-run and short-run marginal costs can diverge considerably. Furthermore, the differences can persist for long time periods. Although a standardised pricing policy with its attendant cross-subsidisation was followed by the railways in the United Kingdom for many years, the years since 1968 have seen the emergence of price discrimination among routes, passengers and times of day and week prompted by an analysis carried out by the National Board for Prices and Incomes (1968). The objective of the discrimination is to maximise revenue from the services provided, and it takes advantage of differences in elasticities among passengers. For instance, students and pensioners who, *a priori*, would be expected to have a high price elasticity can travel on most trains at half adult fares, and numerous special tickets reduce fares for other price-sensitive groups (e.g. families travelling together). At the other end of the scale the relatively price-inelastic business-travel market is to a great extent insulated from fares reductions by confining them to second-class travel.

This still leaves railways with the problem of whether to continue a service or not. Their philosophy here is only to do so when revenue exceeds long-run marginal costs, which is consistent with the pricing principle suggested here. Joy (1971) has outlined the application of this policy to freight services.

Cross-subsidisation has nevertheless been a problem in the railway industry as well as in the bus industry. The Beeching Report (British Railways Board, 1963) gives ample evidence of this although, as shown in Chapter 4, Joy (1964) has subsequently challenged the cost base on which the calculations were made. Much cross-subsidisation was eliminated between 1963 and 1968 by the widespread closure of lines, and more has been eliminated since 1968 by specific government grants to cover losses on unremunerative but socially beneficial services under sections 20 and 39 of the Transport Act 1968. The latter payments were merged in 1974 into an overall passenger-deficit grant – not tied to specific services – under the Railways Act of that year, which again opened the door to potential cross-subsidisation on the railways.

This, however, takes the analysis into the related area of subsidies, which are better discussed as part of the final section on the relationship between public and private transport prices.

PRICING FOR TRANSPORT AS A WHOLE

The analysis of the two preceding sections has shown that for neither roads nor public transport is the suggested pricing principle currently followed. Perhaps the most serious problem is that, because the price of road space is not equal to marginal social cost, the price of private transport will diverge from this level also, and this in turn can affect the balance between private and public transport.

This is most severe where price is below marginal social cost for private transport. In this case Figure 5.2 shows that as long as demand is not completely inelastic with respect to price more private transport trips are being undertaken than would be so if price equalled marginal social cost. If some of these trips would have been made by public transport in these circumstances – implicitly assuming that the cross-elasticity of demand between the modes is non-zero – then the misallocation is compounded because public transport often adds less to road congestion per passenger-mile than private transport. The rationale of this statement should be self-evident for railways; for buses, if a bus adds as much to congestion as, say, three cars and if the cars carry two people each, congestion cost per person will be lower by bus so long as the bus has more than six passengers.

In response to this it has been argued that public transport fares should also be reduced below marginal social cost in order to remove the bias in resource allocation caused by the lack of marginal social-cost pricing. The argument has often been stated simply as a case for subsidising public transport. (Tyson, 1972b, has discussed the issues in more detail.) This was first given official recognition in the White Paper *Railway Policy* (Ministry of Transport, 1967), and subsidies to urban railways were given under the Transport Act 1968. Another part of the Act also created Passenger Transport Authorities and Executives, who were allowed to finance the bus and rail services in their areas from subsidies. Subsidies to public transport have increased substantially since 1974 and in 1975 were about £750 million (Department of the Environment, 1976).

It can be seen that these arguments at first sight run counter to those mentioned earlier in which increased peak fares were suggested. However, the main argument there was that off-peak users should not be subsidising peak fares, not necessarily that peak fares should not be subsidised (Tyson, 1977, has given fuller details of this argument). If they are to be subsidised, however, the community as a whole and not a small sector of it should meet the cost.

The case for subsidising public transport in congested areas as an alternative to road pricing rests heavily on the arguments that the cross-elasticity of demand between private and public transport is non-zero and that as a result of the policy the reduction in congestion costs will exceed the extra public-transport-operating cost. A formal model of these conditions has been developed by Sherman (1972), who has concluded that the subsidies would be beneficial in the United Kingdom in congested areas and/or at congested times. A more recent study by Glaister and Lewis (1977) concludes that in London there is a modest case for subsidies to public transport.

In the Consultation Document (Department of the Environment, 1976) public transport subsidies, particularly for bus services, have been considered much more critically. To begin with, it has there been argued that urban traffic congestion is not so serious a problem as was thought ten years ago. At that time estimates of £200–£500 million per year at 1966 price levels were being made for the economic losses resulting from congestion (Ministry of Transport, 1968). On the basis of surveys showing little difference in the average speeds of peak and off-peak traffic in urban areas, and on the implicit assumption that off-peak traffic is uncongested in the economic sense, the study concludes that benefits from reduced congestion may be measured in tens of millions of pounds rather than hundreds of millions.

The Consultation Document then analyses alternative ways of reducing congestion and broadly favours physical restraint and increased parking charges despite the theoretical objections to the latter, summarised above. Bus subsidies have not been considered to be effective in most circumstances, for two reasons. First, the cross-elasticity of demand was found to be very low indeed; although this was not studied directly the conclusions were drawn from several indirect sources (e.g. response to reduced fares experiments on buses). Second, subsidies also attract traffic to buses from other sources (e.g. walking, generated traffic); this traffic has to be carried at resource costs, which far outweigh benefits from the trip.

This analysis is consistent with many of the conclusions reached in this chapter and Chapter 4. In particular the high marginal cost of peak bus provision and the low responsiveness of peak passengers to higher fares stand out. However, the analysis in the Consultation Document apparently ignores the fact that the basis of its analysis is one in which peak bus passengers already receive substantial subsidies from other sources. Before determining whether further subsidies were justified it would have been better to analyse the consequences of removing existing subsidies and to use this situation as the base. In addition, the analysis does not consider the uses to which subsidies should be put (e.g. reduced fares, improved service quality). Finally, in considering alternative restraint measures their effects on bus-operating costs have seemingly been ignored. Clearly, further analysis is needed to justify policy action in this area.

The Consultation Document considers subsidies to urban rail services to be effective in London but not, on the whole, in provincial conurbations, largely because in the latter the railways offer an alternative mode of transport to and from work to only a minority of commuters. Even so it argues that, for long distance trips to work in London, rail has such an advantage over cars that the services could break even without subsidy by charging higher fares. However, this analysis also has shortcomings, which cannot be discussed here.

CONCLUSION

Overall, the picture is one of considerable confusion. No mode of transport currently conforms to the pricing principle. How much this affects the distribution of traffic among modes is open to question because relatively little work has been done to establish the relevant elasticities in the passenger field and even less in the sphere of freight operations. The proposals in the 1976 Consultation Document go some way towards clearing the confusion in some areas, but even here some issues have been left untouched. What policies will emerge is impossible to predict, however, and a rational pricing policy in the transport sector is doubtless a long way off.

FURTHER READING

Several sources of further reading are available. Those amplifying matters raised in the chapter have been referred to there. Others (e.g. Foster, 1975b) have discussed problems of pricing in much more detail. Munby, D. L. (1968) contains several papers on pricing problems. Beesley (1973) has analysed both subsidies and road pricing in considerable depth and provided probably the best recent survey of both issues. The much neglected area of income distribution has received attention in the journals (e.g. Richardson, 1975; Foster 1975b). Finally, the Consultation Document (Department of the Environment, 1976) includes an interesting appraisal of policy options and the results of considerable research on matters such as the allocation of track costs and their implications for pricing.

CHAPTER 6

Investment

INTRODUCTION

The importance of investment analysis is obviously critical in transport economics, for the investments are usually long lived and commonly exercise a decisive influence on the way in which communities live and grow. The essence of such analysis is the comparison of a future stream of receipts from a project with the future pattern of costs, so that a decision can be made on which of several projects is financially most attractive or whether indeed society may prefer to reject all the projects in favour of expenditure elsewhere. Whether the investment is undertaken privately by an individual or company, or employs public funds, it involves the fundamental issue of choosing allocations for scarce funds.

There are very significant differences between public and private investment criteria, but they share a common characteristic in the use of discounting methods since both public and private enterprise has to relate the value of income at some time in the future to the cost of outlays in the present. We shall therefore examine discounting techniques briefly before proceeding to consider investment analysis. Fuller expositions are readily available elsewhere (Merrett and Sykes, 1973; Bromwich, 1976).

The logic of discounting depends upon the phenomenon of compound interest. Suppose that someone invests £100 at an interest rate of 10 per cent reckoned each year. After one year he will be credited with £100 + (£100 × 10%) = £110, and after two years the amount will rise to £110 + (£110 × 10%) = £121. Knowing the original sum and the rate of interest (i.e. rate of return) we can calculate future values, S, by the formula

$$S = P(1 + r)^n$$

where P is the principal or starting amount, r is the rate of interest and n is the number of periods. Hence, from the simple two-year case it can be seen that

Principal	*Year*	$P(1+r)^n$	*Sum*
100	1	$100(1.1)^1$	110
100	2	$100(1.1)^2$	121
100	3	$100(1.1)^3$	133.1

It is of course possible to reverse the calculation. So, knowing the sum of money that we wish to accrue at a given time in the future and the rate of interest, we can calculate how much money will have to be invested currently to yield that future sum. For example, if a project will yield £110 after one year, and a further £121 after two years and a further £133.1 after three years; and if the rate of return on the project is 10 per cent, the principal or present value of each of those future sums will be £100, and the total present value of the investment will thus be £300. The formula for the calculation is

$$P = \frac{S_1}{1+r} + \frac{S_2}{(1+r)^2} + \frac{S_3}{(1+r)^3}$$

$$= \frac{110}{1.1} + \frac{121}{1.21} + \frac{133.1}{1.331} = 300$$

Thus, a series of future sums can be reduced to a present value. Alternatively, knowing P and S we can calculate a value for the rate of return, r. If r exceeds the rate that must be paid for capital in the project, the project will be profitable.

In practice investment decisions will be more complex than this, because outlays as well as returns may be necessary at different times and because of risk and uncertainty, but the discounting principle underlies any comparisons through time. The annual series of figures for net revenue (i.e. income minus costs) may be estimated and discounted by an appropriate rate of interest – usually one that represents the cost of capital to the enterprise. If the resultant net present value is positive, the project will be worthwhile to the enterprise; this is called the *net present value (NPV) method.* Alternatively, the *rate of return or yield method* may be employed by calculating the value of r that equates outlay and returns. If the value of r, shown as a percentage figure, is less than the cost of capital to the firm, the project will be rejected; but if r exceeds the cost of capital, the project will be viable.

The application of discounting methods is much simplified by electronic calculators and by the availability of discount tables, which list the factors by which a future sum must be divided to give a present value. For example, if an income of £1,000 in ten years' time were estimated and we wished to discount at 15 per cent annually, we could read off in a table of discount factors the figure 0.247, which means that the present value of £1,000 is £247.

Clearly the timing of investments and returns is critically important. Discounting, especially when high rates are used, diminishes future returns very severely. Hence, where an investment project necessitates several years of capital outlay before any returns are forthcoming it will be heavily burdened by its early capital charges. Likewise, if an investment project earns relatively low revenue in its early years but traffic and revenue build up substantially in later years, the discounted future revenue will be likely to be much less impressive than a layman would expect. High rates of discount usually militate against capital-intensive projects, especially where their gestation period is long; low rates of discount are more favourable to capital-intensive projects and to those where the generation of high levels of traffic is slow. The selection of an appropriate discount rate will be discussed later in this chapter.

COST–BENEFIT ANALYSIS

Private investment decisions involve the issues that concern the individual or firm in allocating its capital outlays. Typically, a firm of road hauliers assessing the purchase of extra trucks or a commercial airline contemplating the replacement of its jet airliners would conduct such an analysis; and if all the markets of the world were perfect, we could abdicate all of society's allocation decisions to the invisible hand, confident that the perfection of markets would yield perfection of resource allocation. However, very few markets are perfect; oligopoly and monopoly obtrude almost everywhere, price diverges from marginal cost, and in certain cases there are no effective markets at all.

Where the private investment decision seeks the optimum allocation of capital from the viewpoint of a private individual or group, cost–benefit analysis aims to secure the optimum allocation from the point of view of society as a whole, so as to maximise the social welfare function of the whole community. Since the function of public investment is to advance social welfare, cost–benefit analysis is employed in public investment decisions where market imperfections require that a wider viewpoint be adopted than that of the private profit-maximising investor. It attempts answers to a variety of questions: Is a given investment worth undertaking? Is one project preferable to another? When would be the best time to start a project or to close an existing facility? Cost–benefit analysis is the logical extension of the investment decision to take account of market imperfections and of the interests of all those people who will be affected by the decision. Clearly this makes the judgement of the full extent of benefits and costs critically important if the analysis is to have any validity, and it is by its very nature likely to be more searching than a typical private-investment decision.

PROBLEMS IN THE DISTRIBUTION OF BENEFITS

A major difference between the private investment decision and cost–benefit analysis is the nature of the beneficiaries. The profit- or growth-maximising firm is much more likely to have a unique goal with relatively little conflict of aims, but society as a whole includes people with very disparate aims. For example, the user of a motorway may wish to minimise his travel cost, but residents near urban motorways may attach much greater importance to the minimisation of traffic noise and exhaust fumes. In ideal circumstances it may be found that everybody is better off on balance (i.e. that to every individual the benefits of the investment more than compensate for the costs to him). This represents a *Pareto improvement*, where everybody is manifestly better off. In practice the outcome of the investment is unlikely to satisfy the Pareto condition, and the best that may be hoped for is potential Pareto improvement, where the gains accruing to the beneficiaries exceed the costs to the losers by a margin that is comfortable enough for the gainers to compensate the losers satisfactorily yet to remain net gainers themselves. In theory such a position might be desirable enough to warrant the investment under consideration; if some citizens experienced gains of such magnitude, society might be seen as somehow better off even if the compensation were not actually paid. Under the Hicks–Kaldor criterion an investment yielding a *potential* Pareto improvement would be justifiable even if compensation did not actually take place; but it is a politically explosive criterion, conceived against the background of debate on the repeal of the corn laws albeit almost a century after that event. It was argued that, after repeal, the gainers (i.e. consumers) could have more than compensated the losers (i.e. landlords). Moreover, the direction of the redistribution of welfare was progressive since consumers were on average poorer than landlords. It was a situation in which the Hicks–Kaldor criterion would have seemed reasonable to all but the most reactionary observers. However, the application of the Hicks–Kaldor criterion in the contemporary cost–benefit analysis of transport investment would be more likely to create regressive effects if compensation were not actually paid. As shown in the chapter on demand, travel is a function of income; it is the richer people who tend to travel most and the poor and old who travel less. Much transport investment is directed towards time saving, to which travellers impute a high monetary value. Hence, urban motorways, supersonic airliners and advanced passenger trains tend to favour travellers who are relatively wealthy but may bring little or no benefit to poorer people who do not use them. The latter, however, may lose from these innovations, either because they pay taxes that finance the introduction or operation of the innovations or because they suffer through the inherent characteristics of the innovations (e.g. traffic or aircraft noise). Similarly, subsidised urban transport schemes may often tend to favour commuters from wealthier dormitory areas at the expense of the poorer inhabitants of inner areas.

Hence, in setting out the basic rationale of cost–benefit analysis it must be conceded that there are serious problems concerning income distribution that can be critically important in the decision-making process. The economist who conducts the analysis may conclude that the investment offers a potential Pareto improvement. However, the ultimate decision is political; and if the political decision must take account of the social equity of the investment, the economist should make explicit the likely distributional consequences of the investment.

Cost–benefit analysis seeks to reduce as many of the disparate social costs and benefits to a common measurement as a means to comparison and ultimate decisions. The most convenient common measure is money, which although imperfect is a more versatile measure than it might appear at first sight. This is because the economist can measure changes in the welfare of individuals by asking them what they would be willing to pay for benefits received and what they would be willing to pay to avoid the costs, or he may infer these relative prices from the actual behaviour of consumers. Objections are sometimes raised to cost–benefit analysis on the grounds that it is a shallow and mercenary tool, but this criticism tends to be stereotyped and oversimplified as Williams (1973) has shown, although some critics (e.g. Self, 1975) have remained thoroughly sceptical. Not every item can be simply reduced to monetary terms, but it may be possible to question values by imputation. Suppose, for example, that a public investment can be confidently calculated to yield benefits of £20 million but will involve the demolition of an historic building. Then it may be asked whether the building can be valued as highly as £20 million or, possibly, whether the investment project (e.g. airport, motorway) can be marginally resited, involving a small loss of benefit yet preserving the building. However, if the decision makers refuse to acknowledge that choices are involved and that opportunity costs must be counted, the decision process will sink to a combination of slanging match and power struggle with different factions advocating policies with incommensurable outcomes. At the extremes 'progressives' or 'developers' may dismiss the value of historic features or environmental beauty, while environmentalists and preservationists may describe such factors as priceless, outweighing the undoubted positive value of public investment.

Cost–benefit analysis stresses the importance of considering all the relevant elements of the investment. It requires skill and judgement in its application and interpretation, with acknowledgement that some of the monetary values are only approximations, and it should not be treated as sacrosanct calculation. Yet its detractors often overlook its virtues. It *is* imperfect, but the appropriate yardstick is not perfection but the decision process as it existed before cost–benefit analysis. It is seen as evidence of the powerful bureaucracy, yet it can assist decentralised decision making since, once the discount rate has been standardised, the acceptability of investment projects does not require assessment by central government.

However, it would be quite erroneous to suggest that cost–benefit analysis could solve all problems of allocation. It has inherent limitations, and we must therefore examine some of the basic principles. It must necessarily be a cursory account, and any reader who is likely to become involved in the detailed construction or criticism of a cost–benefit study should consult one of the many texts that are available (e.g. Mishan, 1975; Harrison, 1974).

CONSUMERS' SURPLUS

The concept of consumers' surplus is fundamental in cost–benefit analysis because it draws a distinction between what consumers pay for a commodity or service and what value they attach to it. The concept was first expounded by Dupuit as long ago as 1844, and it has been widely illustrated at the level of the individual consumer by numerous economists. For example, Jevons (1871) and Marshall (1890) both suggested that the successive consumption of units of a particular commodity or service will eventually lead to diminishing marginal satisfaction to the consumer. Reverse this phenomenon, and it can be suggested that, if the consumer purchases several units of a commodity such that the utility of its marginal unit corresponds to the price that he is willing to pay for it, the utility of the first or early units will be higher than the price paid. In that case the sum of satisfaction will exceed the actual price paid; and if the consumer were threatened with the withdrawal of the commodity or service, he would be prepared to bid more for it than he had been paying. The increase in petrol prices during 1973–74, for example, caused only a modest reduction in petrol consumption as most consumers were willing to pay the surcharge rather than to forgo the advantages of motoring; clearly, during the earlier years of low petrol prices they had enjoyed extensive consumers' surplus.

Consumers' surplus may apply differently among different people or groups. Suppose that a suspension bridge between two cities has a toll charge of 10p to motorists. A private investment analysis would assess the revenue earned by the bridge and compare it with the cost, but the social benefits are more complex. The bridge saves motorists both time and running expenses in varying degreees according to the origins and destinations of their journey. Hence, some motorists reckon it as just worth 10p to use the bridge, while others save much more by using it and would be willing to pay a toll of 15p or even 20p. In this case consumers' suplus is the difference between the total sum that motorists would be prepared to pay and the sum that they actually pay. In Figure 6.1 it can be seen as the area *PAB* between the demand curve and the

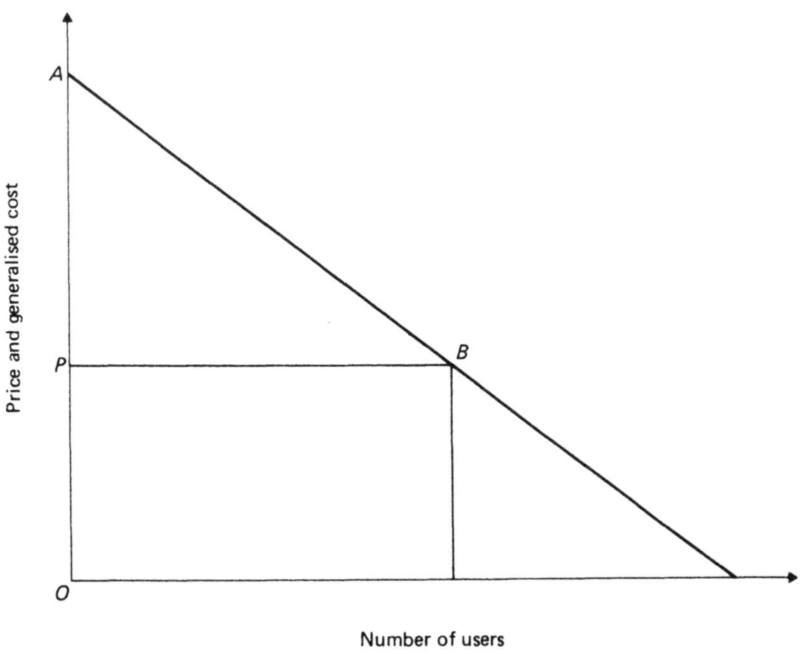

Figure 6.1 *Consumers' surplus and the market demand curve.*

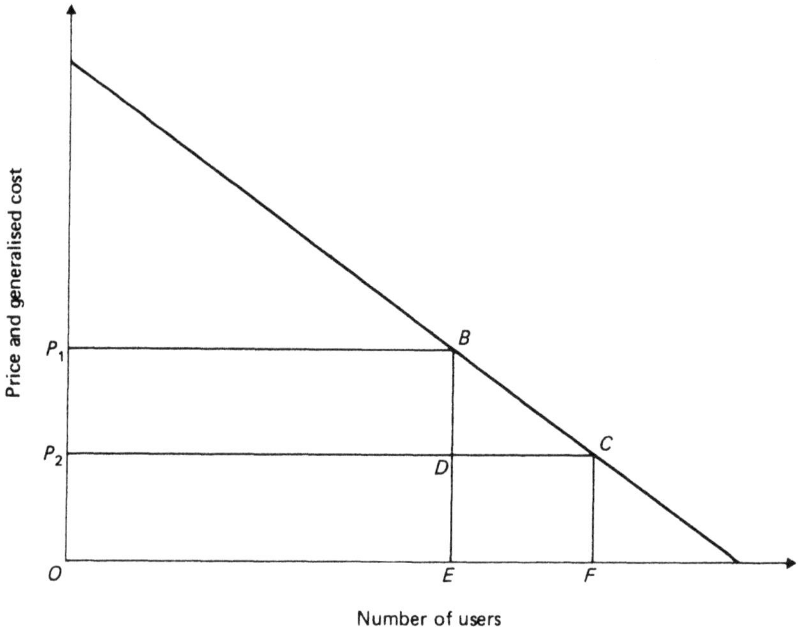

Figure 6.2 *Consumers' surplus with changing costs*

horizontal price line. This surplus is a benefit enjoyed by society, even though it is unpaid.

Often transport investment produces improvements to existing routes, and the calculation of benefit becomes more intricate. More realistically, suppose that before the bridge was built some motorists already travelled between the two cities by an earlier lengthier route. For them, the effect of the bridge has been to reduce their journey costs, adding to consumers' surplus. However, the fact that the bridge has made the real cost of the journey cheaper has induced some people to travel who previously found it too expensive in terms of time and money. This additional traffic is said to have been *generated* by the improvement and is shown in Figure 6.2 as *EF*. These extra travellers value the journey at any sum between OP_1 and OP_2 such that some of them enjoy a measure of consumers' surplus, which amounts for the generated traffic as a whole to the area *DBC*. The total benefit in this case is given by a combination of cost reduction (area P_2P_1BD) and consumers' surplus (area *DBC*).

While this measurement is superficially straightforward the practical problems raised are formidable. It is extremely difficult to assess the exact nature of the demand curve since the curve below the existing price level involves forecasting the extent of generated traffic, and the degree of consumers' surplus depends especially upon the value that travellers attach to savings in travel time – a value that, as we shall see presently, involves problems.

Another problem of cost–benefit analysis, which imposes restrictions on its use, is that it employs partial-equilibrium analysis. Consumers' surplus in one market is defined only for a specific income level and distribution and for given resource-allocation decisions in other markets. Unless there is spare capacity in the economy an increased demand for one commodity or service may cause reductions in the output of another and change the level of consumers' surplus in other sectors. Thus, it is legitimate to neglect these lost surpluses only if the marginal effect of changes following the investment are extremely small – indeed virtually infinitesimal. If the price of a commodity falls, there will tend to be an increase in the sales of the commodity, but an income effect is also possible because the fall in the price of the commodity tends to increase real income. Yet these macroeconomic effects are beyond the direct compass of the analysis. In effect, this restricts the use of simple cost–benefit analysis to relatively small projects; for larger projects it may be necessary to consider non-incremental changes.

Market imperfections may give rise to *rents*, which have to be considered in cost–benefit analysis. Rent may be defined as the difference between what a factor is actually paid and the minimum payment that would induce its continued employment there. Suppose that, before the construction of our hypothetical suspension bridge, a ferry operated between the two cities and exploited its monopoly to earn monopolistic profit that was well above the level of normal profit. If the bridge rendered the ferry uneconomic and put it out of business, it would be necessary to consider several factors. The loss of monopoly profit would not be a loss to society, since it was not a payment for real service in the first place but a transfer payment in the form of rent paid to the monopolist ferry owner. If the ferry boat were scrapped, there would be a loss to society of the value of its service, excluding the monopoly profit, but this would be made good by the use of the bridge, so that the loss would be cancelled out; the gain would simply be the lower cost to existing traffic and the consumers' surplus of the generated traffic. However, if the ferry boat could be employed elsewhere and need not be scrapped, its discounted stream of revenue in that use could also be allowed for, and there would be no net loss.

TRANSFER PAYMENTS

Transfer payments may crop up in various guises. Where the private investor must allow for profits tax or income tax, from the point of view of society these are merely transfer payments. Thus, tax revenue from the income earned by a public authority investment must be ignored. Sometimes, lack of appreciation of transfer payments may cause serious errors in cost–benefit analysis through double counting. If a new urban commuter railway line opens up urban job opportunities to people who would not hitherto have commuted, the rents in their new urban jobs should *not* be included as benefits because they are already subsumed within the consumers' surplus in using the railway line. The increased salaries that they could earn would bid up what they would be willing to pay to travel on the line, and this clearly adds to consumers' surplus. On similar grounds a cost–benefit analysis of the Victoria line on the London Underground system, Foster and Beesley (1963), rejected the supranormal increase in the value of houses adjacent to the Victoria line as an element of benefit; if the increase in values was due to the convenience of the new service, it was simply a reflection of the increased consumers' surplus. However, the calculation of consumers' surplus may be very difficult in practice, and where resources formerly unused are employed a direct estimate of the net income gained by factors may be used as an approximation.

The example of the bridge and the ferry is a very simplified one. In practice the issue may be very much more complex as Table 6.1, involving the withdrawal of a bus service, shows. In it the costs and benefits are itemised for the various parties involved. The acceptability of the withdrawal of a bus service may be a matter not simply of showing aggregate net benefit but of persuading all the parties involved to accede to it. The case shown involves the proposed withdrawal of the peripheral section of a bus route linking a residential area with a suburban shopping centre and railway station; but the balance of the route, into central London, would continue to operate. In this case the table shows that the withdrawal of the service would be attractive to London Transport, which would save £39,000 a year, and to the local authority, which would gain £8,000 in extra parking revenue. The net effect, column G, has been calculated as

$$G = A + B + C + D + E - F$$

SHADOW PRICES

The existence of market imperfections can sometimes be mitigated in cost–benefit analysis by using shadow prices, which simply means that goods or services are valued by a price that is more realistic to society than the ostensible or nominal price currently set upon the item. Sometimes the issue is fairly straightforward, as in the case of unemployment. If our hypothetical bridge is built by workers who would otherwise be unemployed, the real cost to society may be zero because unemployment has no opportunity cost in as much as the workers would be idle if they did not build the bridge, although they would place a leisure valuation on their idle time. Their wages in this case, while a cost to the private contractor, may be counted as a benefit to society. Unemployment benefit is not a part of their opportunity cost since it is merely a transfer payment. However, the amount and duration of unemployment benefit can be influential for it may be necessary to offer higher wages to induce those receiving benefit to accept a job than would be necessary if benefit were lower or zero. A potential Pareto improvement could be achieved if the worker's output in a job exceeded the minimum wage that he would accept, minus the unemployment benefit.

We have already mentioned briefly the distorting effects of monopoly prices; any deviation from the perfectly competitive rule, by which price must equal marginal cost, can cause deviation from the social optimum. If price exceeds marginal cost in a wide spectrum of the economy, the costs of production of an item may estimate wrongly the value of output forgone in other areas of the economy, since the price may exceed the marginal cost of the factors of production involved. Suppose that a transport investment requires the use of a factor of production whose price exceeds marginal cost. Which cost is appropriate: the market price of the factor or its marginal cost of production? This will depend upon the effect of the new investment on the production of the factor concerned. If the new demand does not alter the output of the factor but diverts sales of the factor from erstwhile consumers, the value of the factor will be its market price since this reflects the opportunity cost, namely, the amount that previous consumers were willing to pay for it. If the new demand does increase the output of the monopolist or oligopolist, the cost to society will be the marginal cost of the factors required for the increased output since these factors will no longer be available for use in other areas of the economy. The shadow price is the price employed in our calculations, which, as we have just seen in the case of expanded output by a monopoly, is marginal cost rather than market price.

Shadow prices have a variety of applications in transport economics. We have seen that if there is unemployment the shadow price of labour, reflecting a real resource cost, may be well below the wages actually paid; this can be a particularly significant factor in investment projects

Table 6.1 *Effect of the withdrawal of a specimen bus service: social cost–benefit assessment, measurable items (all figures relate to £'000 per year to the nearest thousand).*

	London Transport *A*	*British Rail* *B*	*Local authorities* *C*	*Central government* *D*	*Users of withdrawn bus service* E^j	*Users of road and parking space indirectly affected by withdrawal* F^j	*Change in social costs and benefits* *G*
Withdrawn bus service							
(1) Value to users					−63		−63
(2) Revenue	−40				+40		0
(3) Cost effect	+68			− 1[a]			+67
Other bus services							
(4) Value to users					+10	+ 1[b]	+11
(5) Revenue	+11				−10	− 1[b]	0
(6) Cost effect	nil						nil
British Rail[c]							
(7) Value to users					− 3	+ 1[d]	− 2
(8) Revenue		−2			+ 3	− 1[d]	0
(9) Cost effect		nil					nil
Road Users							
(10) Value to users of withdrawn bus diverted to car					+52		+52

(11) Cost to users of withdrawn bus diverted to car				+ 9[e]	−52		−43
(12) Congestion				+10[f]		−120	−110
(13) Value to car users diverted because of increased congestion						− 5	− 5
(14) Cost to car users diverted because of increased congestion				− 1[g]		+ 5	+ 4
Parking[h]							
(15) Value to users					+10	− 2	+ 8
(16) Revenue			+8		−10	+ 2	0
(17) Congestion						− 2	− 2
Other considerations							
(18) Change in indirect taxation receipts on non-transport expenditure				− 4			− 4
TOTAL	+39	−2	+8	+13	−23	−122	−87

Source: National Board for Prices and Incomes (1970).
Notes: + = *Increase* in benefits or reduction in costs.
− = Reduction in benefits or increase in costs.

(continued)

table 6.1 continued

General: In the case of columns E and F it is to be noted that there are several pairs of adjacent rows with equal figures but opposite signs; for example, in column E rows 4 and 5 show respectively the benefit of £10,000 per year that former users of the withdrawn bus service enjoy from the other bus routes to which they divert and the money cost of £10,000 that they pay for using these services.

(a) Reduction in government revenue from the taxation of bus fuel.

(b) Relates to other people who divert from car to bus owing to increased congestion on the roads.

(c) The specific section of bus route withdrawn feeds a rail head in the suburban centre, which caters for a substantial number of peak period commuters. Therefore, following the withdrawal of this particular section of bus route there will be a reduction in the number of people travelling by rail from the rail head in question. There is no rail service that passengers can use as a substitute for the withdrawn bus service in this case.

(d) Relates to other people who divert from car to rail owing to the increased congestion on the roads.

(e) Tax on petrol consumed by the users of withdrawn bus service who now travel by car. Note that, if this figure can be calculated directly, the introduction of the £52,000 and £43,000 will be unnecessary for the analysis. They are included here only in order to make the logic clear.

(f) Of the extra time costs and running costs imposed on other road users by the additional car traffic, £10,000 constitutes extra fuel-tax revenue.

(g) Loss of fuel tax revenue from previous road users now diverted from the roads owing to the increased congestion (cf. (b) and (d)). Here too the £5,000 and £4,000 only enter into the final result by difference but are included to make the logic clear.

(h) In this particular case there will be enough parking space for commuter users of the withdrawn service who shift to travelling by car. The displacement of existing users is due to the extra road congestion on weekdays, and the parking congestion is due to an excess demand for parking space confined to Saturdays in the suburban centre.

(i) Travellers will spend more on travel by public and private transport combined after the withdrawal of the bus service than they did while the bus service still operated. Assuming the same level of savings they will therefore spend correspondingly less on other personal consumption, with a consequent reduction in indirect taxation receipts to the government. The average rate of indirect taxation for all personal consumption has been assumed to apply to this reduction in the consumption of non-transport items.

(j) Where figures are shown in *both* columns E and F in any one row and also in rows 10 and 11 on the one hand and 13 and 14 on the other, the split between columns E and F is unnecessary for the analysis. All these figures cancel out in the column totals, and they do not of course affect the overall estimate of social loss. They are included here only to make the logic clear. The split between columns E and F in these cases should be regarded as illustrative only. Further research would be necessary to determine firm quantative estimates of the allocation between the two columns.

For example, the basic figures necessary for the analysis as regards railways are shown in column B (rows 8 and 9). These show a net loss of £2,000 per year in the 'producers' surplus' for British rail. Columns E and F (row 8) show users of withdrawn bus services and users of roads respectively saving £3,000 by shifting away from railways and spending £1,000 more by shifting to railways. This latter figure arises because some original motorists are diverted to railways due to increased road congestion. Row 7 (columns E and F) cancels out with row 8 (columns E and F) by showing the benefit forgone or secured corresponding to the extra money saved or spent.

in developing countries where labour is very plentiful. If an economy is in difficulties over its external balance of payments and its currency is maintained at an exchange rate that would not prevail if free currency markets operated, shadow prices will be advisable in evaluating its investment projects. Suppose that the currency is overvalued and that balance-of-payments equilibrium is maintained by quota or exchange control; then the demand price for foreign exchange exceeds the price that holders of import licences pay. Common practice is to use a shadow price for foreign exchange reflecting the demand price rather than the official rate of exchange. Thus, imports and exports are valued above their nominal prices, reflecting their social opportunity cost in terms of domestic goods. Import values are high because, in order to buy the imports at the high demand price, local production is forgone. Export values are high since each pound's worth of exports permits a corresponding amount of imports. The official rate of exchange will not reflect the real value of imports under quota because the imports are scarce. Thus, even if the imports are costed at the nominal rate of exchange, their opportunity cost will be higher because of their scarcity, and there may be either a black market or very high profits to import licence holders. Shadow prices for foreign exchange may be appropriate in various instances of investment in transport; for example, imports may be necessary for a wide range of transport investment in developing countries, or for the purchase of airliners or ships by developed nations, which will earn foreign exchange by their subsequent operation.

TIME SAVING AND THE VALUE OF TIME

One of the most important areas in transport economics in which we seek to establish a value that is not explicit in the market is the value of time saved by travellers. Examples where time savings are important are legion, ranging from the hypothetical suspension bridge discussed earlier to urban rapid-transit systems, airport sites, the Channel Tunnel, motorways, faster cargo ships and supersonic airliners. In view of its pervasiveness and its intrinsic importance as a crucial factor that may make or break an investment proposal we shall devote rather more space to this issue than we have in the rather sketchy outline of cost–benefit analysis so far.

The basis for the valuation of time saved is that time spent in travelling has an opportunity cost. Journeys made by an individual during his working hours usually subtract from the time in which he is able to work and therefore from his product; journeys spent during leisure hours likewise restrict his pursuit of pleasures that are more enjoyable than travel, which in any case usually involves disutility. Economists usually draw a distinction between time valuations depending on whether *working time* or *leisure time* is involved. In the case of leisure time it may be appropriate to apply different valuations to different parts of the journey since disutility varies according to circumstances. Travellers tend to attach greater disutility to time spent waiting for public transport than to time spent travelling upon it, and this implies that even where the overall journey time may be unchanged the customers' valuation of the journey may vary according to the characteristics of the mode. Recent empirical analysis of the valuation of travel time has therefore taken account of a variety of characteristics, subsumed under headings such as walking time, waiting time and in-vehicle time, and attributed different values to each.

Working time journeys comprise all journeys undertaken during working time; leisure journeys, perhaps more accurately called non-working journeys, comprise journeys made during the time for which the traveller is not paid. Hence, travel to or from work is a non-working journey as time saving here affords more leisure to the traveller rather than more working time to the employer. A variety of interpretations has been offered for the value of working time saved. The commonest is that savings should be valued at the average gross wage rate of the traveller, but deviations from this may be expected. The manufacturers of Concorde have suggested that the business executive has overhead capital associated with his job, which is substantially idle when he is absent, so that his travel time savings should be valued at three times his salary rate. On a similar basis British Airways has reckoned twice the salary rate, but both these estimates seem to be rather speculative. However, in the cost–benefit analysis of the Third London Airport, the (Roskill) Commission on the Third London Airport (1970) followed the practice of the Ministry of Transport in calculating figures based on salary levels plus overheads of 10 per cent, but it recognised that such calculations were controversial and therefore adopted upper and lower values for time valuation in both business and leisure time savings.

If the analysis is to be accurate, it is desirable that the composition of the travelling population using a transport facility be known. Normal practice is to value the savings of working time as some proportion of the wage/salary rate, but it could be misleading to take the national average figure if the composition of travellers were in some way unrepresentative. For example, business travellers by air have higher than average incomes, and their time savings will be of above average value, but they will involve judgements about income distribution mentioned earlier in the chapter; indeed, people who travel during their working hours tend to receive above average remuneration. There may also be regional income inequalities that imply time valuation differences.

A further problem arises over minor time savings. A saving of 1 hour has fairly obvious benefits for much can be done in that time; but how significant is the saving of 5 minutes, and is the saving of 5 minutes each by a dozen travellers equivalent to one traveller's saving of 1 hour? No unique and simple answer is possible. If the 5 minutes has a clearly perceived opportunity cost, it may be valuable, and this is most likely if the time saved applies to working time and may be incorporated into a regular schedule. The Roskill Commission on the Third London Airport opted to treat small time savings as additive and therefore significant in principle, although in that particular case the aggregated value of small time savings turned out to be very small in relation to total costs and benefits.

In principle the value imputed to working time savings can be calculated from wage rates plus an appropriate weighting for overhead costs, as the Department of the Environment (1976) does, adding 18 per cent to the gross earnings rate. The valuation of time saved for leisure purposes requires a more empirical approach since there are no established market prices. If the market for leisure were perfect, the marginal valuation of working time, minus any intrinsic disutility of work, might be expected to equal the marginal value of leisure time from the individual's viewpoint. However, the market is imperfect because the length of the individual working week is not generally flexible, and the individual's valuation at the margin is subject to marginal tax rates since from any income forgone must be deducted the amount that would be lost to the tax. All these reasons (i.e. disutility of work, tax effects, the relative absence of overheads) lower the implied valuation of leisure time saved.

Studies of actual behaviour or *revealed preference* among travellers are probably better sources of analysis than questionnaires asking people to assess their likely behaviour in imaginary situations. Several behavioural approaches are possible. Behaviour where travellers are faced with a choice between a long slow cheap route and a short but more expensive one may be compared, typified by the choice between a long journey round an estuary and the use of a suspension bridge where a heavy toll charge is made. Relative monetary costs can be calculated, including motoring costs, and the differential related to the time saving. However, as Thomson (1974, p. 61) has pointed out, suitable cases are rare and complicated by car occupancy rates and non-monetary items.

Cases involving modal choice on given routes have proved more fruitful. At the simplest level the values of two groups of travellers can be illustrated using a method employed by Beesley (1965). Let T represent time, C the cost of travel, subscript A the preferred mode and subscript B the rejected mode. Now suppose that the traveller has the choice of a $2\frac{1}{2}$-hour rail journey to London for £6 or a 4-hour bus journey for £3. Then the minimum valuation of a rail traveller will be, if non-speed qualitative differences are ignored,

$$V_R(\text{min}) = \frac{C_A - C_B}{T_B - T_A} = \frac{6-3}{4-2.5} = \frac{3}{1.5} = 2$$

or £2 per hour. For the bus traveller the maximum valuation of time will be (with his preferences altering the subscripts)

$$V_B(\text{max}) = \frac{C_B - C_A}{T_A - T_B} = \frac{6-3}{4-2.5} = \frac{3}{1.5} = 2$$

or again £2 per hour. The rail traveller's valuation must be a minimum of £2; otherwise he would travel by bus, and he is essentially a time saver. The bus traveller's valuation must be a maximum of £2; otherwise he would travel by rail, and he is a money-saver.

Clearly, this is a simplified model that merely serves to measure certain limit values rather than average values. In practice Beesley examined journey choice among urban office commuters such that no necessary identity was implied between the maximum and minimum values, and he sought to derive the value of time that could explain the largest number of modal choices, stratifying his sample into three different income groups. His results suggest a leisure time valuation of about half the earning rate.

The basis of Beesley's method is to fit a line, as a simple form of the discriminant analysis mentioned in Chapter 3, that minimises the number of choices on the inappropriate side of the line. Several limitations of the method are evident. It can treat only two variables; but what are we to make of qualitative differences, of the question whether the opportunity cost of a marginal loss of time is greater than the value of a marginal saving in time, and of how people value different segments of their journey time?

Several variations on the simple theme outlined above have been attempted. Lee and Dalvi (1969), for example, have used a notional diversion charge in assessing the value of travel time (i.e. the change in time or price of the preferred mode that would be just enough to induce the traveller to change to the alternative mode). In terms of the equations above, given a diversion charge CD, it is possible to establish a minimum value of travel time for travellers choosing the faster mode:

$$\frac{C_A + C_D - C_B}{T_B - T_A}$$

and a maximum value for those preferring the slower mode:

$$\frac{C_B - C_A + C_D}{T_A - T_B}$$

With suitable empirical data these expressions would make it possible to attempt answers to the following questions: what reduction in the price of the rejected mode would induce a switch to it, what increase in journey time would induce the traveller to switch away from it, and what reduction in journey time would be just enough to persuade the traveller to change mode?

Lee and Dalvi then employed the new values, which incorporated the diversion element, as dependent variables in a series of regression equations designed to show how various indexes of quality employed as independent variables influenced the valuation of travel time; data were collected from users of buses, trains and private cars commuting into Manchester. In examining transport users they found that people who preferred the train to the bus had a higher time value than those preferring the bus to the train and that the latter set had a higher time value than those who travelled by bus rather than by a combination of bus and train. Rather unexpectedly in-vehicle travel time and walking and waiting times were not separately important as determinants of valuation, implying that travellers did not attach more disutility to walking and waiting time than to time spent travelling in vehicles; this conflicts with the findings of other studies, as we shall see later. Personal income levels were positively related to time valuation, especially in the minimum value set (i.e. time savers), but at a diminishing rate as income rose. Slow travellers, from the maximum value set, valued time savings proportionately more on long journeys than on short ones. Significantly, it was evident that among groups with common income, personal and household characteristics there were differences in the valuation of time savings. The average value of time savings, which involved additions to leisure time in effect, was about 30 per cent of gross hourly earnings.

In a second report Dalvi and Lee (1971) have examined modal choice among car users travelling to the same urban offices as the public transport users. In analysing the determinants of demand for motor travel, there are discrepancies between average cost per mile, marginal cost per mile and perceived marginal cost per mile. Average costs include *all* motoring costs, some of which do not affect the marginal cost of any particular journey; for example, any fixed cost of motoring (e.g. car licence, insurance, interest on the capital cost of the car) has no effect on marginal journey costs. Actual marginal costs include items that are paid for intermittently but do not enter the user's day-to-day calculations, such as maintenance expenditure (e.g. oil, tyres, servicing, repairs) and depreciation costs, where these relate to the mileage covered by the car rather than its age. However, motorists often ignore some of these marginal costs, and their behaviour follows from their perceived marginal cost, which may fall as low as their petrol cost plus any parking charges. Harrison and Quarmby (1969) found that marginal cost ranged from 4d to 7d (1.7p to 2.9p) per mile but that the perceived element ranged from 2d to 4d (0.8p to 1.7p). Dalvi and Lee (1971) have estimated travel time values for car users on the basis of all three types of cost averages (i.e. actual, marginal and perceived marginal), but they found the actual marginal cost to be the most useful. Estimates for the valuation of time saved were calculated for maximum and minimum value sets on all three cost bases, yielding a value of about 40 per cent of earnings if actual marginal costs were employed and only 10 per cent if perceived costs were used.

A limitation of the Dalvi–Lee type of analysis is that it employed questionnaires rather than revealed preference. One method that employs revealed preference is discriminant analysis, in which a value is established that successfully explains the maximum number of modal choices made by travellers. Beesley (1965) has employed this method, and Quarmby (1967) has used a more elaborate version in his Leeds study. Quarmby's model examined seven explanatory variables to account for modal choice: relative overall travel time, relative excess travel time, relative cost, relative income, car demand ratio (i.e. the ratio of driving licences to cars in the household), the use of car for work and the ownership of cars by firms. Of these, travel time difference, excess travel-time difference, cost difference and the possibility of using the car at work emerged as important influences on modal choice. His study concluded that walking and waiting times were valued at between two and three times in-vehicle times and that the average value of time was valued by both bus and car users at between 21 and 25 per cent of the wage rate. Quarmby's study is also interesting for the policy prescriptions that he has offered to diminish private car usage in the (Leeds) city centre.

Research into the valuation of travel time savings continues, although the Department of the Environment has standardised a valuation of the wage rate plus a small variable overhead for working time savings, and 25 per cent of the wage rate for leisure time savings, and a third of the adult amount for children. Obviously, such valuations are crude expedients, and recent research (Heggie, 1976) suggests that there may be non-linearities in time valuation; but Harrison (1974) has rightly emphasised that we will usually have to be satisfied with an average value that is representative of most travellers. The values used by the Department of Transport are shown in Table 6.2, the different working time rates reflecting the observed average wage-rate of the users of different modes.

Table 6.2 *Department of Transport time valuations, 1982.*

Time category	*Pence per hour*
Working Time	*(1979 prices)*
Car drivers	411.2
Car passengers	328.8
Rail passengers	440.4
Bus passengers	272.9
Underground passengers	400.0
Goods-vehicle occupants	300.0
Light-goods-vehicle occupants	258.4
Bus drivers	276.8
Bus conductors	270.6
All workers	393.4
Leisure time (behavioural value)	
In-vehicle time	65.3
Walking and waiting time	130.6

Source: Department of Transport.

ACCIDENT COSTS

Another problem in shadow pricing is the valuation of losses through accidents. The costs of accidents to society have reached significant levels in relation to gross domestic products; and as transport usage increases these costs may be expected to rise in proportion to gross domestic product unless positive steps are taken to limit the growth of accidents. The national significance of accidents is shown in Table 6.3. Fouracre and Jacobs (1976) have shown that developing countries suffer high accident costs despite their low vehicle ratios because of a high incidence of fatalities in road accidents.

Any accident valuation figures involve attributing a value to human life and estimating losses due to incapacity arising out of injury. Although it may seem macabre and unfeeling to impute a cash value to

Table 6.3 *Road accidents in selected countries*

Country	*Year*	*Vehicles per 10,000 persons*	*Fatalities per 10,000 persons*	*Fatalities per 10,000 vehicle-kilometres*
Australia	1979	5,004	2.33	3.1
Eire	1980	1,640	1.64	2.8
France	1981	4,267	2.29	4.4
Great Britain	1981	3,064	1.05	2.1
Japan	1981	3,358	0.74	2.3
New Zealand	1981	5,002	2.10	4.0
South Africa	1981	1,563	3.74	17.0
USA	1981	6,812	2.12	2.0
West Germany	1981	4,088	1.91	3.6

Source: International Road Federation, *World Road Statistics*, 1983.

the life of a human being it is an absolutely unavoidable issue; for if an explicit value is not put on life, an implicit one will be put on it in all those investment decisions in which human lives are at risk. In the absence of enough investment funds to finance every project society makes choices (e.g. between schools and hospitals, between extra roads and safety barriers on motorways, between ambulances and buses). Where one investment will on known probabilities save life and an alternative investment will not, an implicit valuation of life is revealed. Suppose, for example, that by erecting barriers on the central strip of a section of motorway a predicted ten lives could be saved over a given period of time. If its proponents urge that the investment be made at a cost of, say, £3 million, their implicit valuation of human life will be £300,000. Likewise, all investment choices involving risk impute a value to life and limb. If the valuation is not explicit, there will be a danger of misallocation between these projects; and in not establishing the most accurate criterion of the value of life investors are likely to misallocate, either by overspending or by underspending, between projects involving safety and those where risk to life and limb is not involved. At the extreme it may be claimed that human life is invaluable, but logically this entails that all investment should be devoted to life-saving projects.

Even so the establishment of a monetary valuation is difficult and probably defies ideal solution. Mishan (1975, Chapter 45) has examined four possibilities. One is to impute a value from investment decisions in the manner described above, but this really avoids the issue and is unlikely to yield a unique value. A second is to calculate the discounted future earnings-stream of a person, possibly augmenting this by allowances for suffering to the victim and the bereaved and for loss of utility from ceasing to be alive. A third possibility is to restrict the earnings stream to an amount net of his consumption, measuring in some sense his contribution to society. Neither the second nor the third criterion appeals. The third ignores the victim and considers only the interests of the rest of society, while the second also emphasises contribution to economic growth without regard to consumption and suggests that the elderly are a net drain on society. In a productive sense this may be so; but the ultimate ethic of economics is to facilitate consumption as well as production, in which case the future consumption stream of the person is as valid a criterion as the future earnings stream. A fourth possibility is to apply some kind of insurance principle. Mishan has rejected the notion of equating the value of life with the value of insurance policies since it is a function of concern for others rather than an expression of the value of life to the insured. In any event decisions such as to take out insurance or to use seat belts are subject to ignorance or the miscalculation of risk on the part of potential users; and even if perceptions were perfect, their use would be unlikely to proceed to the socially optimal level, so that risk takers would ignore the consequences to people outside their family circle.

Mishan has objected to all the above methods on principle, in as much as they neglect the basic tenet of cost–benefit analysis that economic arrangements should be ranked according to the Pareto criterion. However, consistency with this criterion would require that a person's life be valued according to the compensating variation principle. Any project involving risk to life would have to demonstrate that benefits would exceed costs after compensating the losers. Yet in a subjective sense it may be suggested that the consumer's surplus from life is infinite: no sum of money could compensate adequately for the loss of life. As an aid to decision taking this is hardly a useful conclusion, and in practice economists tend to accept the valuations made by individuals as guides to their welfare. It may therefore be proposed that people accept the generalised risk that x persons may die from the use of a particular transport facility and, by accepting the generalised risk, make an implicit judgement that the gains from using the facility offset the risks. However, personal perception of risk may be defective, through ignorance of accident rates and through the optimism of users who are unable to translate the impersonality of accident rates to the realistic probability of their own injury or death.

No wholly satisfactory assessment of the value of life exists then at present. The Department of Transport employs a method that values life according to gross consumption rather than net output. The distinction is important for investment decisions. If we wish to know the loss to society *after* the death of a victim, the net or *ex post* figure will be the appropriate one; but if we wish to invest in safety measures to prevent deaths and make calculations while the potential victim is alive, the potential victim's future loss of consumption will be a loss to existing society and the gross or *ex ante* figure will be preferred. However, there is criticism in the Leitch Report (Department of Transport, 1977c, Chapter 21) that the value of life has been underestimated, because victims have been assumed to be average income receivers whereas in fact travellers at risk have above average incomes. The Department of Transport employs a discount rate of 10 per cent to yield present values from the stream of future incomes.

The value of life is the most controversial element in the cost of accidents, but it is only one of several contributors to the total cost. Some recent figures for the breakdown of total costs in Great Britain are shown in Table 6.4. It has been estimated that £650 million of the total cost of accidents was borne by private individuals and the balance of £225 million by the state in 1974.

Table 6.4 *Total accident costs in Great Britain, 1982.*

Cost	*£ million*
Damage to property	903
Medical and ambulance costs	73
Administration costs	124
Pain, grief and suffering	560
Lost output	715
Total	2,375

Source: Department of Transport.

The basis of calculation for pain and grief appears to be somewhat arbitrary and more tenuous than that for the valuation of life. Another breakdown of accident costs is also possible according to the venue and severity of the accident. More fatalities usually occur in typical motorway accidents although the chances of having an accident there are lower than on other roads. The figures employed in 1982 by the Department of Transport are quoted in Table 6.5.

Table 6.5 *Road accident costs, 1982 (£).*

Type of cost	*Urban*	*Rural*	*Motorway*	*Weighted average*
Cost per accident				
– Fatal	158,210	168,260	166,760	158,630
– Serious	7,640	10,050	10,130	8,400
– Slight	990	1,750	1,900	1,150
Average cost of injury accident	7,730	14,360	14,110	9,280
Average cost of damage-only accident	470	570	670	490

Source: Department of Transport.

POLLUTION COSTS

In recent years public awareness of the social costs of pollution has grown. These costs are not reflected in the market mechanism and are therefore appropriate subjects for shadow price calculations. Transport creates pollution in the form both of noise and of unwanted chemical-effluents. If the pollution affected transport users alone, the economic problem would be much diminished, but the noise and fumes all too commonly inconvenience people who are not travelling. The most extreme case, if the worst fears were borne out, would be the destruction of the earth's ozone layer by high-flying supersonic aircraft. At more down-to-earth levels aircraft noise near airports and the effect of traffic noise in conurbations are issues that cost–benefit analysts have sought to incorporate into their calculations. Incidentally, it must be noted that certain apparently clean forms of transport may involve pollution elsewhere; for example, the electric train may draw its power from electricity sources that themselves create pollution, as may the battery-driven car.

If the problem of noise as one manifestation of pollution is studied it will be clear that there is no unique market for peace and quiet. However, there is an implicit market; one can buy more or less quiet houses, for example. Hence, the analyst aims to determine how much house prices change because of changes in the prevailing levels of noise with the expectation that house price differentials will reflect, *inter alia*, perceived noise nuisance. Some economists have been critical of this approach. Mishan (1975, p. 335) has claimed that it is 'doomed to failure', and his qualifications merit the attention of any analysts concerned with pollution assessment that assumes that house values can capture the effect of pollution changes. Several attempts have been made to quantify the intrusiveness of noise, usually involving the measured level of noise and how often the noise occurs. The noise and number index (NNI) used by the Roskill Commission (1970) was calculated in this way using the formula

$$\text{NNI} = \overline{\text{PndB}} + 15 \log N - 80$$

where $\overline{\text{PndB}}$ is the mean perceived noise in decibels of the average peak noise of aircraft and N is the number of aircraft heard per day. The NNI has been criticised for emphasising N and understating the significance of loudness and also for failing to differentiate between different fractions of day and night noise, being based upon the pattern prevailing around Heathrow in 1961. An alternative measure widely used in the United States is the composite noise rating (CNR), formulated as:

$$\text{CNR} = \overline{\text{PndB}} + 10 \log N - 12$$

with some adjustments for night and day peaks and for the duration of noises. Walters (1975, pp. 18–19) has noted a convenient coincidence in that the indices are ordinal, such that an NNI of 50 is known to be more unpleasant than one of 45 and one of 55 to be more unpleasant than one of 50, but the successive increments of 5 units do not imply equal increments of displeasure. However, in practice the public behaves as if the index were cardinal, and the increments of 5 units just noted tend to elicit similar volumes of complaints. Typical reactions to different NNI levels are a little annoyance at 32, moderate annoyance at 42 and very much annoyance at 60. Different indices are used in France and West Germany, and work continues on more sensitive measures (e.g. the noise exposure forecast, NEF).

Any increase in noise levels increases the number of noisy houses, depressing their relative price, and reduces the number of quiet houses, forcing up their relative price. However, the housing market is imperfect, and the problems in deciding the implicit value of quiet are rather like those of evaluating time savings; we know that buyers of quiet houses value the lack of noise at more than the amount implicit in the house price, and that those buying or content to remain in noisy houses may value quiet at less than the market price suggests. Calibration by observing movement is difficult, but attempts to assess consumers' surplus in occupancy by surveys of householders are in Walters's judgement likely to produce an upward bias.

Noise increases affect three categories of household: those who would have moved anyway, who lose by the depreciation of their property; those who remain, whose loss may be measured by the discounted future stream of the annoyance; and those noise avoiders who move, suffering their noise depreciation and incurring search and removal costs. It is possible, although complex, to calculate the costs that are relevant to each group. Empirical studies, for example, show that in the United States an increase of 1 unit in the CNR (equivalent to a 0.7 increase in the NNI) is associated with a 1 per cent drop in house prices, while near London an increase of 1 unit in the NNI (equivalent to a 1.4 increase in the CNR) is associated with a 1 per cent drop in house prices. British data also suggest that the elasticity of 'demand for quiet' to permanent income is between 1.7 and 2.0 which in turn suggests that as real income grows over time so will the demand for quiet houses. This expectation assumes that calculations based on cross-section studies can be used to forecast future trends, but careful interpretation of a permanent income model gives a reasonable prospect of accuracy. However, the probability that the cost of noise will increase in the future emphasises the need to devise sensible policies towards it.

While it should be emphasised that the economic assessment of noise is in its infancy, the customary approach in cost–benefit analysis is to attempt to measure the implicit cost through valuation changes. Starkie and Johnson (1975) have adopted Millward's (1971) 'exclusion facilities' approach, in which they examine the prospect of reducing noise levels by insulation. Their approach has the advantage of coping directly with the problem of householders who do not or cannot move; but it fails to offer guidance on the valuation of noise outside insulated buildings, so that while it produces potentially useful information for compensation policy it cannot offer a general solution.

A radically different approach to the problem of noise is through planning, in what Walters (1975) has called the 'authorities' approach. This appeals to many people who misunderstand the market (i.e. prices) approach or feel that it cannot take account of the many imponderables of information, valuation, movement and compensation. A major weakness of the planning approach is that its blanket restrictions on land use exclude people who may have no objection to noise; it is a blunt instrument lacking the discriminating finesse of a properly constructed pricing mechanism. To achieve the latter, however, is often politically as well as theoretically difficult as airport authorities are typically government or quasi-government agencies and have other goals or constraints than economic rationality. Walters has suggested that a compromise may be necessary in which the authorities should at least attempt a cost–benefit approach. As things stand, all too often the present pricing and accounting systems produce perverse social results. For example, aircraft landing fees reflect aircraft weight although the type of engine used is a prime determinant of noise. Furthermore, older urban airports that are close to built-up areas are often ostensibly low cost because of their older written-down assets, and this low cost attracts traffic and makes them efficient in private accounting terms, whereas newer greenfield sites are high cost and require longer surface journeys but involve far fewer households in noise nuisance. Incorporating some charge for aircraft noise into landing fees would eventually yield a pattern of airport sites that was more socially desirable and hasten the replacement of noisy aircraft by quieter ones and the development of quieter designs. The revenue generated by noise fees could be employed to compensate local residents when there was an unanticipated rise in noise levels; and although such compensation might be imperfect in the sense that an average figure derived from local NNI or similar readings would undercompensate some and overcompensate others, it has been argued that such compensation could be pitched on the generous side if the opportunity cost were a protracted and expensive planning wrangle. Moreover, there would be some beneficiaries from rises in air traffic who would live outside the noisy area, which tends to be elongated along the runway(s), but benefit by the improvement in opportunities for employment. The value of their properties would, *ceteris paribus*, increase.

Thus, the valuation of pollution costs remains, like the valuation of time savings, an area of controversy and a very suitable subject for further research.

THE CHOICE OF A DISCOUNT RATE

Once costs and benefits, including those accounted by shadow prices, have been estimated there arises the problem of converting them to a present value by using a discount rate. The choice of rate is, as Peacock (1973) has noted, a matter for furious debate. Several possibilities have been advanced although some can be dismissed summarily, such as the rate of interest on long-term government securities, which is too volatile and offers no real reflection of the community's real state of preference between present and future consumption. Feldstein (1972) has examined two possibilities: the social time-preference (STP) discount rate, and the social opportunity-cost (SOC) rate. The STP function establishes current values for future consumption. Henderson (1965) has advanced three reasons why the STP rate should be expected to be positive. First, the future involves risk and uncertainty, but strictly this should be accounted for separately in terms of specific risk premia. Second, it can be argued that the inevitability of death puts a premium on tangible income today; this may seem somewhat arbitrarily to favour present rather than future generations, but it is after all the contemporary generation that sacrifices current consumption to finance the investment. Third, Henderson has suggested that, if consumption levels per head rise over time, the phenomenon of diminishing marginal utility will yield lessening increments for successive equal additions of income; hence future increases may be valued at less than their nominal amounts.

The derivation of a unique value for the STP rate is a task bordering on the impossible, as Feldstein (1964) has shown. Hirshleifer (1961) has advocated the use of the SOC rate of interest; any investment has an opportunity cost, measured by the returns forgone on projects that could have been undertaken in its stead. Unfortunately, the derivation of the opportunity cost is far from easy. It may be advocated that, if public investments displace marginal private investment, a common rate should apply in both sectors. However, the private rate itself may be non-optimal and difficult to quantify at the margin and may not represent the communal concern for future generations that Marglin (1963) has invoked to justify a social rate of discount below the private one. Readers interested in the controversy will find ample literature on the subject (e.g. Layard, 1972), and we cannot detain ourselves further here. As long as the methodological controversy continues the choice of any rate may be criticised as somewhat arbitrary and 'dangerous', since high rates penalise long term projects with high initial expenditures and very low rates overencourage them; but Henderson (1965) has stressed the need for the government to establish a single rate as a necessity for consistent choice and to obviate inferior methods of project appraisal. At the time of writing the Treasury applies a test discount rate of 7 per cent in its assessment of public expenditure proposals, though 5 per cent is used by the nationalised industries.

SOME PRACTICAL PROBLEMS OF INVESTMENT EVALUATION

The ideal practice in an investment appraisal is to discount all the costs and benefits to yield a unique net present value, but it is not always possible to calculate such a sum. One obvious problem is that the future is uncertain, so that the analyst must accept the possibility of a range of outcomes rather than a unique solution. Since transport investments are typically long lasting it is especially important to take account of risk and uncertainty – an area that is a major subject in economics with extensive literature (e.g. van Horne, 1977; Bromwich, 1976). The commonest means to deal with risk and uncertainty is the use of sensitivity analysis, by which the items of cost and benefit that are most subject to uncertainty are selected and figures for a range of potential outcomes are calculated. In transport economics this technique might well be applied to demand projections (e.g. the studies of the Channel Tunnel and the Third London Airport), to the valuation of travel time (e.g. the Third London Airport studies) or to the discount rate (e.g. the study (1963) of the Victoria underground line by Foster and Beesley). The selection of items for sensitivity testing tends to become evident as the cost–benefit analysis advances and it becomes clear which costs and which benefits are numerically important. Moreover, if the analysis proves sensitive to their variation, it may be worth conducting research into a more satisfactory valuation of the items concerned.

However, sensitivity tests have some limitations. The selection of items for sensitivity testing rests upon the competence or bias of the analyst, and there may be limitations on the amount of testing that can be undertaken or comprehended if a vast array of components are treated as variable. It may even be cynically alleged that some cost–benefit analyses are produced *after* the political decision has been made and that the quantities are manipulated to yield a politically desired result; but this is a criticism more of the abuse of the system than of the system itself, and, properly publicised, such abuse would be apparent.

Uncertainty also surrounds the unquantifiable elements in an analysis (e.g. national prestige, defence potential). These are often appended to the quantified section of the analysis and may tilt the balance of a finely argued case. If the nature of the intangible items appears very significant, there may be a case for investigating its implications in some depth (e.g. moving and reconstructing an historic building in the path of a proposed airport runway). Political views may fall into this area of uncertainty, especially the problem of income distribution, from either the regional or hierarchic point of view. It may be possible to attach weights to costs and benefits according to the income levels of the payers or recipients, but often this is impractical; certainly, the distributional issues are an area that merits further analysis.

There may be computational difficulties in calculating all the figures required for a net present value figure across all the periods required in a transport cost–benefit analysis, where a thirty-year appraisal period is quite typical. A discount rate of 10 per cent may be expected to scythe the figures thirty years hence down to trivial proportions; but if there is a growth element in the traffic predicted, the net impact of estimates thirty years later may still be very significant. With the development of modern analyses of urban networks, which may have hundreds of area nodes and a multitude of links, even the capacity of contemporary computers may be incapable of accommodating all of the data for a thirty-year period, or the cost–benefit analysis itself may be subject to a budget that limits its use of the computer. In these circumstances the expedient of a single-year rate of return may be employed. Most commonly the first-year rate of return is calculated as the ratio of benefits accruing in the first full year to the capital cost of the scheme. Clearly, such a simplification is fraught with dangers, but it may be reasonably employed if the time profiles of early costs and benefits are consistent over the life of the project. If it is used as an arbiter between two schemes, the profiles of the two will have to be similar, since once that involved large but diminishing benefits would yield an apparently different result from one with modest but rising benefits.

Where the model is so complex that a single-year rate of return is necessitated it may become a matter of judgement for the analyst to decide whether the complexity of the model should be lessened to permit estimates of benefits and costs at, say, five-yearly intervals. If their pattern over time is expected to be regular, the model may be constructed over a very disaggregated network; but if the time profiles are at all erratic, it may yield more meaningful results if the network is coarsened to facilitate the computation of values at different times.

SUGGESTIONS FOR FURTHER READING

Fuller exposition of the principles of cost–benefit analysis has been given in Mishan's *Cost–Benefit Analysis* (1975). Layard's *Cost–Benefit Analysis: Selected Readings* (1972) is an extremely useful collection of some of the key issues. Harrison's *The Economics of Transport Appraisal* (1974) provides a useful link between theory and the practical application of cost–benefit analysis to transport investment. Sugden and Williams's *The Principles of Practical Cost–Benefit Analysis* (1978) is an introductory text that includes problems for readers to attempt. All four works are available in paperback.

Shortage of space precludes our reproducing case studies, but students should examine several if possible in order to appreciate the essentially practical issues faced. The following are possible candidates:

(1) *The Report of the Commission on the Third London Airport* (Roskill Commission, 1970) – the celebrated and emotive Roskill Report – is a massive work; it has been summarised by A. D. J. Flowerdew and attacked by E. J. Mishan in Layard (1972).

(2) The Channel Tunnel has twice been analysed: first in the Ministry of Transport's *Proposals for a Fixed Channel Link* (1963), abridged in Munby (1968); and more recently in *The Channel Tunnel: A United Kingdom Cost–Benefit Study* Cooper and Lybrand Associates Ltd (1973).
(3) The M1 motorway has been discussed in Foster's *The Transport Problem* (1975b, pp. 259–283).
(4) For the Victoria line see Foster and Beesley's 'Estimating the social benefit of constructing an underground railway in London' (1963), abridged in Munby (1968).
(5) Pearce and Nash's 'The evaluation of urban motorway schemes: a case study' (1973) is worth reading.
(6) Barker and Button's *Case Studies in Cost Benefit Analysis* (1975) gives brief analyses of five cases including the Victoria line and the Third London Airport.

Finally, there is the *Report of the Advisory Committee on Trunk Road Assessment,* under the chairmanship of Sir George Leitch (Department of Transport, 1977c). It is neither a general text nor a specific case study but offers a most lucid analysis of the problems in applying cost–benefit analysis to trunk road schemes. It includes a number of examples of sensitivity tests and makes recommendations for improvements in a number of the Department of Transport's evaluation procedures.

CHAPTER 7

Spatial Equilibrium

INTRODUCTION

This chapter attempts to bring together a range of issues concerning where people earn and consume their incomes. These issues can be classified as follows. First are considerations that determine the location of individuals and firms as *producers*. Second are factors that govern the location of individuals as consumers (i.e. where they like to live and spend their incomes). The decisions of producers and consumers together determine the overall distribution of activities on both the regional and the urban scale. The purpose of the chapter is not to provide a detailed description of the specific distributions of industries or populations nor even to outline a comprehensive theory of the location of firms or individuals; rather, it is to present some insights into how locational decisions are governed by transport cost considerations and how the producer's decision of *what* he wants to produce is linked with *where* he wants to produce it or the consumer's decision of *what* he wants to consume is linked with *where* he wants to consume it.

Spatial problems have been neglected in economic theory, and the field of spatial economics is relatively uncharted. Historically, the theory of firm location was first developed by Weber (1909), whose work went unnoticed until Hoover drew attention to it in the later 1940s. Hoover (1948) improved many aspects of the theory and introduced a greater measure of reality. During the 1950s further additions were made to the structure of this theory, of which the most noteworthy contribution came from Isard (1956) who demonstrated the unity of the theory with classical economics-of-substitution analysis and also extended its scope to cover regional analysis. This led to the development of theories of market areas such as Perroux's (1950) growth poles, which bear a close relation to the work of Lösch (1944), who developed the theory of central place in order to explain the empirical regularities of economic regions.

While these developments have occurred motivations for locational decisions by individuals have hardly received attention. Hoover (1948), for instance, has argued that producers' motives are much more significant than consumers' motives in shaping overall locational patterns. Hence, he has thought it appropriate to admit consumer motivations through the back door in the form of labour costs and their effect on producer location; but consumers' spatial decisions (i.e. those relating to the questions of where they would like to work and live) have not received attention as part of formal location theory.

In the urban context an individual's locational decisions fall into two categories: first, once he has found a job, and hence his workplace, an individual must decide where to live; second, he may already have a home and be looking for a better job, in which case his locational decision is to determine the best site for his workplace. These, in a sense, are static locational decisions although they play a crucial role in the determination of journey-to-work lengths (Beesley and Dalvi, 1974). The more dynamic decisions entail changes in the location of workplaces as well as in that of residences. This happens when individual workers move out of their existing locations in search of better opportunities elsewhere. These latter decisions, which explain in large part interurban migrations, determine the shape of urban patterns in the long run.

In recent years urban analysts have developed theoretical models to explain the residential locations of households. The pioneering work in this field is that of Alonso (1964a) who has applied conventional consumer utility theory to explain household location and the determination of urban rents. His work has been extended through contributions by later writers (Herbert and Stevens, 1960; Senior and Wilson, 1973; Wilson, 1969), but these developments have mainly focused on the sophistication of Alonso's original residential-location model. Apart from the paper by Beesley and Dalvi cited above the factors and motivations affecting households' workplace locations have not been fully explained. Similarly, more long-run changes in household locations involving shift in both workplaces as well as residences have received only cursory attention.

Despite recent interest in household locational decisions the focus of attention in this chapter will nevertheless be on producer location and firm behaviour. In the first place, ultimate household locational patterns are determined by the geographic distribution of opportunities, which in turn depends primarily on the location of production. Second, consumer locational preferences seem to be more stable and less susceptible to change in locational costs or geographic patterns than producer preferences. Producer motives, as Hoover (1948) has emphasised, are more compelling; he who ignores them risks bankruptcy rather than a diminution of utility.

The plan of the chapter is as follows. We shall first examine the nature of transport costs and their effect on the locations of business enterprises. We shall then outline the salient features of the location theory, depending mainly on the work of Hoover (1948) and Alonso (1964b). These sections will deal with explaining the locational behaviour of business firms via free markets, but in recent years attention has turned to national regional development. Increasingly, the question of the optimal distribution of activities is being considered by a government agency as part of its overall economic plan rather than as a profit-making venture by a private firm. In this regard there have been two distinct developments. First, there is the Hitchcock–Koopmans formulation of the transport-cost minimisation problem, whose purpose is to determine an optimal pattern of commodity flows over a given transport network. We shall discuss this briefly in a subsequent section. Second, there is the more general approach to spatial equlibrium problems, which not only deals with the inter-regional commodity flows and inter-regional input–output linkages between two or more spatially defined economies but also probes into the determination of competitive prices in the spatially separated markets. This is the Enke–Samuelson spatial price-equilibrium problem, which we shall discuss briefly in the final section. Inter-regional input–output relationships, which in a sense treat the Hitchcock–Koopmans transportation problem as a special part of a general activity-allocation problem, will be left out of the present discussion partly because they deal with more complicated spatial relationships and partly also because they involve complex mathematics. Interested readers may, however, refer to Takayama and Judge (1971) for a more comprehensive treatment of these models.

THE STRUCTURE OF TRANSPORT COSTS AND THE LOCATION OF ECONOMIC ACTIVITY

THE STRUCTURE OF COSTS

The most obvious basis for the distribution of industries and people is the disposition of natural resources. A productive enterprise wanting to produce and sell a particular product must take into account the expense and inconvenience of producing materials, transforming them into the product and finally selling to its customers. In principle the firm's productive activity falls into three stages:

(1) procurement (i.e. the purchase and assembly of necessary materials and supplies at the production site);

(2) processing (i.e. the transformation of materials into final products); and
(3) distribution (i.e. the sale and delivery of products).

In a competitive market a profit-maximising firm wants to minimise the price charged to the final consumer by saving costs on each of these three stages. For present purposes we shall assume that demand is fixed, that processing costs are locationally independent and that there are no risk and uncertainty associated with particular locations. Under these conditions the firm attempting to minimise the price of its product will select a location that will minimise the total procurement and distribution costs.

There is always a difference between the costs of performing a transport service and the charges that a shipper or consignee has to pay to have that service performed. The difference arises mainly because the rates charged by a transport agency do not usually reflect the assignable costs of the service. In this discussion we shall ignore this and focus primarily on the cost characteristics of different transport agencies. Generally a producer can choose between carriers to procure materials or distribute products, depending on his particular requirements. No matter what mode of transport he chooses, in general the longer the distance the greater the transport expenses that he must bear. However, it is a common characteristic of all transport agencies that cost does not increase in direct proportion with distance. In the first place there are terminal costs: the costs of loading and unloading and of packing and insurance. These in general will not vary with distance. Second, it is common practice in the transport industry to charge a lower rate per mile for longer hauls, so that the slope of the curve of transport costs flattens with increasing distance. The tendency of transport costs to taper off with increasing distance is, however, more marked in agencies that need heavy investment in terminal facilities. Usually trucks have lower terminal costs but higher per-mile costs than railways, as do railways with respect to ships. Figure 7.1 shows the relation of transport costs to distance when alternative carriers are considered. The user will choose the carrier with the lowest costs for a particular distance, so that his effective curve of transport costs will be the heavy line in Figure 7.1, which is more curved than that of any one mode.

THE LOCATION OF A FIRM WITH ONE MATERIAL AND ONE MARKET

The profit-maximising firm responds to transport costs by seeking to minimise them. It can reduce procurement costs by moving to a point

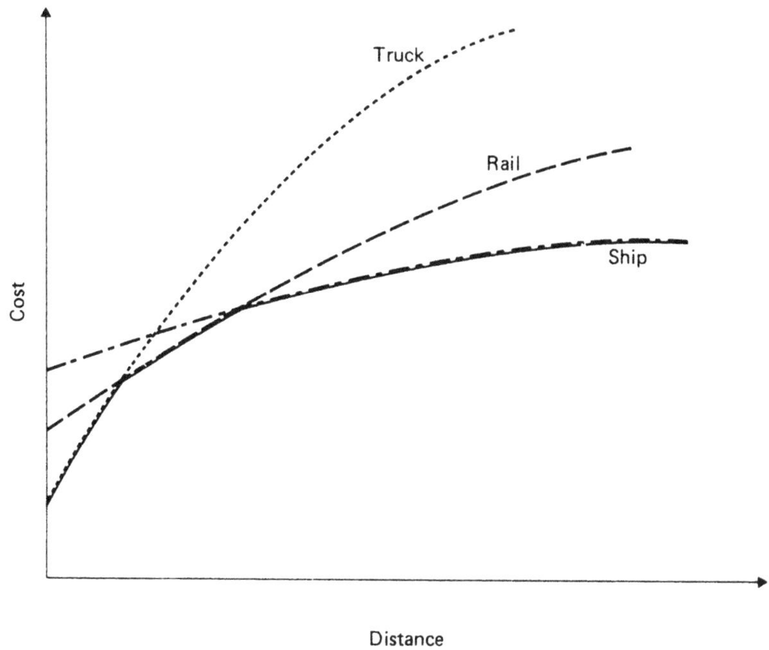

Figure 7.1 *Transport costs by alternative carriers*

with better access to materials or can lessen distribution costs by moving to a point nearer markets. These two considerations are quite likely to lead in different directions, so that the firm must strike a balance of relative advantages by choosing a location that will minimise total transport costs.

To illustrate this principle let us examine the simplest case by considering an activity that uses only one material and produces only one kind of product, sold in a single market. In Figure 7.2 the base line measures distance along the most economic route between the material's source and the market, and the gradients *a* and *b* show procurement costs and distribution costs respectively for all production locations along the route. Note that because of the curvature of the procurement and distribution costs the total transport-cost curve is also curved with the costliest point occurring at an intermediate point.

In Figure 7.2 the firm obtains its raw material at *M* and sells its product at *C*. The curve of procurement costs is steeper than that of distribution costs, meaning that it is more expensive to move the raw material than the product. For this particular case the curve of total

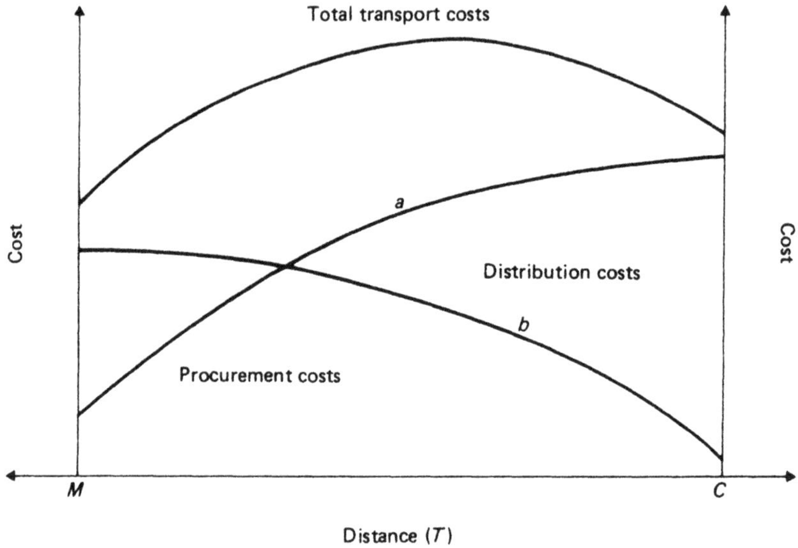

Figure 7.2 *The transport costs of a firm with one material and one market*

transport costs has a minimum point at *M* (i.e. the material source), indicating that this is the best location for the firm. Had the curve of distribution costs been the steeper, the curve of combined transport costs would have been lowest at *C*, indicating that the pull of the market was the stronger and that the ideal location would be the market location.

It is apparent from Figure 7.2 that, as long as the gradients of procurement and distribution costs show their characteristic convexity, the combined transport-costs curve must dip at both ends, generally with one end lower than the other, indicating that the best location will usually be found either at the material's source or at the market location. Although this conclusion needs some reservations it is part of the explanation for the spatial concentration as opposed to the dispersion of activities.

One special case, however, deserves attention as it accounts in large measure for the growth of many cities (e.g. London, New York). This is the use of trans-shipment points (e.g. seaports). Here, goods brought in by ship must be taken off and put on trucks or railways for onward movement and vice versa. This provides an excellent opportunity to process materials after they are unloaded from one carrier and before

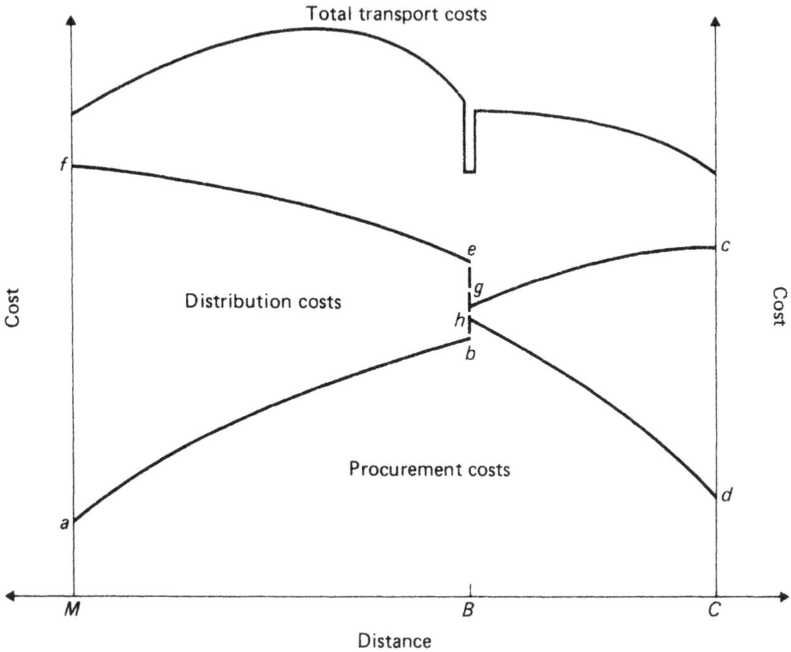

Figure 7.3 *Transport costs involving a trans-shipment point*

they are loaded on another. In such a case it is clear that the total transport costs will be minimised by locating the production process at the trans-shipment point. The case is illustrated diagrammatically in Figure 7.3. Assume that the raw material, which is available at *M*, is brought in by sea to *B*, from which it is carried by rail to the market at *C*. For this movement the procurement costs are shown in the figure by curve *Mabgc*. If the material were processed at the source, *M*, the costs of distributing the product first by sea and then by rail with trans-shipment at point *B* would be shown by curve *Cdhef*. As trans-shipment is involved in either case, the curves of procurement and distribution costs both show a vertical jump in the gradient at *B*. Consequently, the curve of total transport costs dips at *B*, indicating that this is the best location from the point of view of transport. Ports owe their existence to the fact that they often prove to be the best location.

THE LOCATION OF A FIRM WITH MANY RAW MATERIALS

When considering the location of a firm with more than one material or market a two-dimensional diagram is not enough. For each additional

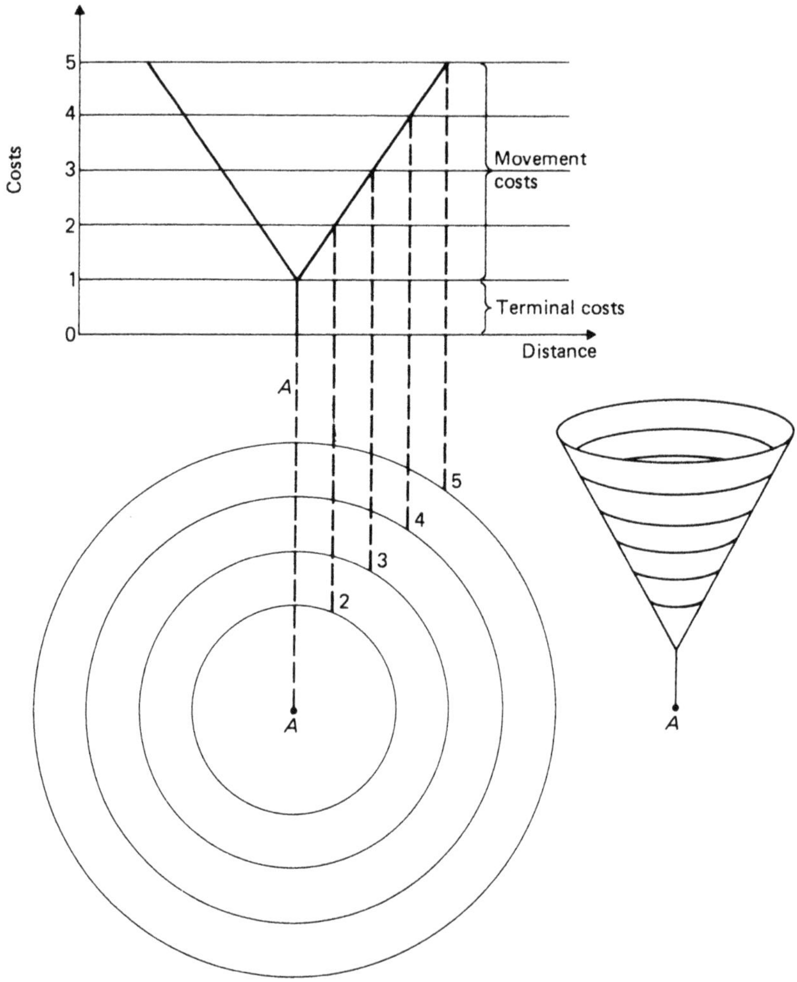

Figure 7.4 *Transport costs: alternative diagrammatic representations* (adapted from Alonso, 1964a, b)

raw material or market considered an additional dimension is needed to represent its location. For instance, to analyse the case of the firm with two materials and one market a three-dimensional model is needed. Although it is possible to draw three-dimensional diagrams it is extremely cumbersome to work with them, but locational theorists such as Alonso (1964a, b) have shown a simpler way of handling such cases. In the upper part of Figure 7.4 the transport costs from some point A are shown much as in Figure 7.2 except that the possibility of movement in both directions from A is being considered. In fact movement in every direction from A may be considered, so that the transport costs will look like a windblown umbrella as shown in the diagram on the right, where the stem represents the terminal costs and the rings above it the movement costs. The meaning of each circle in the lower part of Figure 7.4 is that one unit of whatever is being shipped from A can be carried to any other point on the circle at the same cost.

Consider now the location of a firm that uses two raw materials, M_1 and M_2, and sells its products at a single market, C. It is necessary to standardise the quantities per unit of product. Let us assume that 2 tons of M_1 and one ton of M_2 are needed for one unit of product. It can be found that the terminal costs of M_1 and M_2 are the same (i.e. £1 per ton) but that the movement costs per ton differ, with M_1 and M_2 costing respectively £0.67 and £1.00 per 100 miles to move. Movement costs per unit of product will therefore be £1.34 for M_1 and £1.00 for M_2. Terminal costs for the product are £3, and the movement costs are £1 per 100 miles.

With these cost details the analysis can be carried out as in Figure 7.5. Around M_1 are drawn a series of circles, each representing the transport costs of carrying the 2 tons needed per unit of product at a given distance; these curves are called *isotims*. Similarly, the transport costs of moving the necessary quantity of M_2, shown by another series of circles, are drawn. Finally, isotims for the product are drawn, centred on C. The total transport costs at any point will be the sum of the isotims. For example, at point X the costs of carrying 2 tons of M_1 are £10, the costs of bringing 1 ton of M_2 are £4, and the costs of delivering a unit of product to C are £8; total transport costs are thus £22. As total transport costs are calculated over the map, points with the same total costs may be joined. The resulting lines, shown by the heavy solid curves in Figure 7.5, are called *isodapanes.*

To locate the plant it is necessary to find the point of least transport costs (i.e. a point on the isodapane with a minimum transport cost). In many cases the least cost isodapane may indicate the true minimum at some intermediate point between the raw material sources and the market (e.g. point A in Figure 7.5). It is also a normal feature of isodapanes to get closer and closer to a single point as the total transport costs are reduced, so that there is not a multiplicity of intermediate locations to choose from. It must, however, be pointed out that the intermediate location determined by isodapane mapping (e.g. point A in Figure 7.5) is nevertheless a relative minimum. Locations at material

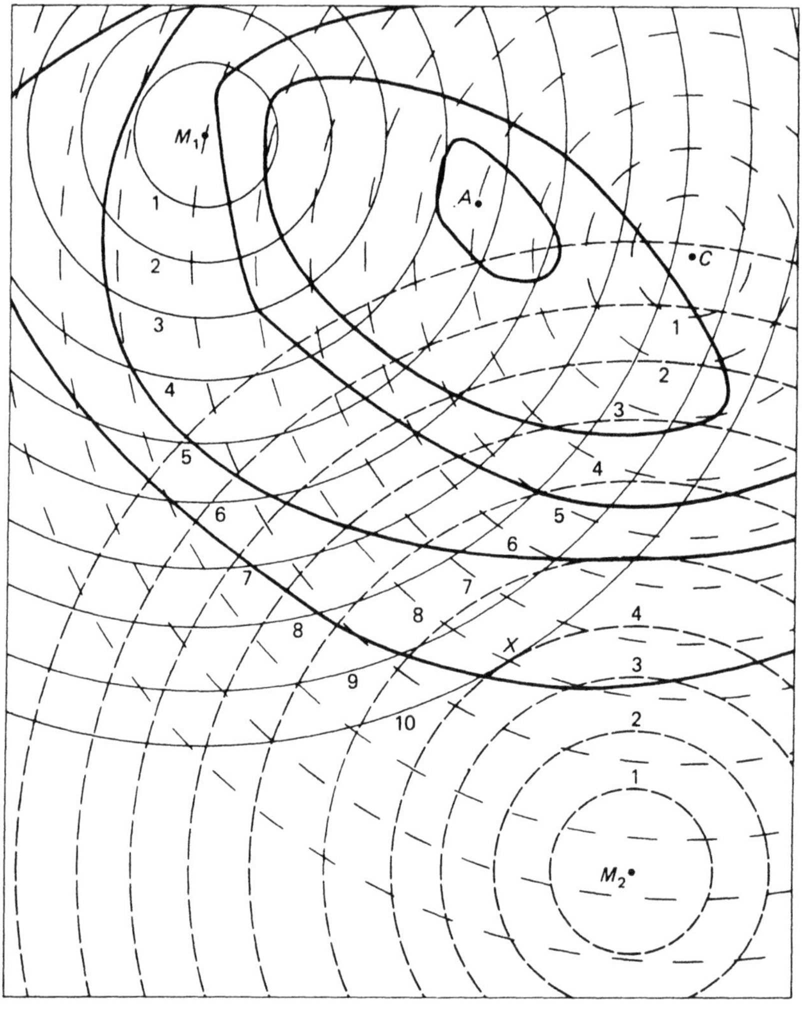

Figure 7.5 *Isotims and isodapanes for a firm with two materials and one market* (adapted from Alonso, 1964a, b)

sources M_1 and M_2 or at market C may be equally efficient or even better. Consequently, the minimum found by isodapane mapping should be checked against location at the sources of materials or at the market to ensure that the true minimum is found.

In the preceding illustration it has been assumed that transport is equally possible in all directions. Hence, isotims have been constructed in the form of evenly spaced concentric circles. However, roads and railways exist only in certain directions, so that rather than perfect circles isotims will take forms more similar to starfish with arms extending along the transport routes, as shown in Figure 7.6, where *AA* and *BB* are roads and railways and a single isotim is shown. Although point *D* is nearer than point *C* to source *M* it is more expensive to reach, since part of the travel must be over routes inferior to *AA*.

The analysis presented above can be extended to cover a problem involving any number of points and any number of routes. All of this will complicate the geometry of isotims but not their logic, which is based on location theory.

TRANSPORT–COST MINIMISATION MODELS

As mentioned in the introductory section, transport-cost minimisation models are essentially planning rather than explanatory tools whose purpose it is to ensure an 'optimal' distribution of activities within a regional or urban area subject to certain supply and demand constraints. The original model, first formulated by Hitchcock (1941) and later analysed by Koopmans (1949), aims to find a pattern of shipments that involves minimum total transport-cost. The model has been extended by later writers to incorporate a number of specific aspects of spatial interactions such as spatial price equilibrium (Samuelson, 1952), inter-regional flows and trade analysis (Isard, 1956) and inter-regional input–output analysis (Leontief, 1963). To these may be added the work of

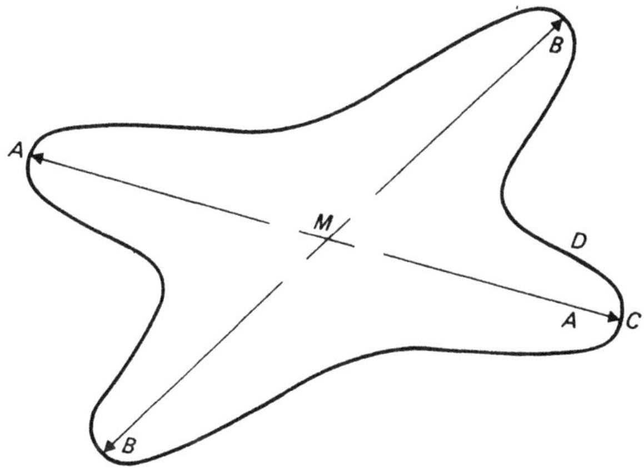

Figure 7.6 *Isotim considering the transport network*

Wilson (1970) who has developed entropy-maximising models to explain spatial interactions in both urban and regional contexts. It is not possible to deal with these models satisfactorily here as we can use only elementary tools to analyse them; so our attention will be centred on explaining the basic rationale underlying their structure. For a more comprehensive understanding readers should refer to the original authors. In this section we shall deal briefly first with the Hitchcock–Koopmans cost-minimisation model and then with Samuelson's formulation of spatial price-equilibrium model.

THE HITCHCOCK–KOOPMANS COST-MINIMISATION MODEL

The essence of the model can best be conveyed by a simple example. Suppose that a homogeneous product is produced at three spatially separated factories and supplied to five spatially separated markets. Suppose also that the costs of shipping 1 ton of product from each factory to each market are given, the capacities of the factories are known, and the number of tons to be supplied to each market is fixed. The problem then is to find a pattern of shipment that minimises total transport costs and is consistent with these conditions. This calls for a decision regarding the number of tons to be shipped by each plant to each locality. Clearly, total shipments from each plant must not exceed its capacity while shipments received by markets must equal their requirements. There are many possible routings that meet these conditions, the transportation problem being to find the one that does so with the least possible total transport-cost.

The data used for this kind of problem are commonly displayed in the form of a rectangular array as in Table 7.1. The capacities of the plants are shown in the last row. The quantities required by each market are given in the last column. Transport costs are given in the body of the table. Thus the cost of shipping 1 ton of product from factory 1 to market 5 is £40. An important feature of this problem is that the total capacity of all the plants just equals the total needs of all the markets.

In empirical studies problems of this kind are solved with the aid of computers by setting them up in linear-programming form. Although economists have recently taken increasing interest in linear programming the technique requires a good knowledge of matrix algebra to comprehend it fully, and we do not advocate this approach to the solution of the 'transportation problem'. Readers should consult Dorfman, Samuelson and Solow (1958) for the simplest description of this approach. In this section we shall merely set up the problem in standard linear-programming form in order to outline the nature of its solution and the

Table 7.1 *Typical display of data for transport cost minimisation*

	Factory 1	*Factory* 2	*Factory* 3	*Requirement (tons)*
Market 1	£10	£20	£30	25
2	15	40	35	115
3	20	15	40	60
4	20	30	55	30
5	40	30	25	70
Capacity (tons)	50	100	150	300

logic behind it. We shall first state the problem for the numerical example of Table 7.1 and then describe its general structure.

Let X_{ij} denote the non-negative number of tons shipped from factory i to market j, and let C_{ij} denote the transport cost per ton for shipments between these termini. Total transport cost – the sum to be minimised – is then

$$T = \sum_i \sum_j C_{ij} X_{ij} \qquad \begin{array}{l} i = 1, 2, 3 \\ j = 1, 2, 3, 4, 5 \end{array} \tag{1}$$

for the example in Table 7.1. To achieve this minimum any values of X_{ij} that satisfy three main restrictions can be selected. First, the shipments planned for each factory must not exceed the capacity of that factory. Second, the total shipments to each market must equal the requirements of that market. Third, the amount shipped cannot be negative. Symbolically, the problem is to find the values of X_{ij} that minimise equation 1 subject to the following constraints:

$$\sum_j X_{ij} \leqslant K_i \qquad \begin{array}{l} i = 1, 2, 3 \\ K_i = \text{capacity of factory } i \end{array} \tag{2}$$

$$\sum_i X_{ij} \geqslant D_j \qquad \begin{array}{l} j = 1, 2, 3, 4, 5 \\ D_j = \text{requirements of market or locality } j \end{array} \tag{3}$$

$$X_{ij} \geqslant 0 \qquad \begin{array}{l} i = 1, 2, 3 \\ j = 1, 2, 3, 4, 5 \end{array} \tag{4}$$

If it is also specified that total supply exactly equals total demand, i.e.

$$\sum_{i=1}^{3} K_i = \sum_{j=1}^{5} D_j \tag{5}$$

constraints 2 and 3 can be turned into equalities, so that any standard method can be used for solving limited linear programmes of this kind.

These equations suggest that the computations required by the transportation problem are exceptionally simple; all the choice variables enter the restraining equations with the same coefficient, namely, unit.

It happens that all mathematical linear-programming problems come in pairs; the original problem as set up in equations 1 to 4 is known as *primal,* which is ultimately related to another problem called its *dual.* The structure of the dual to the transportation problem is rather simple. For the dual it is necessary to define two new sets of variables:

U_i = the shadow price on capacity at factory i ($i = 1, 2, 3$)

V_j = the shadow price on demand at market j ($j = 1, 2, 3, 4, 5$)

The dual problem is to maximise

$$Z = \sum_{j=1}^{5} D_j V_j + \sum_{i=1}^{3} -K_i U_i \qquad (6)$$

subject to

$$V_j - U_i \leqslant C_{ij} \qquad \begin{aligned} i &= 1, 2, 3 \\ j &= 1, 2, 3, 4, 5 \end{aligned} \qquad (7)$$

In location theory shadow variables U_i and V_j have an interesting interpretation. In value terms the constraining equation 7 expresses the requirement that the value differential between origin and destination cannot exceed the transport costs involved in making the shipment from factory to locality. This condition is closely related to spatial price equilibrium. Let us assume a price, P, that expresses production costs, including normal profits, and call this the *base price* of the product at all locations. This base price can be incorporated into constraint 7 by writing it as

$$(V_j + P) - (U_i + P) \leqslant C_{ij} \qquad \begin{aligned} i &= 1, 2, 3 \\ j &= 1, 2, 3, 4, 5 \end{aligned} \qquad (8)$$

without in fact altering the constraints.

Now $(U_i + P)$ may be spoken of as the f.o.b. price at production point i and $(V_j + P)$ as the delivery price at market j. Constraining equation 8 then expresses the usual conditions of spatial price equilibrium, as we shall see below (for further discussion see Stevens, 1961).

We shall now return to the primal problem as defined by equations 1 to 5. Considering this as an ordinary linear-programming problem, it is necessary to minimise a weighted sum, T, of fifteen choice variables, K_{ij}. There are fifteen variables because i takes on three values, j takes on five values and all combinations are permissible. These fifteen variables are subject to eight restraining equations – one for each of three supplying factories and one for each of five consuming markets. However, by virtue of equation 5 one of the constraining equations is redundant. Effectively, there are therefore seven rather then eight restraining equations. A general principle of linear programming states that an optimal solution exists in which the number of choice variables (i.e. shipments) at positive levels is no greater than the number of restraining equations (in this case, seven).

The strategy of solution is the same as that used in ordinary linear programming. A *basic solution* is a set of routes in which the number of routes used at positive levels is equal to the number of restraining equations (i.e. the number of origins plus destinations less one). We start with any basic solution and then by an iterative process derive from it successively better solutions until an optimal one is obtained (for further discussion see Dorfman, Samuelson and Solow, 1958).

To state this problem in general form, assume that there are m points of origin and n points of destination. We define an *activity* to be the making of a shipment from a specific point of origin to a specific destination. There will then be mn activities to be considered. The levels of these activities will have to satisfy m restrictions relating to origins and n restrictions relating to destinations – a total of $(m + n)$. However, in view of the condition that the total supply must equal the total demand (equation 5 above), if any $m + n - 1$ restrictions are satisfied, the remaining restrictions will also be satisfied. Thus, only $m + n - 1$ restrictions will be effective, and a minimum cost set of shipments will exist in which only $m + n - 1$ of the choice variables (i.e. activities) are used at positive levels. The argument and the solution procedure for the general case are similar to those for the special case but are beyond the scope of this book.

SAMUELSON'S SPATIAL PRICE-EQUILIBRIUM MODEL

In the preceding section we showed how the dual variables of the Hitchcock–Koopmans linear-programming problems are related to spatial equilibrium prices (equation 8). From an economist's point of view a more instructive way of establishing this relationship is to construct the spatial equilibrium problem on Enke–Samuelson lines, in which instead of minimising total transport cost the objective function is to maximise a net social payoff (NSP) to be defined shortly. The data requirements are similar except that, while in the linear-programming transportation problem total shipments to or from a locality (i.e. local demands and supplies) are given, in the Enke–Samuelson problem they are unknown. In this sense the latter problem is the more general one and encompasses the former. In fact originally Enke (1951) did not construct the spatial equilibrium problem as a maximum problem; this was left to Samuelson (1952) who, by introducing the concept of net social payoff, first cast it mathematically into a maximum problem and then related it to the minimum transport-cost problem. Our discussion depends primarily on Samuelson's formulation.

As in the Hitchcock–Koopmans problem, at each location domestic demand and supply curves are given for a given homogeneous product (e.g. wheat) in terms of its market price at that locality. Note, however, that although demand and supply curves for each locality are given the amounts shipped to or from each locality are determined in the solution of this problem. Also, as in the transportation problem, constant transport costs for carrying one unit of the product between any two of the specified localities are given. The problem is to determine the final competitive equilibrium of prices in all the markets, of amounts shipped from each locality to any other locality and of exports and imports at each locality.

Samuelson has examined this problem diagrammatically for a two-variable case and mathematically for the general case. For simplicity we shall confine our discussion to the former. Figure 7.7 shows the usual back-to-back diagram determining the equilibrium flow of exports from market 1 to market 2. Before trade equilibrium is at $P_1 = A_1$, where supply and demand in market 1 just meet or where the excess supply function ES_1ES_1 – equal to the demand curve subtracted laterally at every price from the supply curve – is at its zero point. Similarly, $P_2 = A_2$ if no trade is possible.

Suppose that goods can move from market 1 to market 2 for T_{12} pounds per unit and from market 2 to market 1 for T_{21} pounds per unit. By construction pretrade price is lower in market 1 than market 2; so trade will obviously never flow from market 2 to market 1, and hence only the T_{12} cost is relevant. Because the initial differential in prices exceeds the transport costs there will be a positive flow of exports from market 1 to market 2, and P_2 will exceed P_1 by exactly T_{12}. Note that the axes of market 1 have been lifted upward relative to those of market 2 by distance T_{12}. The new equilibrium is shown at B, where the excess supply or exports of market 1 exactly equal the negative excess supply or imports of market 2. The distances E_{12}, $-E_{21}$ and CB are all exactly equivalent depictions of those flows.

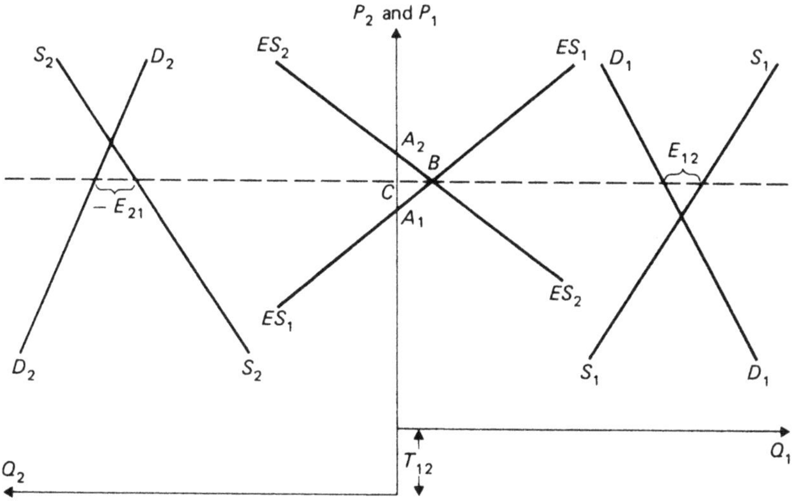

Figure 7.7 *Spatial price equilibrium: a two-market case* (adapted from Samuelson, 1952)

If the price differential between the two markets (i.e. the distance between A_1 and A_2) had been smaller than the transport costs T_{12} (or T_{21}), no trade would have existed, and the separate equilibria would be at A_1 and A_2 prices. Had A_2 been lower than A_1 by more than T_{21}, the flow of exports would have reversed automatically.

How may these price equilibrium conditions be related to the Hitchcock–Koopmans problem? Rewriting the constraining equation 7 of the dual problen. from the last section gives

$$V_j \leqslant U_i + C_{ij}$$

which states that for any origin–destination pair the value at the destination must be no greater than the value at the origin (i.e. factory) plus the transport cost. According to the basic principles of linear programming, if any constraint is satisfied with exact equality in the solution to the dual problem, the corresponding primal variable (in this case, shipments) will have a positive value in the primal solution; and if a constraint is satisfied with an inequality in the solution to the dual problem, the corresponding variable in the direct solution will equal zero (see Dorfman, Samuelson and Solow 1958, for further details).

Applying these rules to our diagrammatic example yields rather complicated non-linear equilibrium conditions. If

$$P_2 = P_1 + T_{12} \tag{9}$$

any non-negative E_{12} may flow. $E_{12} > 0$ implies that the dual constraint $P_2 \leqslant P_1 + T_{12}$ is satisfied with exact equality $P_2 = P_1 + T_{12}$.

Similarly, if both

$$\left.\begin{array}{l} P_2 < P_1 + T_{12} \\ P_1 < P_2 + T_{21} \end{array}\right\} \tag{10}$$

that is, if the dual constraints are satisfied with inequalities, $E_{12} = 0$ and $-E_{21} = 0$.

Finally, if

$$P_1 = P_2 + T_{21} \tag{11}$$

$-E_{21} \geqslant 0$ and $-E_{21} > 0$ imply that $P_1 = P_2 + T_{12}$.

These conditions can be restated in economic terms by depicting them as in Figure 7.8. The same excess supply curves are shown, but this time prices in the two markets are measured from the same level. The final equilibrium is determined at *JK*, where the two excess supply curves differ vertically by the amount of transport costs, T_{12}. The equilibrium determination of exports, E_{12}, and imports, $-E_{21}$, is shown

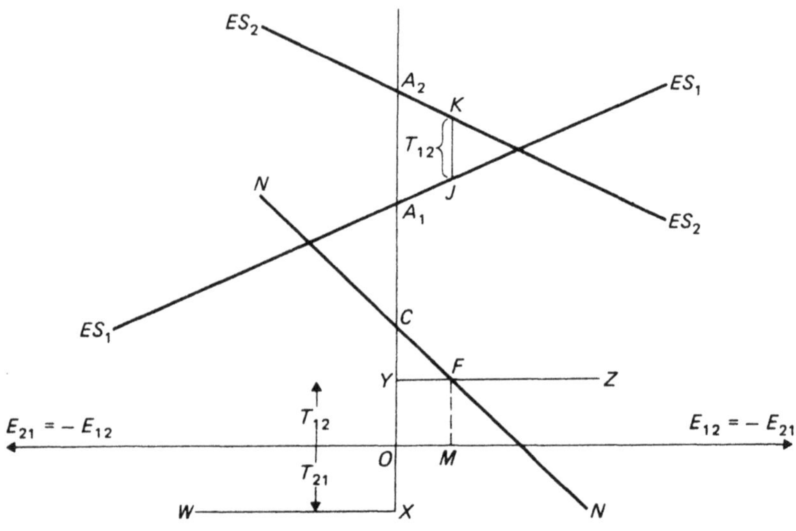

Figure 7.8 *An equivalent depiction of spatial equilibrium: a two-market case*

by the *NN* curve, which represents the vertical differences between the two excess supply curves. The final equilibrium is at *F* where the net excess supply curve hits the curve of discontinuous transport costs, *WXYZ*.

In Figure 7.8 the NSP is represented by area A_1JKA_2 or its equivalent area *OMFC* minus the area under the transport curve, *OMFY*. It consists of three components: NSP = social payoff in market 1 plus social payoff in market 2 minus transport cost, and in this sense bears close resemblance to consumer surplus concept. The social payoff of any market is defined as the algebraic area under its excess demand curve, which is equal in magnitude to the area under its excess supply curve with opposite algebraic sign. Since market 2 has been put back to back in market 1 the area under market 2's *ES* curve does not measure that market's payoff and from it must be subtracted the area – negative in algebraic sign – under market 1's *ES* curve. Hence the area under the net curve *NN* in Figure 7.8 does perfectly measure the combined social payoff of both markets.

To complete the two-variable case, in Figure 7.9 curve *NȮN* has been drawn to show how the combined payoff of the two markets varies with algebraic flows from market 1 to market 2. From this is subtracted the curve of total transport cost, *UOU*. Equilibrium is found where the vertical distance between the two upper curves is maximised.

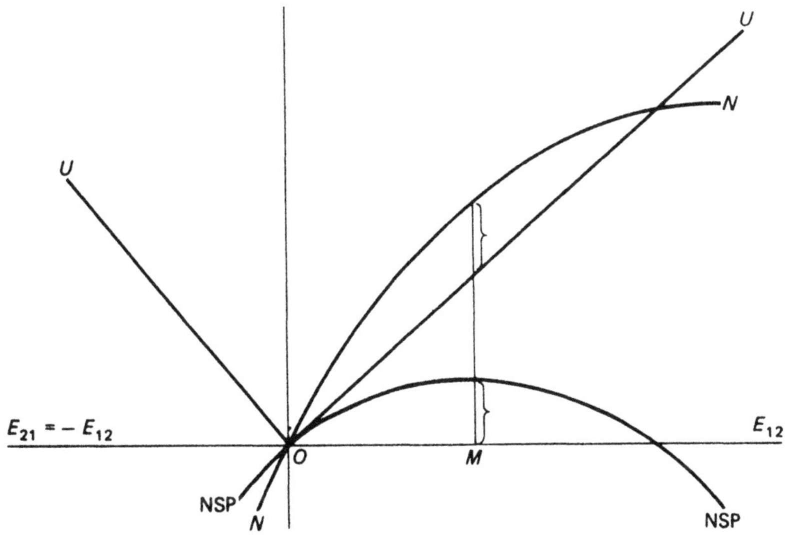

Figure 7.9 *Spatial equilibrium: the maximisation of net social payoff*

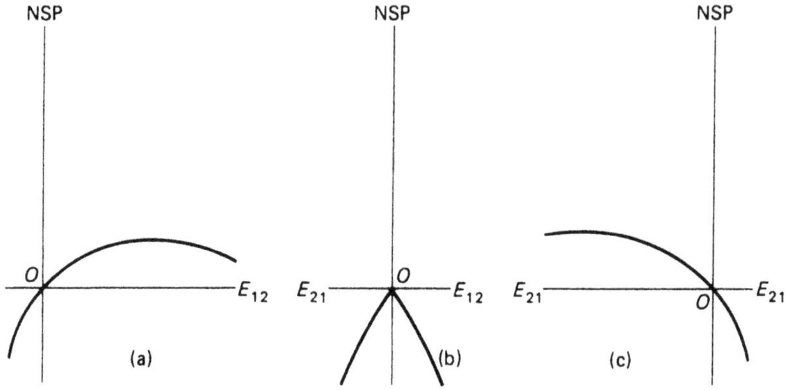

Figure 7.10 *Types of maxima for net social payoff* (Samuelson's, 1952, representation)

This optimal level of exports, E_{12}, or imports $-E_{21}$, is also shown at the maximum point of the NSP curve, which measures the vertical distance between the upper two.

Figure 7.10 illustrates the three possible cases that could emerge, corresponding to equations 9 to 11. In Figure 7.10a market 1 exports to market 2 so that the maximum point is smooth; the corner in the curve, due to the discontinuity in the transport cost curve as shown in Figure 7.9, is on the vertical axis and does not affect the maximum. Similarly, Figure 7.10c shows a smooth maximum without corners when market 2 exports to market 1. Figure 7.10b shows the intermediate case where the maximum point is a cusp with a corner; no trade takes place as transport costs exceed the price differential between the two markets.

CONCLUDING OBSERVATIONS

In this chapter we have outlined briefly the salient features of the location theory, mainly from the point of view of the firm or of the project. We have concentrated on transport costs as a factor affecting the locational behaviour of firms, partly because the expense and inconvenience of procuring the required inputs and delivering the products to customers are often the most important consideration governing a firm's location decision but partly also because the transport costs vary in a patterned way over space. However, there are other factors that may also influence the firm's locational behaviour and hence the distribution of activity patterns, the most important of which include labour costs, technical know-how, taxes and other government policies affecting industrial location. Of course these factors do not vary systematically over space, but there is no difficulty in dealing with them theoretically. All that is necessary is to compare the savings in real costs per unit of outlay among alternative locations on account of these factors and to offset them against the extra transport costs incurred at more distant locations.

The minimisation of transport costs is also the most important criterion governing the decision of a government agency that wants to optimise the location of a factory as part of its overall development plan, as long as the decision turns on the project maximising its own returns. However, the locational decision of the government agency may not be based on maximising the financial returns of the particular enterprise. In the first place the location theory has little force in considering costs and benefits occurring outside the books of the enterprise. Regional economics is concerned with these external or multiplicative effects within the region, and national regional planning is concerned with these effects among regions. The investment criteria adopted for efficient regional planning need not therefore be tagged to minimum transport-cost consideration alone but must take into account the wider external effects associated with the proposed investment.

Second, the government may be concerned as a policy to ensure a balanced regional development of the economy; but if the transport-costs minimisation approach were strictly applied to locational decisions, many disadvantaged regions with poor industrial opportunities might not be candidates for investments. Thus, the purely allocative efficiency criteria underlying the conventional location theory are likely to lead to regional imbalances unless corrective actions are undertaken to direct investment into economically more backward regions. Of course we do not suggest that regional imbalances are not optimal – only that the social consequences of such imbalances may not be politically acceptable. For this if for no other reason it is important that the solution given by the conventional location theory be qualified for purposes of national spatial planning in order that long-term regional development may proceed along desirable lines.

Despite these limitations of the location theory there is much to be said for the formal properties of the spatial equilibrium solution based on transport-costs minimisation principle. For the purposes of spatial planning the following general principles may be stated with a certain amount of validity:

(1) Prices of commodities and of services must reflect real costs at the place of production and the place of consumption.
(2) Prices of homogeneous goods must be the same at a given location without regard to origin and should differ from location to location by the marginal cost of transportation.
(3) The present discounted value of net returns from the investment at the optimal location must be larger than or equal to the present discounted value of the net returns from the same investment project computed for any other locations, basing the computation on real costs and interest.

These principles are equally valid in a free market as well as in a socialist economy, and their violation would result in the misallocation of resources and the loss of future savings and growth potential. The above principles are implicit in the solution to the dual of the transport-costs minimisation problems and are in fact symbolised mathematically by the constraining equation 8.

All the same the formal theory, as Alonso (1964b) has pointed out, has little to say on some important aspects, which remain matters of judgement rather than of scientific analysis. The more important of these aspects relate to: first, forecasting regional demand for the product concerned, which for the purposes of locational analysis is taken for granted; second, dealing with external economies or diseconomies, which, as we have observed, are taken into account within a broader regional development context but are neglected in the locational theory; and third, accounting for risk and uncertainty in locational decisions. Some interesting new work is being done in spatial economics to incorporate these considerations and also, as has been observed earlier, to integrate the 'producer' side of location theory with its 'consumer' side (i.e. with household residential and employment locations), but so far only a small beginning has been made. Finally, there is the most difficult question of spatial dynamics (i.e. how to forecast with certain accuracy future land use and activity patterns on the basis of behavioural parameters and technological relations simulated for the base year). Transport planners nowadays are increasingly being required in practice to tackle such dynamic issues, but with little guidance from formal theory. Spatial dynamics is still a totally unexplored territory.

CHAPTER 8

Government Transport Policy

INTRODUCTION

This chapter aims to introduce the reader to some of the economic problems of transport policy. A detailed analysis even of only one country would occupy a book in itself and use advanced areas of economics. The more modest brief of this chapter is threefold. First, the scope of government transport policy will be described. Second, the reasons for government intervention will be analysed. Third, an analysis will be made of transport policy in the United Kingdom and an attempt to judge its efficacy. Although attention will be focused on the situation in the United Kingdom, readers from other countries will doubtless be able to see the areas where their transport policies are similar to and differ from policy in the United Kingdom and, hopefully, to appreciate the rationale for their countries' policies.

THE SCOPE OF GOVERNMENT TRANSPORT POLICY

It is possible to identify four main spheres of influence of government transport policy although the emphasis among them has varied from time to time, from mode to mode and from country to country. They are:

(1) control of quality;
(2) control of quantity;
(3) control of the organisation of the transport sector; and
(4) control of resource allocation.

The instruments used as part of the policy again vary. In the United Kingdom considerable use is made of legislative powers in the first three spheres while financial/fiscal powers are also used to influence resource allocation.

Quality control encompasses a wide area although the emphasis is usually on safety. Controls are both general (e.g. speed limits, vehicle safety standards), applying to all traffic whether public or private using a mode, and specific to particular aspects of public transport. Examples of the latter are standards set for the construction of buses and aircraft, the control of railway-operating practices and standards for transport operations, both for those in charge of vehicles (i.e. pilots and drivers) and for managers in charge of businesses.

Quantity regulation usually applies to public transport and, as its name implies, seeks to limit the quantity of transport services offered. This usually entails a reduction of supply compared to the uncontrolled situation, and regulation is generally achieved by some form of licensing.

The organisation of the transport industry has been a concern, with differing degrees of reluctance, of governments in many countries. It is not confined to situations where the government itself owns part of the industry; for example, in the United Kingdom railways were reorganised in 1921 by legislation but remained in private ownership. Recent government reorganisation of US railways has also stopped short of full public ownership, but ownership by the state and reorganisation by government policy are highly correlated.

Finally, government policy seeks to influence the efficiency of resource allocation in the transport sector. Indeed, this can be considered the ultimate objective of the first three spheres of policy, but in more recent times some aspects of government policy have been directly concerned with resource allocation. Of particular relevance here are the way in which governments use their fiscal powes in taxing road users and the way in which they use their financial powers by providing assets for the transport sector and subsidising its operations.

THE RATIONALE OF GOVERNMENT INTERVENTION IN THE TRANSPORT SECTOR

In an ideal world there might be no need for government intervention in transport policy. A perfectly functioning market could be left to determine the quantity, quality and price of transport services according to consumer preference and subject to resource constraints. The government's role in the transport sector would be confined to that of a producer and a consumer. Such an ideal does not exist, and government intervention has been necessary in the transport sector since the earliest days of the railways. Even in the *laissez-faire* era of the first half of the nineteenth century transport policy was evolved on an *ad hoc* basis by Parliament when determining which of several rival railway schemes in an area to authorise.

Indeed, railways provided the initial impetus for transport policy for to some extent each railway was a technical monopoly. Clearly, it would be very wasteful to have, say, four capital-intensive railways serving a route – a fact appreciated by early promoters. In some areas, therefore, once one railway had been established there would be no economic case for a second. Given the technical superiority of railways at that time the railway company had in these circumstances a monopoly, and in the United Kingdom at least some control was exercised by Parliament to prevent abuse. A similar situation arose with street tramways, which became common from the 1870s onwards.

The safety of railways also became a matter of public concern when it was appreciated that fatalities and serious injuries in a railway accident could be very great. Railway-operating practice left much to be desired, and eventually government policy on railway safety evolved to the point of using legislation to control certain aspects. Here is an instance of an industry allocating insufficient resources to safety under unconstrained conditions and of consumers being technically unable to appreciate the degree of safety offered by the operator. This argument led to controls on the safety of other modes of public transport, which still exist today in many countries.

When road transport developed as a less capital-intensive form of transport problems of overcapacity arose in both the bus and road haulage industries, and these became acute in the depressed years of the late 1920s and early 1930s. Many governments, including those of both Britain and America, responded to this problem by introducing some form of capacity control by licensing, which also had the objective of protecting railways from some effects of road competition. In principle, however, there is no reason why this aspect of policy should not have been left to market forces, and many economists have argued that this should be the case (e.g. Hibbs, 1971a, and Walters, 1968, in the United Kingdom; Friedlaender, 1969, in the United States) so long as appropriate safety standards are met by the different modes.

The development of road transport has involved governments in road provision and road-user taxation system. Chapter 5 has already shown that the present road-pricing system is unlikely to lead to an optimal allocation of resources. In particular it may allow journeys to be made that result in a benefit that is less than marginal social cost, even though benefit exceeds marginal private cost (see Figure 5.2, p. 81), and some trips to be made by private transport that could be made by public transport at lower resource cost (see Tyson, 1972b, for a fuller explanation). Thus further intervention in the transport market is needed in order to achieve optimal traffic flows and modal split, especially if direct road pricing is not feasible. As discussed in Chapter 5, this can range from increases in other elements of private-transport generalised costs (e.g. extra parking taxes) to subsidies of public transport. Again, however, the market alone cannot bring about an optimal allocation of resources without road pricing; hence the need for government policy to overcome the problem.

These examples show that the market in the transport sector is a far from perfect allocator, and governments of most political persuasions have needed a transport policy affecting the four areas described above. The rest of this chapter will discuss the economic implications of government policy in the United Kingdom in each sphere and try from this to draw general conclusions.

THE EFFECTS OF GOVERNMENT POLICY

THE CONTROL OF QUALITY

This area of policy has had profound influences on transport systems and has a long history. In many ways it is surprising that governments took an interest in railway safety because at the time *laissez-faire* was the dominant theme influencing government economic policy. On the roads the UK legislation of the early 1930s, particularly the Road Traffic Act, 1930, provided for government supervision of the standards of vehicles, crews and operators in both the passenger and freight sectors although licensing was more thorough and comprehensive in the passenger sector. Both these elements of policy survive today and have undergone evolution rather than revolution.

Their effects are difficult to identify partly because they have been present for so long. One major objective of policy is public safety, and it has been argued – quite rightly in our opinion although others may disagree – that, for example, the average passenger cannot distinguish a safe bus from an unsafe one other than by experience. It is a legitimate aim of government policy to protect citizens in this way. Its success is difficult to quantify because there can be no clear and objective standards by which to judge it, but the figures given in Table 8.1 for deaths and injuries in the United Kingdom show the accident record.

Table 8.1 *Deaths and injuries by transport in the United Kingdom 1982 (per 100 million passenger-kilometres).*

	Buses and coaches	*Trains*	*Cars*
Deaths	0.08	0.07	0.54
Serious injuries	2.33	13.74	6.98
Slight injuries	22.47		25.64

Source: Department of Transport (1983).

The good record of public transport in particular can only be obtained at a price. 'Quality' regulations have driven bus operators out of business and thus deprived the community of the benefits of their services. Both now and in the past the attitude of the railways inspectorate may have stifled innovation on safety grounds. Complying with safety laws uses scarce resources and is reflected in fares. The balance sheet is a notoriously difficult one to draw up and is probably worthy of further investigation, especially now that progress has been made in evaluating the economic costs of accidents as discussed in Chapter 6.

THE CONTROL OF QUANTITY

There are two possible arguments that an economist could advance in favour of quantity control in transport. First, it can be argued that in some circumstances free competition, particularly freedom of entry into the market, will result in overcapacity and that resources will be wasted in consequence. This argument only appears justified where operators are unable for some reason to forecast the future competitive situation and/or where the expansion of capacity requires expensive infrastructure that cannot easily be put to alternative uses. Second, some form of quantity control may be needed in order to ensure that existing capacity is fully utilised. Thus, it can be argued that control of a competing bus service is needed in order to ensure that a railway is fully utilised. In this case, however, it needs to be shown that the short-run marginal cost of the railway is less than that of the bus service and that the railway cannot price accordingly (e.g. if it had a financial constraint requiring it to cover average and not marginal costs). In both cases the arguments for quantity control will only be valid in particular circumstances, and on economic grounds it is difficult to justify the extensive controls still existing in many parts of the transport sector.

In this sphere government policy has for many years been to control the level of service with a view to preventing wasteful competition. This has applied to railways, bus services and road haulage. The last-mentioned will be discussed first as experience in the United Kingdom gives a useful lesson.

The main instrument of policy in the road haulage field has been legislation, and the Road and Rail Traffic Act 1933 provided for the control of both quantity and quality in the road haulage industry. The details of control need not detain us, but in outline all haulage for 'hire or reward', as opposed to 'own account' haulage, was controlled by a system of licences. Existing hauliers and the railways could object to applications for new licences. Initially, the protection of railway business was one objective, which it failed to achieve given the economic advantages of road haulage for much traffic and the 'own account' loophole. The system continued until 1963 when a Committee of Enquiry (the Geddes Committee) into its functioning was established, reporting in 1965 (Ministry of Transport, 1965). It concluded that a licensing system did not offer 'a useful way to achieve what we think might be the main aims of government policy in regulating the carriage of goods by road'. The Geddes Committee agreed with critics of the system that it reduced efficiency while giving no compensating benefits.

Although it was not the intention of the government the Transport Act 1968 effectively abolished quantity licensing in road haulage while at the same time strengthening quality licensing. The Act freed all vehicles with a plated weight of 3.5 tons or less from any licensing. Above this weight quality licensing only applied, but quantity licences were to be necessary for vehicles of over 16 tons laden weight, which would require a permit to operate more than 100 miles or, if engaged in the carriage of certain products (e.g. coal, iron, steel), over any distance. This was to apply both to hire-or-reward and to own account haulage. In the event the government changed before the relevant sections of the Act introducing the regulation could be implemented although after the sections removing the old licensing were. By default, therefore, quantity licensing was abolished.

An official study carried out since 1968 looked at the effects of removing quantity licensing (Department of the Environment, 1973). Its main conclusions were:

(1) There was some diversification of operators formerly confined to own account operation into public haulage, but the scale of this had been very small.
(2) There was no evidence of increased exit from the industry by public haulage firms. This confirmed the results of Walters's (1968) analysis of bankruptcies in road haulage prior to 1933, which were that bankruptcy was no more prevalent in road haulage than in other low capital industries (e.g. retail shops) that had similar entry 'qualifications'. Walters has discussed this further, but it should be noted that road haulage is not an industry requiring heavy infrastructure costs and that quantity licensing thus seems inappropriate on these grounds.
(3) There was no evidence of chaotic conditions of competition nor of increased abstraction of railway traffic.
(4) There was no reduction in investment by the road haulage industry.

Statistics for the period since 1970 reveal that the proportion of ton-miles carried by 'mainly public haulage' as opposed to 'mainly own account' haulage increased from 50 per cent in 1969 to 58 per cent in

1975 (Department of Transport, 1977a). This indicates that the own account sector did not make significant inroads into the public haualge market as a result of the deregulation.

Thus a sector of the transport industry can survive without licensing and controls. This has been noted by the EEC, whose means to achieve its policy of efficient resource allocation in freight transport – with each mode carrying the goods that it most efficiently can and all goods therefore going by the most efficient mode – have recently changed from means based on regulation to means based on competition.

In the passenger transport sector control over bus services still exists. Legislation has again been the policy instrument – first the Road Traffic Act 1930 and then that of 1960. In this case too the system was investigated by a Committee of Enquiry, which reported in 1953 and gave it a clean bill of health (Ministry of Transport, 1953). Interestingly, this was before the start of the decline in the demand for bus transport in 1955.

Control has been wide ranging and covered routes, timetables, stopping places and, significantly, fares. The objectives of introducing controls were to protect the railways from unfair competition and to bring order into the bus market, which had suffered from excesses of competition (e.g. rival buses racing to a stop to pick up the passengers first). Government policy in this form has had three main effects. First, it has influenced the structure of the industry and made it difficult for firms to expand other than by takeover. Whether this is a good or bad thing depends on views on matters such as whether large companies are more efficient than small ones. The facts, however, seem reasonably unambiguous. Hibbs (1975), for instance, has deplored the decline of the independent operator and his replacement in many areas by large companies holding territorial monopoly rights.

Second, licensing has had two major economic effects. One is that it has encouraged cross-subsidisation. A licence for a service gives an operator monopoly rights on the route. Because many operators run over a large area they used to be expected, in exchange for the benefits of protection from competitors, to provide unremunerative services in some parts of their areas. Thus, for many years companies used the profits made on routes in urban areas to pay for the losses made on rural routes. This of course raised urban fares above the level needed to maintain services there while reducing rural fares on a similar basis. Unfortunately, the vast majority of passengers were usually in urban areas with the higher fares and thus were given an added incentive to find other forms of transport. This to some extent contributed to the decline in passengers in urban areas served by such companies. In 1970 this system was largely replaced by a policy based on specific grants for losses on rural services, but remnants of it linger on. There is no doubt that the licensing system has increased the level of provision of rural bus services by operators of this type above what it would have been in its absence and thus enhanced the benefits to public transport users in these areas. On the other hand, besides adverse effects on urban services it can be argued against this benefit that the type of service provided by these operators was and is not what rural areas have needed. This is borne out by current experiments in the United Kingdom with more flexible rural bus-services.

The second major impact of licensing has been via fares control. As Chapter 5 points out, bus operators have always tended to charge the same fare for a given distance regardless of variations in operating cost, which occur even in urban areas. In particular, as Table 4.3 (p. 63) shows, this has resulted in peak services being run at a loss caused by high operating costs, which has been met by a surplus on off-peak services. This has caused a loss in off-peak traffic, which is particularly sensitive to price increases, and a worsening of the peak/off-peak imbalance in demand.

Indirectly, both these effects of licensing have reduced the incentive for operators to consider individual parts of their networks. Instead, decisions on fares, services, etc., have often been taken at the level of the whole undertaking.

It may also be doubted whether the licensing of bus services has had a serious impact on railways. Although the protection offered by the rights of railways to object to bus licence applications may have helped them to retain traffic, the fact that they exploited the monopolies created by bus licensing to take over bus companies rather than specific bus routes tailored to enhance their overall service levels probably offset many of these benefits. It may be argued that free competition with buses would have resulted in the railways concentrating their efforts in the 1930s into services (e.g. long-distance expresses) that they were more efficient in providing, rather than in the 1960s as was the case in practice. Hibbs (1971a) in particular has argued this point.

Third, advocates of quantity control in the bus industry have argued that it has encouraged the orderly development of the industry and freed it from losses resulting from excess capacity. The fact that there is such a strong body of opinion in the bus industry against the relaxation of service licensing may show that it has some benefits. The case, however, has never been researched quantitatively.

Returning to the two principles set out at the beginning of this analysis, it can be seen that the history of quantity regulation in the

United Kingdom contains regulation not fully justified by the economic principles set out. Even in the case of the railways it might have been more efficient overall to expose them to free competition in both the passenger and freight fields and, if necessary, to pay a temporary subsidy that would have allowed them to price down to short-run marginal costs until the assets used in the sectors of their business in which they were unable to compete in the long term (e.g. branch-line passenger services) had reached the end of their useful lives. This would have avoided much capital expenditure on replacing these assets in the late 1950s. Joy (1973) has discussed this in more detail. In reaching these conclusions it must be stressed, however, that a comprehensive quantitative study of the impact of quantity regulation has still to be carried out and that circumstances may differ in other countries.

THE CONTROL OF ORGANISATION

The extent to which government transport policy controls the structure and organisation of the transport industry varies considerably from country to country. In the United Kingdom almost all railways, 72 per cent of buses and a substantial minority of the road haulage industry are owned by central or local government. Even in the United States long-distance passenger railway services are operated by a quasi-nationalised agency called Amtrack, and privately owned railway systems are the exception rather than the rule in most of the world.

The objectives of the control of organisation are as follows. First, it may be necessary in order to promote large undertakings that can exploit scale economies in circumstances when normal economic forces would not bring about a merger. As Chapter 4 shows, scale economies are unusual in any sector of transport operation, as opposed to infrastructure, and it is hard to conceive of a situation where operators would not merge voluntarily if there were large economies of scale to be gained. Second, if large scale subsidisation of an operator is necessary for whatever reason, there may be a political case for assuming control in these circumstances. Third, government control of organisation may be needed to promote the co-ordination of services within an area where numerous small operators exist.

In the United Kingdom the earliest direct influence of government policy on the organisation of the transport industry took place in the early 1920s when many still privately-owned railway companies were merged by the Railways Act 1921 into four large companies. This was meant to promote economy of operation. Similar measures covering bus and rail took place in London in 1933, and much inland transport was nationalised in 1947 although a good deal of road haulage was denationalised in 1953. Further reorganisations occurred in 1953, 1963, 1968 and to a lesser extent 1974. In many ways such reorganisations were symptomatic of the very slow process of learning to control nationalised industries generally, which has not yet been completed. Some trial and error were inevitable given the scale of nationalisation.

The creation of Passenger Transport Executives (PTEs) by the Transport Act 1968, continued by the Local Government Act 1972, has provided a useful case study of a recent reorganisation. The PTEs have, *inter alia*, three functions:

(1) to operate directly all local-authority-owned bus undertakings in their areas;
(2) to assume control over a wide geographical area, which is more logical in terms of present-day traffic patterns than the operating areas of individual undertakings, which were often confined to nineteenth-century municipal boundaries; and
(3) to control local rail as well as bus services – indeed, they have wide-ranging powers to operate most forms of transport and to provide ancillary services (e.g. kiosks, car parks) – a function that is coupled with a specific duty to promote an integrated system of public transport within their areas.

Thus, the objectives of the reorganisation were, on the one hand, to unify control that was diverse both geographically and among operating agencies and, on the other, to secure scale economies. Research already discussed (Lee and Steedman, 1970) has shown that this latter objective was unlikely to be achieved as differences in costs per bus mile among municipal bus operators are nearly all due to factors other than the size of the undertaking. However, all the PTEs have made some progress towards the other two objectives, and in these respects reorganisation has been more successful.

There is insufficient space to dwell on the details of the reorganisations prior to 1968 (see Lee, 1968, for a good summary), but there is no doubt that the influence of government policy in this area has been to waste resources – both those needed to effect the reorganisation and those within the undertakings being reorganised that were not able to function efficiently during the reorganisation (Transport Holding Company, 1969, Chapter 8). It may also have given the transport industry the false notion that its difficulties are those of organisation and thus that reorganisation is a pathway to solving them.

This sphere of government policy has probably been the least successful so far as its influence on transport is concerned. The reason is that many of the difficulties faced by the transport industry have been the result of more fundamental problems than its organisation and structure.

THE CONTROL OF RESOURCE ALLOCATION

Ultimately, the result of the aspects of transport policy outlined above is to influence resource allocation and thus help to determine how much of each form of transport is produced. Two areas of economics are important in this respect: pricing and investment, which have already been discussed in Chapters 5 and 6 respectively. Inevitably, government policy has in recent years given increasing emphasis to both pricing and investment, and it is necessary to consider its effectiveness in these spheres. This is not meant to imply, however, that the other areas of policy such as regulation that have an indirect effect on resource allocation are less important.

Turning first to investment, the most important area of direct government control of resource allocation concerns roads, for which government policy determines the total investment expenditure, the criteria for investment, the standards of construction (which affect costs) and which parts of the network will be improved. In 1976 capital expenditure on roads was £820 million and current expenditure £805 million.

Over the past ten years, within an overall expenditure constraint considerable progress has been made in the investment appraisal of new roads, increasing the efficiency of resource allocation in this sector. As no direct charge is made for road use conventional financial appraisals cannot guide investment decisions. Since the first application of social cost–benefit analysis to road investment in 1959 the technique has been developed to the point where all interurban road schemes are evaluated using a common cost–benefit analysis called COBA, which can be incorporated into a computer if necessary. Thus, interurban road schemes can in principle be evaluated consistently although current practice is not to use COBA for very large and very small (i.e. less than £500,000) projects.

This does not mean that there are no weaknesses in investment policy, and in fact three stand out. First, little systematic attention both in the United Kingdom and abroad has been given to problems of intersectoral appraisal (e.g. how much investment in transport, how much in health), partly because of the enormous problems of comparing investments in different sectors in practice. Political decisions have usually been made with little economic guidance. Examples of the current process in the United Kingdom can be found in the government's annual White Paper on public expenditure (HM Treasury, 1977). Second, within the transport sector the allocation of investment funds between roads and public transport has been haphazard. This has arisen partly because so many different agencies are involved (e.g. central and local government, transport operators) and partly through the grant system used prior to 1975, discussed below. Third, the inter-relationship between pricing and investment and the effects of the different pricing policies used in the transport sector have been ignored. These issues have been discussed in more detail by Harrison and Mackie (1973). In road investment appraisal, for example, no account is taken of the fact that, if price equalled marginal social cost on a congested road, traffic levels would, *ceteris paribus*, be less than current levels and that the benefits from the improvement would thus be changed from those estimated on the basis of current traffic levels. The impact of financing a public transport investment on fares and hence on demand can seriously affect the outcome of an investment appraisal, as Beesley and Foster (1965) have shown very clearly.

Government policy on road pricing and its economic consequences have been discussed in Chapter 5. There it has been argued that in some circumstances public transport subsidies, of either a current or a capital nature, could be a partial substitute for marginal social-cost pricing on roads and that this is one area where government policy could have a profound influence on resource allocation. Policy in this respect developed from simply meeting railway subsidies in the 1950s and early 1960s to a clearer recognition of the reasons for subsidy in the Transport Act 1968. Subsidies here were confined to capital expenditure, rail operations and rural bus operations; urban bus operations were excluded except for the minor effects of fuel duty rebates.

If there is to be such a system of subsidies, however, they need to be integrated with the rest of transport policy to ensure that pricing and investment policies are consistent, that the financial objectives of operators are consistent with the subsidy policy and that the subsidies do not in themselves introduce further bias into resource allocation. In this respect the record in the United Kingdom was far from perfect prior to reform in 1975, largely because subsidies had grown up on an *ad hoc* basis rather than as part of an overall policy for efficiently allocating transport resources.

In more detail the situation prior to 1975 was that, through the media of its policies on road provision and finance (which were one set of financial subsidies) and of helping public transport finance (via another set), government policy was influencing both capital expenditures (and hence the future attractiveness of road- and rail-based transport systems) and the current costs of using public and private transport, which has affected the traffic levels presently carried by each mode. It was realised, however, that the system was not allocating resources in the most efficient way because of bias in the grant system. This occurred in two ways:

(1) Because the rates of grant for capital expenditures varied and generally were higher the larger the scheme, local authorities were tempted to propose large capital schemes rather than smaller ones because these could be cheaper to the local authority.
(2) Bias in favour of expenditures that would attract grants as opposed to those which did not was inevitable. Urban bus services were less attractive from this point of view, and so insufficient resources were allocated to them.

There were many other criticisms of government resource allocation policy in transport as well as these two, but there is no space to discuss them further. Tyson (1975b) has analysed them in more depth. The whole system of financial assistance of local-authority transport expenditures changed in 1975 with the introduction of the 'Transport Policy and Programme (TPP) system'. This has been discussed in more detail by Tyson (1975b); but in essence it has meant that, by replacing a plethora of specific grants tied to particular expenditures with a single grant to cover expenditure in total, the biases have been removed. The system has, however, a major drawback: because it places more responsibility for resource allocation in local authorities' hands it makes it difficult for the government to implement policies on a national scale. Almost as soon as the new system was introduced the need to do this arose because public expenditure had to be reduced on a national scale. This inevitably resulted in considerable control and compartmentalisation of the grant under the TPP system and has led to much unwarranted criticism of the system itself.

Still remaining is the problem caused by the fact that railway subsidies, except in the metropolitan counties, have not been included in the TPP system. To conform to EEC regulations, under the Railways Act 1974, subsidy to railway passenger services was given on a block basis and termed Public Service Obligation payment, the intention being to support the whole passenger network rather than individual services comprising it. This means that it is difficult for decisions on railway services to be taken at local level; non-metropolitan county councils can control the size and nature of the bus network but have to take the railway network as fixed exogenously.

CURRENT DEVELOPMENTS

In 1976 and 1977 there was a significant development in transport policy in the United Kingdom with the publication in April 1976 of a Consultation Document (Department of the Environment, 1976), which sets out current government thinking on transport policy as the basis for discussion and comment. After receiving comments the government published a policy statement in the form of a White Paper in July 1977 (Department of Transport, 1977b). This approach based on consultation was a new departure for transport policy making although it has been in other spheres (e.g. speed limits) in the United Kingdom, but White Papers on transport policy have been a regular feature of the postwar period.

In this context the Consultation Document is also notable in several respects for its contents, summarised by Lee (1977). First, it introduces the question of objectives for transport policy as a whole for the first time into the policy debate. Second, it proposes the continuation of the present market-based situation for freight but suggests that existing vehicle taxes be raised in order to ensure that road haulage vehicles cover their marginal social costs; the issues raised by this have been discussed in Chapter 5. Subsidies to railway freight operations should be ended, but subsidies to railway freight infrastructure (i.e. towards the costs of terminals and private sidings) should continue if individual projects can be justified on environmental grounds. Some relaxation of bus licensing in rural areas is suggested. Third, no major reorganisation of the transport sector is envisaged although a co-ordinating body to deal with broad policy issues is suggested. Fourth, on resource allocation policy it makes several suggestions regarding the effectiveness of subsidies in altering modal choice; this also has been discussed in Chapter 5. In summary, it suggests that subsidies be reduced although not eliminated and that the remaining subsidies be directed towards services providing a 'basic' need (e.g. in rural areas) or towards income redistribution objectives, which the Consultation Document claims, would entail eliminating certain rail subsidies (e.g. those to long distance commuters into London).

It also proposes giving local authorities powers to control private non-residential parking in their areas. This proposal is significant as it is the first recognition of the potential of parking control as a way of restraining traffic coupled with a recognition of the inadequacies of existing powers.

On investment a review of both road-appraisal techniques and vehicle-ownership forecasts is promised; this was commenced early in 1977. The problems of the incompatibility of the appraisal techniques used in different parts of the transport sector are raised, but no serious objections to the *status quo* are envisaged.

Finally, the Consultation Document omits two important issues altogether. First, the transport/land use relationship is given no consideration at all, and in particular the land use implications for some of the policies suggested are ignored. Second, it makes hardly any mention of the grant system and TPP system despite the difficulties, discussed above, from which the system is suffering.

The White Paper of July 1977 (Department of Transport, 1977b) reflects some comment received in response to the Consultation Document. No changes from the Consultation Document suggestions on licensing were proposed, and thus relaxation of passenger transport licensing in rural areas was still part of government policy. However, on the questions of resource allocation and subsidies two significant changes were proposed. First, county councils were given more responsibility for resource allocation, including certain railway services, thus meeting some of the criticisms of the TPP system discussed above. Second, policy on bus subsidies was modified, and it was no longer the government's intention to reduce them as proposed in both the Consultation Document and the White Paper on public expenditure (HM Treasury, 1977).

The White Paper of July 1977 contained many other proposals including a more regular public review of transport policy and at several points stressed the importance of long term commitments to policies particularly regarding subsidies and investments. Perhaps the most noteworthy proposal for the long term future was its suggestion that the transport implications of land use decisions need to be recognised and given serious consideration in land-use decision processes. A Transport Act putting some of the White Paper's suggestions into effect was passed by Parliament in 1978.

The advent of right wing administrations in Britain and the United States has led to deregulation in several transport sectors in the 1980s. Early examples are local air services in the United States and long distance coach travel in Britain, both of which witnessed a fall in fares, and there has been a general trend towards more competition where quantity controls remain.

CHAPTER 9

Sea Transport

INTRODUCTION

Over four-fifths of the international trade of the world, measured by weight of goods, is carried by the shipping industry. In recent years it has witnessed rapid and manifold changes arising from the increasing volume and changing pattern of world trade, from the emergence of new nations with new maritime priorities and from technological change, most clearly seen in the immense increase in the size of certain vessels and in the revolution in cargo handling brought about by the use of containers. There has been a massive increase in the carriage of oil by tankers and a great contraction in the operation of passenger liners as the improving technology and efficiency of airliners has won customers from them.

THE STRUCTURE OF THE INDUSTRY

The structure of the industry may be analysed in a variety of ways: according to function, pattern of trade, nationality of registration, or ownership and control. Ostensibly, the patterns of ship registration have changed markedly over the years; but, as Lawrence (1972, pp. 15–19) has observed, the data available are insufficient to indicate with any precision where the real control of ocean shipping lies. Apart from the use of flags of convenience, whereby owners register vessels in foreign countries to avoid taxes or regulations, shipping companies are increasingly crossing national borders for shipping, personnel and even management, and the use of long-term basic agreements is extending from the original areas of tankers and dry bulk carriers. Table 9.1 gives a breakdown of the nominal patterns of national ownership and a partial indication of long run trends. The two yardsticks are the gross register ton (grt) and the deadweight ton (dwt). Gross register tonnage a volumetric measure, each grt comprising 100 cubic feet of enclosed space; whereas the deadweight is the weight, measured in tons, that brings a ship down from its light to its loaded draught line and is thus an effective measure of the weight that it can carry. Passenger liners typically have a high gross tonnage relative to their deadweight while tankers and bulk carriers have a high deadweight relative to their gross tonnage.

Table 9.1 *Leading maritime fleets, 1950–83*

	Dwt (millions)				*No. of ships*
Country	*1950*	*1965*	*1977*	*1983*	*1983*
Liberia	0.5	29.9	151.2	133.1	1,985
Greece	2.1	10.1	45.7	65.9	2,789
Japan	2.1	17.4	66.2	65.3	5,561
Panama	4.8	6.5	28.8	57.3	4,028
Norway	8.3	23.6	48.8	33.0	1,086
U.K.	23.8	29.2	50.6	29.0	1,217
U.S.A.	46.7	33.0	21.0	25.1	920
U.S.S.R.	1.3	8.2	18.6	22.4	2,584
France	3.9	7.0	19.5	16.5	358
Italy	4.0	8.4	17.5	16.3	899
China (mainland)	n.a.	n.a.	n.a.	12.7	963
West Germany	0.3	8.3	14.9	10.6	1,295
Other	22.9	49.8	138.1	191.4	14,734
World Total	120.7	231.4	620.9	678.6	38,419

Source: General Council of British Shipping.
Note: Figures for 1 July. U.S. fleet includes reserve.

Before the Second World War Liberia had a negligible merchant marine. Its rise to pre-eminence is the most outstanding case of registration under a flag of convenience, for most Liberian-registered vessels are controlled by foreigners. Panama is a parallel example, and the label *Panholib* is sometimes used to describe these cases, being a contraction of Panama, Honduras and Liberia. The rise of certain other nations reflects their economic growth, as in the case of Japan, West Germany and the Soviet Union, although in these instances the Japanese and the Soviet maritime growth rates have exceeded their economic growth rates under the influence of deliberate government maritime policy. The growth of the Norwegian and Greek fleets has been due in large measure to enterprising management. The British and US merchant marines have declined in their relative shares having occupied the first and second positions respectively in 1939. Although in recent years the British fleet had fared reasonably well and some measure of decline from its share of 34 per cent in 1901 was clearly inevitable, a number of influences contributed to its sluggish performance in comparison with countries such as Norway or Greece.

There is a correlation between the decline of Britain's share in world trade and the decline of its share of world shipping. Added to this influence there has been the policy of flag discrimination by several countries, which have obliged shippers dealing with such a country to transport goods in its ships. This practice has become increasingly widespread, so that a diminishing proportion of British trade has been carried in British vessels. Thus by 1976 only 31 per cent of British import ton-miles and 43 per cent of export ton-miles were in British ships. The disappearance of the coal-fired ship in the face of oil-fired steamships and diesel propulsion diminished the need for coal-bunkering stations, and therefore British coal exports in British ships virtually ceased. There were also several internal reasons why the British fleet lagged. For many years after the Second World War its composition was inappropriate to the changing pattern of trade: at a time of expanding air travel it included many passenger liners; its dry cargo fleet was suboptimal with a higher proportion of older, smaller and slower ships than in the Norwegian fleet; until the late 1950s there was inadequate appreciation of the importance and profitability of tankers and supertankers; and in the face of a steamship tradition British ship owners were slow to adopt diesel propulsion, which at sea as on rail was more economical than steam, at least on all but the biggest ships. Management among British shipping liners was very conservative. While Greek owners geared up their profits by extensive fixed-interest borrowing British owners made little recourse to the capital market, either for additional equity or for loan capital; instead they preferred to cloak their inefficiency behind inscrutable company accounts with extensive hidden reserves. Sturmey (1962) has suggested that for some time British owners were reluctant to order ships abroad but persisted in buying ships from the declining and inefficient British shipyards. They were also unenterprising in the face of high taxes, whereas the Norwegians made the most of depreciation allowances to maintain a young and efficient fleet.

In recent years the British have rectified a number of these shortcomings and the government has adopted a much more interventionist role in shipbuilding, culminating in its nationalisation in 1977 (Hogwood, 1979). The US marine has declined proportionately during the 1960s and 1970s, and its ships tend to be somewhat elderly although the Americans pioneered container ships. However, the US picture is misleading since there is a vast amount of shipping owned or controlled by US nationals but registered under foreign flags, amounting to perhaps three times the privately owned domestic tonnage. For example, Lawrence (1972, pp. 16–17) has estimated that, of ships over 5,000 gwt in 1970, almost half of the Liberian fleet and over half of that of Panama were American owned. Almost half of these vessels under flags of convenience were United States owned, and over a quarter were owned by Greeks and so-called London Greeks who control their operations from London in order to be close to the market. The British are the third-largest users of flags of convenience including such bases as Bermuda and the Bahamas. In 1976, 31 per cent of world deadweight tonnage was registered under flags of convenience. The structure of the industry may also be illustrated by the nature of the vessels that comprise it. The composition of the world's merchant fleet in 1977 is shown in Table 9.2. The table reveals that general cargo ships are the most numerous type but that oil tankers are much the most significant in terms of carrying capacity. The figures for average tonnage for each type of vessel show that the most modern types of combination

Table 9.2 *World merchant fleet by type of ship, 30 June 1983.*

Type	*Number*	*Grt (millions)*	*Dwt (millions)*	*Average Dwt per ship*	*Type Dwt as % of total Dwt*
General cargo	21,924	79.0	114.0	5,200	16.8
Oil tanker	6,882	157.3	306.1	44,478	45.1
Ore/bulk	4,737	98.7	171.9	36,289	25.4
Ferry[b]	1,026	4.6	1.6	4,516[c]	0.2
Other dry cargo	707	4.2	5.0	7,072	0.7
Liquid gas carrier	750	9.1	9.5	12,667	1.4
Cellular container	786	14.2	14.6	18,575	2.2
Combination carrier	457	26.1	49.4	108,096	7.3
Chemical carrier	794	3.1	5.4	6,801	0.8
Passenger	219	2.5	0.7	11,517[c]	0.1
Total[a]	38,282	398.8	678.2	17,857	100.0

Source: General Council of British Shipping.
Notes: (a) Includes 137 unspecified tankers totalling 480,000 Dwt.
(b) Excludes vessels below 1,000 Grt.
(c) Grt.

carrier (e.g. ore/oil, ore/bulk/oil) are very large; however, the average conceals considerable variation within types. There are very few general cargo ships of more than 25,000 dwt although ships of 14,000 dwt are quite common. Tankers vary widely in size since their network of distribution calls for some relatively small vessels, but in 1977 there were 329 supertankers of 250,000 dwt or more and 68 of more than 300,000 dwt. Cellular container ships range in size from 10,000 dwt to over 40,000 dwt. Over the past two decades the growth of international seaborne trade has exceeded that of world domestic product. The distribution of cargo is dominated by the major purchasing blocs of North America and Western Europe although the trade of some other areas has recently shown a much higher rate of growth.

Table 9.3 shows the recent development in maritime trade patterns although a much more refined breakdown has been provided by Lawrence (1972, Chapter 6) who has divided the world into fifteen trading regions. He found that 21 per cent of general cargoes were intraregional, and another 10 per cent were relatively short hauls between adjacent regions. General cargo voyages averaged 3,500 miles compared with 4,000 miles for dry bulk cargo and 4,200 miles for oil.

SUPPLY AND DEMAND IN SHIPPING MARKETS

The shipping market can be subdivided into a number of distinct submarkets although the boundaries between some of them are rather grey. The *tramp ship* has no regularly fixed itinerary and usually hauls dry cargo between two ports at a rate negotiated by the shipper and the ship owner. It may be hired on a voyage charter. Alternatively, it may be hired on a time charter for a specified period or number of voyages during which the shipping firm meets the costs of operation from charter fees paid in advance; a bareboat or demise charter is paid monthly in advance and gives effectively complete control of the vessel to the charterers, who meet its operating costs and have the right to appoint the master and crew.

In contrast with the tramp the *liner* sails a fixed route with a prescribed schedule, offering cargo and/or passenger space at fixed and stated rates. In terms of revenue earned by ships exceeding 5,000 grt, liners accounted for about 44 per cent of the total in 1970 compared with 11 per cent for tramps, 17 per cent for bulk carriers and 28 per cent for tankers. The preponderance of the figure for liners is explained by the unit value rather than the volume of their cargoes. Liner operators are almost universally organised in shipping conferences, each concerned with particular routes and effectively controlling the supply of liner shipping that is available.

Bulk carriers are generally large single-deck vessels specially suited to the carriage of large homogeneous cargoes (e.g. grain, ore or coal) to which bulk handling techniques can be applied. They often operate over regular routes. Since their cargoes are somewhat specialised they have been increasingly employed on time charter, although many are owned by large Japanese and German corporations with heavy industrial interests.

Oil tankers are a form of bulk carrier that is distinct and old-established enough to constitute a separate market. About two-fifths of tanker tonnage are owned by the multinational oil companies; but their carriage requirements exceed their tonnage, and so they may charter as much again from independent tanker owners. The marginal nature of independent operation therefore permits high profits to the skilled independent operators, typified by the late Aristotle Onassis; but it puts extreme pressure upon them when capacity is at a discount as it has been since the recession of 1974–75. It is possible to hedge against the latter possibility by negotiating time charters for as long as a twenty-year period, although by so doing the tanker owner forgoes the possibility of high profits when short-charter spot rates are at their peaks. In practice independent operators tend to adopt a composite strategy combining both time and single-voyage charters for their fleets. Charter rates fluctuate widely after the manner of a perfectly competitive market where expectations are imperfect and create a cobweb effect; the mechanism and experience of operation in this market have been analysed in detail by Zannetos (1966).

THE TRAMP MARKET

Tramp shipping is, *par excellence*, a competitive business, for a number of reasons. It displays a lower concentration of ownership than liner shipping, with owners from a wide variety of nations and backgrounds. Although new entry is not absolutely open it is easier than in many other industries, and the small firm plays a distinctive and significant role. The Baltic Shipping Exchange in London is more-or-less equivalent to a tramp auction market.

The demand for tramp services is derived, subject largely to exogenous influences. The price elasticity of demand for ocean freight services depends upon three main factors:

(1) the ease with which domestic products or products from other sources can replace imports if specific freight-rate increases raise the costs of imports;

Table 9.3 *Maritime cargo by region, 1975.*

	Loaded	*Increase, 1959–75 (%)*	*Unloaded*	*Increase, 1959–75 (%)*
Percentage of dry cargo				
Developed market economies of which:	60.4	193	73.4	165
UK	2.7	68	5.3	27
Rest of Europe	17.4	101	31.8	151
North America	21.7	160	11.8	76
Japan	4.9	580	21.6	602
Australasia	12.1	1,308	1.6	188
Developing economies of which:	32.2	159	19.7	207
Africa	7.6	248	3.8[a]	145[a]
Latin America	14.9	177	5.2	204
Middle East	0.6	33	2.6	429
Socialist economies	7.4	222	6.7	370
World total	100.0 (=1,393 million tonnes)	183	99.8 (=1,401 million tonnes)	181

Percentage of tanker cargo				
Developed market economies	8.8	328	78.5	282
of which:				
UK	0.8	56	6.2	92
Rest of Europe	5.7	376	37.4	341
North America	0.3	20	16.3	155
Japan	0.1	—	15.1	1,023
Australasia	0.3	400	0.9	15
Developing economies	86.4	255	19.6	147
of which:				
Africa	13.8	5,925	2.0[a]	89[a]
Latin America	12.0	12	10.4	122
Middle East	55.2	355	1.2	90
Socialist economies	4.8	361	1.7	2,700
World total	100.0 (=1,742 million tonnes)	264	99.8 (=1,640 million tonnes)	250

Source: General Council of British Shipping.
Note: (a) Figures for 1974.

(2) the proportion of ocean freight charges to the total value of the goods; and
(3) the availability of substitute modes of transport (e.g. air, road, rail).

The influence of the income elasticity of demand is more difficult to assess in general although some strong trends have been apparent in the past. Seaborne trade has grown faster than world domestic product, and the growth of demand for traded commodities as a result of rising income levels is manifest in the growth of demand for oil and raw materials among the advanced countries and for foodstuffs among the expanding populations of the developing countries.

The elasticity of supply of tramp shipping tends to be limited in the short run. Ships are capital goods, and the stock at any particular time is almost fixed, for while some laid-up ships may be recommissioned their numbers are usually few. At the end of March 1977 laid-up ships represented 8 per cent of tanker tonnage (dwt) and 2 per cent of dry cargo tonnage, but the figures for end-1974 were more typical at 0.6 and 0.2 per cent respectively. The gestation period of new ships is long – perhaps twelve or eighteen months if the ship can be laid down immediately, but possibly much longer if the order books of the shipyards are full. However, the flexibility of supply is important at the local as well as the global level as in the very short run supply is limited to ships on hand at or near the port of despatch. Given time and a sufficiently attractive voyage rate ships may be induced to come from other ports. However, while the stock of shipping is relatively inelastic ship-owners can and do employ several fine-tuning devices to regulate the supply of shipping available: ships may be slowed; additional ports may be visited; maintenance may be deferred or accelerated. For example, tanker companies regularly slow down their voyages in the slack summer season when demand is low.

The interaction of supply and demand in the tramp market is typified in Figure 9.1. The supply schedule is highly elastic at low levels of demand, but capacity limits and the gestation period of new vessels render it inelastic at high levels. Thus, when the demand is below capacity level, at OQ_1, an increase to OQ_2 produces only a little change in price, from OP_1 to OP_2; but when the tramp market, or indeed the tanker market, approaches full capacity working, a relatively small increase in demand to OQ_3 may provoke a marked rise in the charter rate, from OP_2 to OP_3. The volatility of the rates clearly depends upon the speed with which changes in demand occur. If they are slow, new construction may shift the supply schedule to SS_2 and substantially reduce the rise in rates; but if the change is sudden (e.g. the closures of

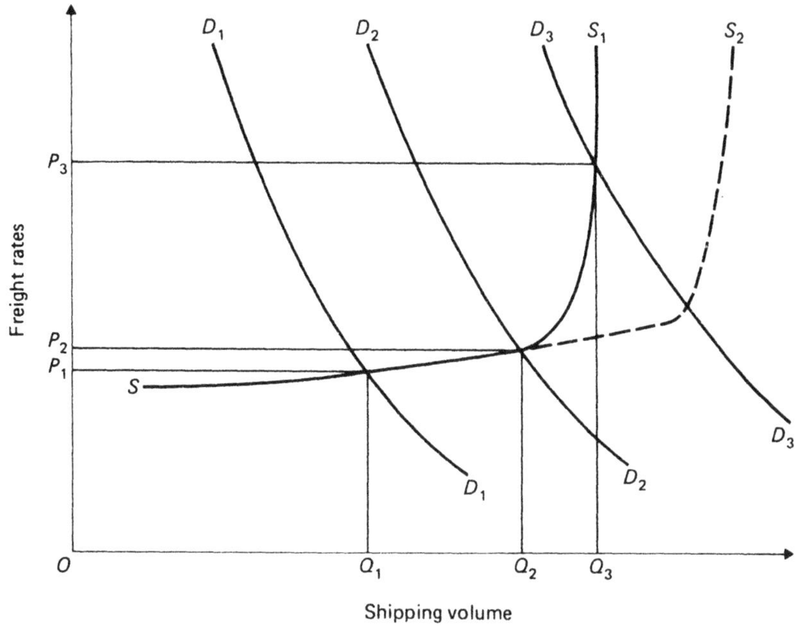

Figure 9.1 *The volatility of shipping freight rates*

the Suez Canal in 1956 and 1967), there can be a dramatic change in the market. The closure of the Suez Canal obliged traffic to take the Cape route, thus causing a major increase in the ton-mileage demanded.

COSTS

At the lower end of the supply schedule the offer prices of services depend on the nature of costs in the shipping industry. The most important characteristic is the very high proportion of fixed cost to total cost. O'Loughlin (1967) has summarised this cost structure for a moderate-sized typical cargo ship (Table 9.4). Clearly there are variations around the averages shown, arising out of variations in the methods of depreciation, the nationality of the crew (which can cause fivefold differences in manning costs), insurance rates (which at one stage were very high on supertankers because of technological uncertainty surrounding the safety of their construction) and fuel costs (which can increase very rapidly at high speed). If a ship is not chartered but lies idle, only a comparatively small part of total costs can be avoided:

Table 9.4 *Cost structure of a typical cargo ship of between 7,000 and 12,000 grt, less than eight years old, on a transoceanic route, 1967.*

Item	*% of total cost*	*Influential factors*
Management and fixed selling costs	7	Size of fleet
Depreciation	17	
Manning and crew	25	
Repairs and maintenance	14	Size; age beyond 7 years
Insurance	8	Cargo value; owners' reputation
Port fees	7	Size
Fuel	17	Speed; type of engine; laden or in ballast
Other vessel costs	5	

Source: O'Loughlin (1967, p.116).

fuel costs will obviously be cut but not eliminated since even at rest the vessel requires power for heat and light; crew costs can only be reduced if the crew is paid off, which is not feasible in the short run. Hence, the variable costs saved by remaining in port are unlikely to amount to much more than a fifth or a quarter of average costs. Thus, when demand is low ship owners may be prepared to accept any cargo as a temporary expedient provided that it makes a contribution to fixed costs (i.e. if it covers the variable costs). In 1975 many tanker charters barely covered fuel costs. The alternative (i.e. laying up) is not costless since there are significant fixed costs in preparing to lay up or recommission a ship and additional costs *per diem.*

This willingness to accept unprofitable work for a short period makes for great variations in tramp and tanker freight rates, and their amplitude creates speculation about future rates. The imperfect anticipation of future rates and the urgency of securing a place in the queue of shipyard orders lead to cycles in activity at the shipyard – not unlike the cobweb theorem or hog cycle of classical economic theory. In 1977 some tankers were leaving shipyards to be laid up immediately.

At the level of individual voyage or time charter expectations also play a part, for in quoting a price for a one-way voyage the tramp owner has to make an arrangement for, or a judgement about, the possibility of a back load for the return journey. An owner may prefer a two-month charter at £300 a day profit to a three-week charter at £450 a day if his vessel is unlikely to be rechartered at the end of that time. In summary, it is a highly competitive market where there is still a place for the individual entrepreneur with acute judgement (Metaxas, 1971).

One of the long run influences on shipping has been the impact of economies of scale in operation. Ships are essentially boxes and accordingly are likely to display economies of scale since volume increases faster than surface area; thermal processes (e.g. ship engines) are also likely candidates for economies of scale; crew size does not increase proportionately with size of ship; and there are hydrodynamic reasons for higher propulsive efficiency with larger vessels. Hence, the size of most cargo ships has shown a steady upward trend over past decades and contributed to a reduction in the real cost of shipping, which is most evident in the case of bulk loads. The economies of scale can be shown in index form as in Table 9.5.

Table 9.5 *Economies of scale in bulk carriers.*

Ship size ('000 dwt)	15	25	41	66	120	200
Index of size	100	167	267	432	793	1,318
Capital cost index	100	140	197	291	457	641
Operating cost index (excluding fuel)	100	121	134	155	201	275
Seagoing fuel-consumption index	100	155	230	353	578	843
Crew size (no.)	31	38	38	38	38	38

Source of data: Goss and Jones (1971).

Similarly, impressive economies have been estimated for oil tankers, as the figures in Table 9.6 show.

Table 9.6 *Economies of scale in oil tankers, 1966.*

Tanker size (dwt)	*Typical rate per ton (£)*
100,000	0.84
200,000	0.57
300,000	0.49
500,000	0.44

Source: Greenwell (1967).

However, there are limits to scale, just as there are with trains, trucks or any other mode of transport.

(1) Technical problems as ships get longer, a 326,000 dwt tanker being about 1,100 feet long. Several tankers broke up in storms in the Sea of Japan in 1970, leading to
(2) Higher insurance costs, which for a time outstripped fuel costs.
(3) Problems of indivisibilities. Only major routes are suitable, and the likelihood of sizable backloads is remote.
(4) Problems over terminals as deep water channels with a draught of 100 feet are essential for a laden supertanker. The subdivision of loads and the entry of part-laden vessels into shallower harbours are expedients.
(5) Long loading times. If loading is anything but very simple, harbour times will become prohibitively long for the largest ships.

Hence, the scope for really massive ships has been limited to bulk carriers and tankers. The latter were all below 150,000 dwt in 1967; whereas several exceeded 500,000 dwt in 1978, and the million-ton tanker has become a real prospect. Consequently, large ships have gained cargo faster than the smaller vessels that typified the traditional conference system. Lawrence (1972) has estimated the relative costs of different types of freight vessel, which are reproduced in Table 9.7.

Tramps and conventional liners usually call at more ports on a given voyage than do bulk carriers or container ships. The economy of the bulk carrier is clearly shown, while the high costs of container ships and liners restrict them to the more valuable cargoes where freight charges bear a smaller relation to the final landed costs. Air freight now competes for some of these cargoes although it remains much more expensive than even liner costs.

THE CONFERENCE SYSTEM

Dry cargo ships offering scheduled services along regular routes are usually organised into shipping conferences, which numbered about 360 in 1973 with about one-third of these regulating major international trade routes. The first recorded conference was formed by seven British ship owners on the London–Calcutta route in 1875 when they became alarmed at excess capacity on the route. It therefore seems to be a typical case of cartel restrictions to maintain prices, and as such it has been the subject of widespread and recurrent attack by economists, whose task has not been made easier by the dense veils of secrecy that have traditionally surrounded conference operations. Yet conferences have proliferated over the past century – there is still one on the United Kingdom–Calcutta route – and government investigations

Table 9.7 *Ship operating costs, 1970.*

	20,000 dwt container ship	*14,000 dwt conventional liner*	*150,000 dwt ore/bulk/oil carrier*	*14,000 dwt tramp (new)*	*14,000 dwt tramp (fully written off)*
Voyage characteristics					
Speed (knots)	20	17	15	16	12
Ports of call	2	4	2	4	4
Distance (nautical miles)	3,500	3,500	3,500	3,500	3,500
Sea time (days)	7.3	8.6	20	13	18
Port time (days)	3.0	10.0	5	4	8
Voyage time (days)	10.3	18.6	25	17	26
Typical voyage costs per cargo ton ($)					
Variable costs:					
load and discharge cargoes and other costs in port	10.55	18.85	1.14	2.14	2.15
Voyage costs:					
crew costs, stores, insurance, fuel at sea	1.81	2.76	0.47	2.08	3.40
Carrying costs:					
insurances, administration	0.48	0.44	0.09	0.31	0.53
Debt service	4.31	2.89	0.98	2.03	–
Total cost per 1,000 dwt of cargo	17.15	24.94	2.68	6.56	6.08

Source: Saguenay Research; cited in Lawrence (1972).
Note: Liner data for measurement tons; tramp and bulk carrier data for metric tons.

have not found against them. The 1964 United Nations Conference on Trade and Development (UNCTAD) formally recognised the need for them, and a decision by the West German government in 1975 permitted them. In the United Kingdom neither the restrictive practice nor the antimonopoly legislation has been critical of freight conferences, although the Monopolies and Mergers Commission (1974) was critical of the practices of cross-channel car ferries. It has been estimated that about 30 per cent of UK trade is regulated by conferences, the main area free from such regulation being trade with the Continent (Monopolies and Mergers Commission, 1976).

Conferences display a number of common characteristics. They comprise a number of shipping lines operating on a common route; for example, there were thirteen members of the United Kingdom–Australia conference in 1971, and two of the thirteen were consortia of container operators. As a minimum they offer an agreed schedule of charges for traffic with no hidden discrimination between shippers using their services, but generally they do not publish these rates, thus lending ammunition to those critics who typify them as covert price setters. They determine which ports shall be served, including 'outports' outside the normal itinerary that the conference will serve by trans-shipment. The conference effectively controls the output of its members by controlling the supply of shipping space, by restricting the number of sailings or the tonnage of shipping that operates the route, or by arrangements to pool the revenue of its members. One or more of these methods may be in use at any given time. Revenue pooling seems to have gained ground in recent years, and the proportion of revenue paid in to the pool can be as high as 100 per cent. Earnings may be calculated either gross or net of certain expenses, and redistribution to conference members is based upon their relative share of traffic in an earlier period.

Conferences may be open to new membership or closed. Open conferences admit new members provided that they observe the common tariff and any other conditions. Following pressure from US antitrust legislation most conferences are now open. Closed conferences may receive an application for membership, which usually requires a unanimous vote in favour. Existing members are generally concerned that the entrant should have a genuine and permanent interest in the trade, but they may exclude the entrant if the latter is small and unlikely to succeed in 'fighting' the conference. Such 'fighting' is by no means uncommon; and if the rival has the financial strength to compete openly with the conference, it may ultimately be admitted.

Conferences do not always oppose incidental outsiders which trespass upon their monopoly, but a variety of weapons may be deployed against outside lines that are judged to threaten the stability of trade on the conference route. Rate wars involve undercutting the rival's rates either generally or on the cargoes that matter most to him. However, such wars are costly; and in the same way that oligopolists dislike a downward move along a kinked demand curve, so conferences have been reluctant to enter into nugatory trials of strength. In the past, conferences have used 'fighting ships' to undercut the rival and match his sailing dates, to be withdrawn if the rival climbs down. Conciliation may be attempted through the Council of European and Japanese National Shipowners' Association (CENSA) Conciliation Committee although this can only recommend solutions. The shipper, as customer, is the other obvious focus of attention of the conference, for without customers the rival would have no future. In normal times, as we shall see presently, shippers usually get a discount or rebate if they are loyal to the conference; these may be increased to make the rival's task harder. Also, the conference may cancel the rebates of disloyal shippers after a suitable warning. Notwithstanding this formidable armoury entry into conferences is by no means a rarity.

The reticence of conferences has made it difficult to analyse the precise details of their rebate systems although an admirable research monograph by Deakin (1973) has advanced our knowledge. Table 9.8

Table 9.8 *Selected conference rebate practices, 1960 and 1971.*

Mode of rebate	*1960*	*%*	*1971*	*%*
None offered; net price quoted	6	12.5	2	5.7
Deferred rebate[a]	11	22.9	–	–
Contract rebate, *c.* 9½% net	10	20.8	3	8.6
Combined contract and deferred rebate	21	43.8	30	85.7
Total of conferences in sample	48	100.0	35	100.0

Sources: Sturmey (1962, p. 341); Deakin (1973, Appendix A).
Note: (a) Net *c.* 10%; 4–6 months' lag before distribution.

shows the types of rebate offered by conferences and their widespread incidence. The deferred rebate is not paid until a considerable period has elapsed, between four or six months after the shipper used the conference's services. Thus, at any time, the shipper may have a considerable accumulated rebate at stake. The contract rebate is payable to shippers who sign an exclusive contract with the conference, which if broken means loss of present and future benefit and possibly even invokes a penalty clause. The rebates offer a clear reward for loyalty;

but there is an added strength for the conference in that interlopers are unable to match the frequency of conference sailing, so that a shipper who decides to transfer his custom to the interloper may find his scheduling much more difficult.

The potential for abuse by conferences is all too apparent and has provoked much criticism by economists at both the general and the particular level. Moreover, the lack of competitive pressure within the cartel may permit an undesirable degree of x-inefficiency; as Sturmey (1962) has noted, for example, 'revenue pooling is a limitation on internal competition ... dangerous to the maintenance of efficient services'. What then are the compensating advantages that the conference can claim to offer to shippers? The classic defence of the system hinges upon the very high incidence of fixed costs relative to total costs. Without regulatory collusion, the argument runs, there would be violent fluctuations in rates as liners would be operated in the manner described earlier in this chapter, up to the point where cargoes yielded anything greater than variable cost minus laying-up cost. Liner companies would chase business, perhaps discriminating against the small shipper, and would be reluctant to adhere to scheduled sailing dates, preferring to sail whenever the ship happened to be full. Much of the argument tends to be speculative, but Deakin's work offers a valuable insight into the *actual* practices of conferences. His studies of price formation and profit are useful checks on whether conferences abuse their power through exploitation or inefficiency. Price discrimination in the monopolistic mould is quite conceivable since conferences provide a service that cannot be resold, because of the imperfect knowledge of the market among shippers and because of the barrier to new entrants. Liners may therefore be expected to charge what the market will bear; and Deakin has estimated that demand-based factors, or 'value of service' relating to the value of the goods, account for two-thirds of the variation in price while cost-of-service factors account for the remaining one-third. Deakin has observed cross-subsidisation both (1) within conferences among shippers despatching goods in one direction, and (2) in favour of shippers sending predominantly bulky lower value products from developing countries as against shippers sending more valuable manufactured products from developed countries, for which the transport demand is less price elastic. Both forms of cross-subsidisation are arbitrary and lack justification on economic grounds; some rates fail to cover even short-run marginal cost. However, the extent of cross-subsidisation can sometimes be more apparent than real because joint outputs are involved, and the marginal costs on certain legs of a voyage may be very low.

Shipping lines display wide variations in their profitability because of variations in their cost levels. The Rochdale Committee (1970) found that British shipping had been earning low post-tax profits by the standard of other British industries and that cross-subsidisation among conference members meant that inefficient firms would survive in effect at the expense of their efficient brethren and of the industry's general level of efficiency. However, no evidence of vast monopoly profit was found.

Clearly, the picture of conference operation is not a model of economic rationality or efficiency. However, the conclusion to be drawn is not necessarily that conferences are undesirable in principle; rather it is that attempts should be made to improve their operations than to eliminate them. At the 1964 UNCTAD it was concluded that 'the liner conference system is necessary in order to secure stable rates and regular services' (UNCTAD, 1964). Goss (1968, p. 17) has stated that 'the shipping conference is not so much an anti-competitive device as a coordinating one'. The Rochdale Report includes a brief review of many national attitudes to conferences and seems generally to accept their existence. The shortcomings of conferences seem in large measure to be matters of omission rather than commission, and it is important to remember that the degree of monopoly exercised is seriously constrained in many cases. Conferences proliferate in mid ranges of international trade. For highly expensive goods, where freight charges are a low proportion of value and slow travel imposes an inventory cost, air transport is an active and growing competitor. Helleiner (1973) has pointed to the critical role of air transport in the spread of labour-intensive subassembly operations in countries with abundant cheap labour. At the other end of the spectrum bulky and inexpensive goods are suitable for charter transport, by tramp or bulk carrier. Disgruntled shippers may even establish their own line as they have occasionally in the past. Finally, in a competitive environment, if high conference freight-rates push commodity prices from one source very high, alternative routes, alternative sources and alternative products will frequently be open to consideration for there is no restriction of competition between different conferences.

On balance then conferences tend to stabilise freight rates although anatomically they are apt to insulate and preserve inefficient members. In the period between the two world wars they seem to have limited the accession of faster ships to the British liner fleet at the behest of the owners of slow ships. To judge the net contribution of the system is a mammoth task, although it need not inhibit economists from recommending improvements as UNCTAD (1975) did in proposing a code of conduct for liner conferences, advocating *inter alia* open conferences, better consultation machinery and the abandonment of 'fighting ships'. As Lawrence (1972, pp. 13–14) has noted, the future of the conference system is an open question; in some ways its power has been whittled away by the growth of national flag carriers, of specialist charter tonnage and of vessels owned by companies without previous maritime interests. In other respects, however, the need for vigilance against monopolistic abuse is all the greater following the growth of container traffic. The massive investment required to introduce container traffic has resulted in consortia of shipping companies pooling their interests so as to afford all the associated onshore facilities, including inland container depots. These consortia are obviously likely to increase the concentration levels of conference membership, with all the attendant dangers of oligopoly or even monopolisation. However, it seems unlikely that the conference system will disappear. Apart from its durability the alternatives are problematic for several reasons: unilateral action by governments is seldom conducive to efficient resources allocation as it usually involves a form of subsidy; bilateral arrangements tend to be narrow and inadequate; and multilateral agreements are difficult to establish and implement. The practical requirements of maritime trade will probably ensure the continuation of the conference, or a close mutation of it, for many years to come.

TECHNICAL PROGRESS: THE CONTAINER REVOLUTION

Technical progress has manifested itself in many ways in shipping during this century. In recent years some of the seemingly dramatic innovations, such as marine hovercraft and nuclear-powered ships, have proved to have little or no economic impact, while other more mundane advances, such as the much increased size and speed of cargo ships and the spread of standardised freight containers, have had immense repercussions.

The increase in vessel sizes and speeds and the growth of container traffic are closely related phenomena. Additional size and speed augment the earning capacity of a ship; but unless a large ship can be unloaded quickly in port, its advantage is lost (Goss, 1974). Carriers of homogeneous cargoes, amenable to bulk handling techniques, can be loaded and unloaded quickly; but many dry cargoes, such as liners might carry, were not suitable for bulk handling. An early advance was the use of pallets, introduced in the 1940s; these are wooden trays with a horizontal space into which a fork-lift truck can insert its prongs and thus manoeuvre loads much more efficiently than by traditional manhandling. After the Port of Manchester encouraged the use of pallets in 1965, the result was a 75 per cent quicker handling of cargoes there. Palletisation is less ambitious than containerisation, though its simplicity and low cost make it a useful first step towards improved cargo handling in less developed countries.

Containers are standarised metal boxes made on a modular principle with a cross section 8 feet by 8 feet, and 10, 20, 30 or 40 feet long, the TEU or 'twenty-equivalent-unit' being the datum for comparison. The first modern containers were introduced by Sea–Land on their US coastal services in 1956, and the Matson Line soon offered a similar service to Hawaii. Associated Steamships – an Australian line – inaugurated its Melbourne–Fremantle service in 1964, and Sea–Land began a successful North Atlantic service in 1966.

Containers can be loaded, possibly with a combination of different goods, at inland clearance depots (ICD) near urban centres. They are then taken by road or rail to the port. At the quayside a special crane lifts the container aboard ship, but extensive parking space and straddle carriers are also needed. Containers can be carried in limited numbers by traditional decked cargo ships, but specifically designed 'cellular' container ships are much more efficient and can dispense with shipboard loading gear. Containers offer a number of savings (Johnson and Garnett, 1971):

(1) More efficient use of capital equipment by improving the utilisation of ships and marine terminals. Some impression of the potential saving is given by the relative times in port and at sea of different types of ship, shown in Table 9.9. The container ship serves cargo liner routes but is much closer to the pattern of utilisation of the tanker.

Table 9.9 *Percentage of time spent at sea and in port for different types of ship.*

	Passenger liner	*Cargo liner*	*Tramp*	*Tanker*
At sea	63	40	57	81
In port	37	60	43	19

(2) Reduction of the time for which cargo is in transit since handling is speeded up. This reduces inventory costs.

(3) More rapid handling between the different modes (i.e. at the 'interfaces') of transport and associated reductions in damage and pilferage.

(4) Potentially lower packing and insurance costs.
(5) Slight crew-cost savings in cellular ships and the prospect of using bigger liners.
(6) Much reduced direct labour costs through automatic-handling techniques. Capital costs of equipment are greater, and labour is also required at ICDs, but the figures in Table 9.10 illustrate the different dockside labour productivity.

Table 9.10 *Dockside labour productivity for different types of loading.*

Mode	*Men*	*Tonnage*	*Time (hours)*	*Tons per man-hour*
Traditional ship	90	1,200	8	1.67
Pallets	50	1,800	8	4.5
Containers	20	6,000	10	30.0

Source: National Ports Council.

Not surprisingly the advantages of the container system have caused a major swing towards container ships on deep sea routes; 90 per cent of Canada–United Kingdom non-bulk dry cargo and 70 per cent of United Kingdom–Canada non-bulk dry cargo is containerised. Rapid turn-round time in port means that fewer and bigger ships are required to provide the same traffic as before and that costs fall. Goss (1974) has estimated that, if time in port can be cut from 60 to 20 per cent (i.e. from cargo liner to tanker levels), costs can be reduced by between 18–35 per cent.

The implications for shipping are composite. On shorter routes (e.g. from Britain to the Continent, from the Australian mainland to Tasmania) service frequency is important and thus constrains the size of ship; roll-on, roll-off (RoRo) traffic with road trucks is often more appropriate than cellular ships. On longer runs between continents sailing frequency is less, and so ships can be much larger; the number of ships required may therefore tend to fall although the growth of cargo in total will limit the degree of the fall.

Apart from the implications for competitive behaviour mentioned earlier in connection with the conference system, containerisation has had very far-reaching effects on ports. Holloway (1971) has written of 'an incipient financial crisis' in British ports whose 'heightening sense of crisis is due to the scope and speed of technological opportunities, of which the revolution in cargo handling is by far the most important'. Within this revolution may be included both bulk carriers and containerisation, and the consequences are several.

First, bigger ships bring problems for ports with shallow approaches, most obviously in the case of supertankers, which may have a draught of over 100 feet. The bigger container ships may also be constrained, being unable, for example, to navigate the Manchester Ship Canal. Together with the much greater capacity of container docks for handling cargo the tendency is for containerisation to concentrate traffic among fewer ports and for many of the traditional packing functions to be carried out at inland clearance depots before the container reaches the ports.

Second, container berths are capital intensive; for example, one berth with two container cranes cost £7.3 million in 1976. Not all ports can afford these facilities, and not all have wharfing suitable for containers. The more suitable locations (e.g. Tilbury) have grown while the disadvantaged ones (e.g. the old London docks) have suffered a massive contraction in traffic.

Third, pricing policies have had to be revised by port authorities. Until recently port charges for vessels were levied per grt for a fixed and often lengthy stay in port. Cargo rates were usually per dwt or package, occasionally *ad valorem*, but seldom positively related to average or marginal costs. Containers brought some progress towards more economic pricing, but in smaller ports the application of more economic pricing systems seems to have been restricted to the elimination of the worst loss makers.

Fourth, one of the most difficult problems of containerisation is the displacement of dock labour. In any industry moving from a labour-intensive to a capital-intensive system the problems of displaced labour are likely to be severe; but labour relations in the docks suffer from the legacy of employment policies that, before the decasualisation of dock labour in the 1950s, verged upon the brutal. Non-recruitment and wastage have been insufficient to bring the labour force towards an economic number, and under the Jones–Aldington proposals of 1972 the government paid £30 million to 8,000 dockers in a voluntary redundancy scheme. Ironically, it was often the younger, fitter and more mobile dockers who left, so that the older ports were left with a relatively old and inefficient labour force. This exacerbated the problems, so that, for example, four men in Felixstowe shift as much cargo as ten in London. The Transport and General Workers' Union (TGWU) sought to protect the dockers' interests through the Dock Labour Act 1976 by securing employment for dockers at ICDs within a specified radius of the docks, although the Act as passed was much less restrictive than the union wished. However, the potential here for restrictive practice through a monopolisitic organisation is, in the judgement of many observers, no less than that in the liner conference system.

However, the legacy of bad labour relations a generation ago and a helter-skelter run-down of the current labour force have made dockers very suspicious of further technical change. For instance, interunion disagreement between dockers and railway men in the mid 1970s effectively blackballed attempts to introduce 'lighter-aboard ship' (LASH) at Hull, although technologically it is a promising development involving lighters or barges that can be carried like containers but floated off the ship to use inshore waterways and canal – in effect a floating container. Expanding Continental and North American ports may be more accommodating, with sobering consequences for the British ports industry, but it does point the clear moral that technological change brings a host of consequences of which the impact on labour is one of the most critical.

CHAPTER 10

The Economics of Airlines

INTRODUCTION

The most distinctive feature of the air transport industry is its rapid development since the Second World War: until the early 1970s passenger-mileage increased annually by over 14 per cent; the speed of airliners rose from 200 m.p.h. to 600 m.p.h. commonly and to 1,350 m.p.h. for Concorde; and the real cost of air travel had fallen significantly. These changes distinguish air transport from many other modes of transport, particularly in the international field, although despite its growth air travel is still used by a minority of the population even in the developed countries.

A second feature is that airlines operating internationally are subject to political constraints imposed not only by their country of origin but also by the other countries to which they operate. Any country may prohibit foreign aircraft from using its airspace, and although conventions about overflight and technical landing rights have been established many aspects of airline operation remain subject to bilateral haggling between the countries concerned. The Chicago Convention of 1944 established the International Civil Aviation Organisation (ICAO) and the first two of the five 'freedoms of the air'. These were:

(1) the right of one nation's airline to fly over a second country to reach a third; and
(2) the right for that airline to land in the second country for fuel or maintenance, although not to transfer passengers there, while *en route* for the third country.

The Bermuda Agreement of 1946 proposed three more freedoms:

(3) the right to set down traffic from the airline's country of origin in a second country;
(4) the right to pick up traffic destined for the airline's country of origin, in a second country; and

(5) the right of one nation's airline to carry traffic from a second country to a third country.

However, these freedoms were ambiguously formulated in the agreement in the hope that informal agreements could be reached over them, and in practice there has been much dispute, arising largely out of the proviso that capacity should be related to the traffic requirements of the area through which the airline passes 'after taking account of local and regional services'. This has been variously interpreted since it permits the expansion or reduction of traffic, but the commonest result has been to restrict airlines of other nations from providing services to nations at intermediate points. In bilateral negotiations over routes politics have often over-ridden economics, and sometimes the desire of both nations to offer a service has created overcapacity. A number of economists have been very critical of the degree of restriction that has followed the agreements (Straszheim, 1969). The Bermuda Agreement was the subject of intense Anglo–American renegotiation in 1977.

THE DEMAND FOR AIR TRAVEL

The determination of demand is extremely important in such a fast-growing sector as air transport; yet, as we shall see, the analysis of demand is beset by many problems. Simple economic theory suggests obvious reasons why air travel has expanded so rapidly. In most countries there have been large increases in real income per head. Changes in relative prices have also favoured the international airliner; between 1957 and 1967 average world air-passenger fares fell by 8 per cent in money terms and air-freight rates by 29 per cent, whereas the general price level and ocean liner fares both rose. The quality of service has also improved markedly, in terms of greater frequency of service, shorter journey times and better travelling conditions (e.g. the reduction in cabin noise and vibration by the introduction of pure jet aircraft; the use of cabin pressurisation enabling aircraft to fly above bad weather).

However, the demand for air travel is not such an attractive proposition for statistical analysis as it may seem at first sight. It is not exactly analogous to the demand for a commodity since transport is a derived demand. For a business traveller the journey is basically an input of his firm – it can be seen as an element of the information process – and for the tourist an airline journey is merely part of a bigger item – the visit or holiday.

Demand can be analysed at a variety of levels. The analyst may be interested in the global demand for air travel; or the demand generated on particular routes; or the variables, especially price and income levels, that influence demand on specified routes; or the demand for a distinctive mode of air travel (e.g. supersonic flight, where a rational evaluation would have to try to determine the imputed value of time saved).

Global estimates are subject to very obvious difficulties. Not only do they involve aggregating the demand for a myriad of different 'products' (i.e. journeys over many different routes), but also they cannot easily separate the business from the leisure traveller. Such estimates have therefore tended at best to be little more than simple extrapolations of past growth. ICAO (1968), for example, has spoken of a probable annual increase in passenger-kilometres of 12 per cent until 1980, with an upper limit of 16 per cent; the consideration of income elasticity is limited to a footnote. Such extrapolations were shattered by the colder economic climate of the 1970s and the impact of the policies of the Organisation of Petroleum Exporting Countries (OPEC) on aviation fuel prices after 1973. In the late 1970s and early 1980s growth rates of 6–8 per cent are expected. Gravity models of the sort mentioned in Chapter 3 may be used to attempt an explanation of the total demand on specific routes. These were first applied to the demand for air travel in the early 1950s (Harvey, 1951) and are essentially cross-section studies taking one or two cities. Several of these have been conducted in the United States, and a few outside it, employing a number of variables to explain differences in the demand for air travel between pairs of cities. The simplest models are restricted to population and distance as variables, but others have incorporated journey time, fares, indices of competition or service on the route, income levels of the linked pairs of cities, measures of the 'community of interest' of linked cities (e.g. the number of intercity telephone calls, or the number of hotel registrants in the city of destination who come from the city of origin).

No uniquely satisfactory determinants have emerged from these studies, which often suggest significant geographical influences not subsumed in the independent variables, although it is clear that income, distance and population are influential in varying degrees. The basic difficulty of such cross-section studies is that the demands for trips along different routes vary according to the 'attractiveness' of the destination; the cross-section does not compare like with like, and the cross-section observations are essentially points on *different* demand curves. Added complications arise on international routes once the gravity model is elaborated beyond the simple population and distance function, in that it is difficult to incorporate fares because, under the pricing policies of the International Air Transport Association (IATA) cartel, fares are correlated with distance. It may also be necessary to introduce some criterion of 'attractiveness', and to this end Straszheim (1969, pp. 116–118) has employed a dummy variable to signify whether or not the destinations of flights from Paris were capital cities.

There are virtually no published gravity models to explain the pattern of demand for flights to and from Britain, although an unpublished paper by Hanlon (1970) has constructed gravity models for business travel between the United Kingdom and fourteen to twenty-nine overseas countries. His three explanatory variables are gross national products, trade flows between the respective nations and distance, with fares and flying times sometimes used instead of distance. However, the results are disappointing statistically, and no meaningful estimates of demand elasticities can be derived from them.

An attractive approach is to analyse time-series data for traffic on specified routes. Here, however, a major problem arises because of the rapid rate of change in the airline industry. A linear regression model presupposes stable coefficients. Hence, if a simple model were used to investigate the influence of price and income changes across two decades on the demand for air travel on a given route, it might be specified thus:

$$D_t = a + b_1 P_t + b_2 Y_t + u_t$$

where D = demand at time t; P = the relative cost of air travel; Y = the level of real income; and u_t = an error term.
The results would yield coefficients b_1 and b_2, which supposedly would be constant across the period observed. In practice, however, this constancy is open to question. Over two decades so many important characteristics of airline service have altered that it is inadequate to employ price and income changes alone to explain the growth of demand. This is called an *underspecified model* because it omits certain important explanatory factors. Such an equation will yield estimates based on price changes that are subject to a specific set of other influences that may not apply in the future. These changing influences include shorter journey times, greater comfort, more frequent flights, decline in competitive surface modes of transport and other factors.

A problem known in econometrics as *multicollinearity* arises, in which it is impossible to observe changes in one of the variables without simultaneous changes occurring in one or all of the others. The explanatory variables are very highly correlated with each other, and it is very difficult to isolate their individual importance as would be necessary if income and price elasticities were to be derived from the data. In this case price and income changes are highly correlated with time, and a time trend inserted into the regression will 'explain' almost all of the variation in demand; the addition of price and income variables barely improves the fit of the equation to the data and sometimes yields implausible coefficients for the price and income variables (e.g. the *negative* income coefficient calculated by Straszheim, 1969, pp. 125–6). A negative income coefficient does not necessarily mean that rising demand is associated with falling individual income levels; rather it means that with falling prices lower income groups can now afford to fly. The weakness of presuming that coefficients are constant may be illustrated by considering prices; over the postwar period the class of service has changed significantly, and it seems that the price elasticity of demand differs between each class – first, tourist and economy.

The finer specification of models requires finer data, which at present are difficult to obtain. For example, differences are likely between business and leisure travellers, but traffic statistics such as those issued by IATA do not generally distinguish between the two. Further desirable breakdown between scheduled and charter flights has also been difficult. A number of expedients may be used to overcome some of the difficulties. The methods employed by economists have used outside information or prior knowledge to constrain the estimates within specified boundaries to produce either a 'constrained regression' model or a more sophisticated Bayesian model. Straszheim (1969) has fitted data to both these models, obtaining better results from the latter. It takes all prior information about the parameters, arranged as a probability distribution, and applies sample data to that distribution to yield new estimates of the parameters. Straszheim formed his probability distribution from case studies, cross-section data and survey data and analysed traffic on the North Atlantic route. He calculated an income elasticity of demand for tourist travel of +1.82 and a price elasticity of −1.42, but about one-third of the growth of traffic remains unexplained by either price or income changes. The Bayesian technique avoids the problems of multicollinearity but is open to the criticism that there is a subjective element in constructing the probability distribution. More recently Ellison and Stafford (1974) have surveyed British and Continental cross-sectional studies, including that of the Roskill Commission (1970) on the Third London Airport. They noted that income elasticity of demand is not constant but increases with income levels and that meaningful elasticities can only be estimated after allowing for changing income levels, service frequency and competition from alternative modes.

Finally, within the area of demand analysis the advent of supersonic passenger aircraft has emphasised the importance of the valuation of time savings by airline customers, for with Concorde in commercial operation there is a choice between cheap subsonic flights and supersonic flights at a premium charge usually 15–20 per cent above first-class fares. Although vast investment programmes have been authorised for the development of Concorde the analysis of demand for its service has been extraordinarily limited. Gronau (1970) in the United States has investigated the effects of time valuation among airline passengers, on the assumption that valuation is a function of annual earnings. The demand for supersonic travel then depends upon the length of journey and the degree of surcharge levied in supersonic airliner fares, using a modal difference method of assessment that is similar to that outlined in Chapter 2. Short stage lengths clearly militate against supersonic operation, and Gronau projected that by 1975 time valuation at 1960 prices would range approximately from $4.40 to $5 with a 10 per cent supersonic surcharge and from $22 to $25 with a 50 per cent surcharge depending on stage lengths. Time valuation below these figures would yield a preference for subsonic aircraft. One interesting finding by Gronau is that the price elasticity of demand for both demand for personal and business travel by air is less than one, so that a reduction in fares by airlines would tend to reduce total airline revenues despite the increase in traffic thus generated. Other studies have confirmed a figure below one for business elasticity but suggested a personal figure of around two. Clearly, arguments for lower air fares as a means to increase traffic would benefit from explicit calculations of the price elasticity of demand. Cooper and Maynard (1971) have argued persuasively that lower fares would solve many of the industry's difficulties, although Doganis (1973) has suggested that the benefits of increased competition would be limited in scope and area – notably to the densest routes.

COSTS

Fortunately, information about costs is easier to obtain. Costs may be considered in two forms: the costs of operating particular aircraft and the costs of operating a fleet of aircraft. It must also be noted that the marginal cost of carrying one more passenger may be virtually zero if an existing aircraft is operating at anything less than full capacity.

Different aircraft have widely varying operating characteristics. Their carrying capacity differs; for example, a Boeing 707–320B may carry up to 189 passengers and a Boeing 747B up to 490. Moreover, the carrying capacity of the same aircraft varies over routes of different length. The carrying capacity of an aircraft, exclusive of the fuel carried, is called the *payload*, but fuel is a considerable item of the all-up weight of an aircraft. Hence, the further an aircraft flies the more fuel it uses at the expense of payload. The relationship can be shown graphically as in Figure 10.1 with certain practical constraints illustrated. An aircraft can usually take off safely at a higher weight than it can land at because the impact of landing stresses the structure more, and fuel reserves are necessary for diversions, head winds and variations in stacking time while circling airports. There is also a slight performance gain as the aircraft loses weight through fuel consumption. From this relationship can be derived an output function as in Figure 10.2. Then, allowing for the direct operating costs of the aircraft, which we shall discuss presently, it is possible to derive the operating costs of different aircraft over different stage lengths as in Figure 10.3.

It is apparent that the efficiency of aircraft has increased over time from the DC-3 of the late 1930s to the Boeing 707 of the 1960s. The two important determinants of aircraft are operating costs and stage length. The components of direct operating costs are: direct flying expenses, which include crew costs, lodging, fuel and oil; landing and navigation fees; and insurance, maintenance and depreciation.

The succession of designs in Figure 10.3 illustrates the nature of operating costs. Piston-engined aircraft increased in size and speed as technology advanced. Both size and speed augmented their revenue capacity since an airliner flying at 300 m.p.h. can produce twice as many seat-miles as one that is capable of only 150 m.p.h. Moreover, bigger aircraft have physical advantages of scale (Wheatcroft, 1956, p. 3): scale brings aerodynamic advantage; structural weight increases less rapidly than capacity, as does crew size; and larger aircraft can use bigger and more efficient engines.

Piston-engined aircraft were succeeded by turboprops such as the Viscount and Electra, in which a jet engine drove a propeller, and eventually by pure jets. These have higher capital costs than piston-engined aircraft, but they have the benefits of high speed and low maintenance costs since jet engines can work for twice as long between overhauls. Thus, between 1957 and 1967 the flight operation of airlines in ICAO fell as a proportion of total cost from 30 to 26 per cent, but the share of depreciation rose from 9 to 11 per cent.

Competing airlines commonly fly similar aircraft on the same route, so that the cost in running a given service may be expected to be similar. However, differences can arise through variations in the utilisation of capacity, which naturally affects cost per seat-kilometre. Scheduling can make all the difference between getting 8 hours' work a day out of an airliner or 10 hours', and this is clearly important where the capital costs of the aircraft are high, as they are with modern jets and especially

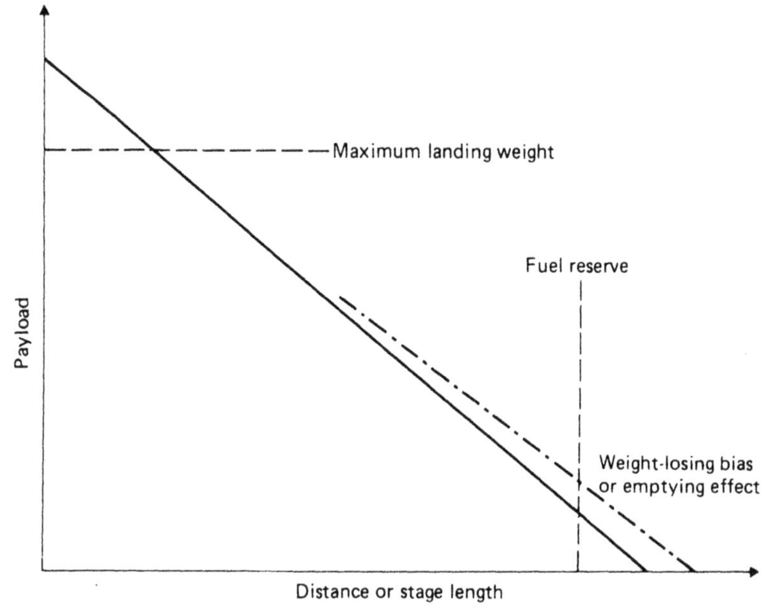

Figure 10.1 *The relationship between payload and distance*

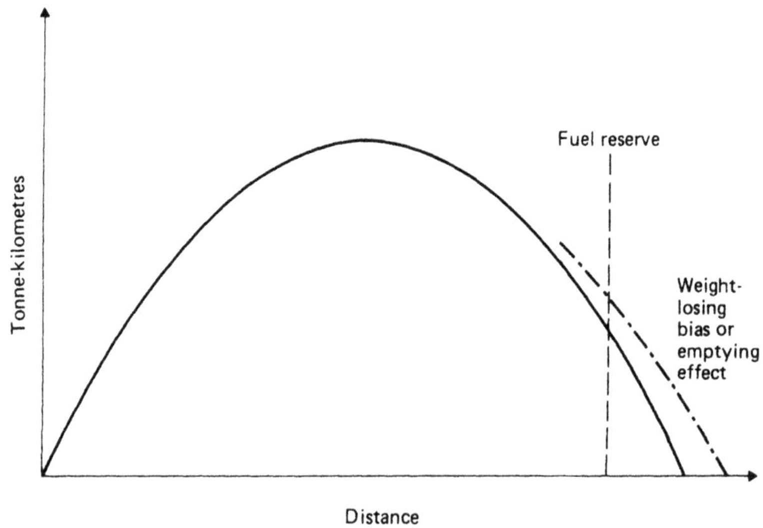

Figure 10.2 *The output of an aircraft*

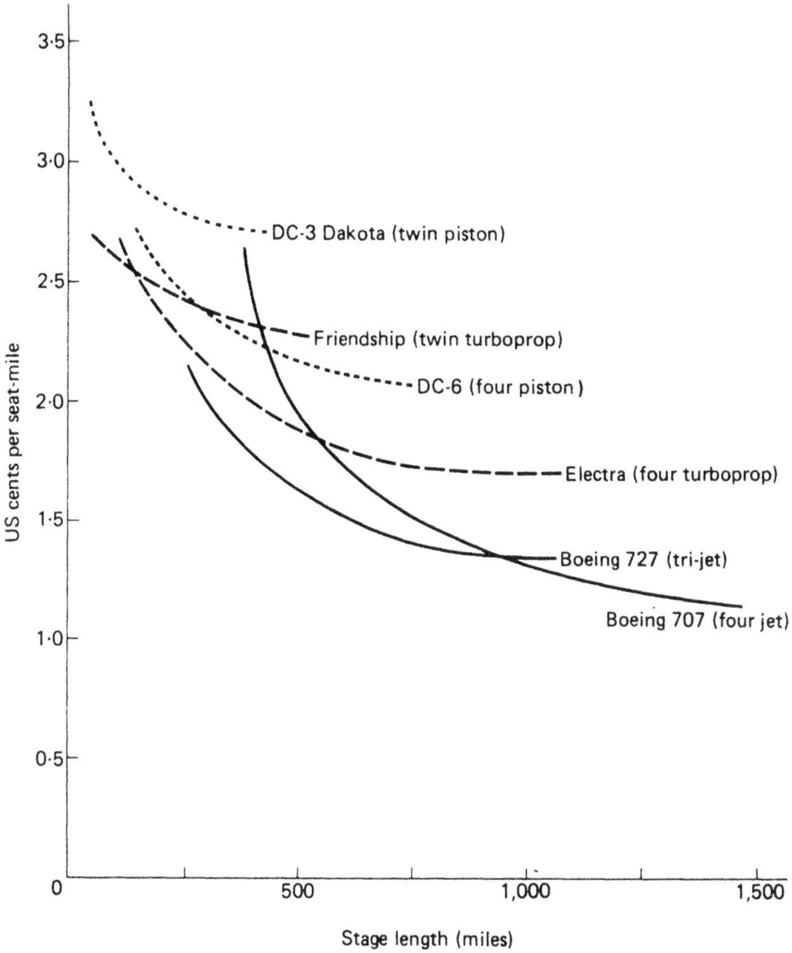

Figure 10.3 *Direct operating costs in the United States, 1965* (after Straszheim, 1969).

with supersonic airliners. There are also significant variations in the manning costs of aircraft since even among internationally operating airlines there are salary differentials, conditioned partly by living standards and partly by other professional salaries in the country of origin. Thus, in 1967 pilots of the US company Eastern Airlines earned an average of $22,800, those of BOAC $12,800 and those of Lufthansa $11,700. There are similar variations among other personnel costs per man, which during 1967 ranged across $1,034 for Pakistan International Airlines, $4,000 for the British Overseas Airways Corporation (BOAC) and $7,500 for Eastern Airlines. In practice, Straszheim (1969) has observed, high wage-cost operators have tended to have better scheduling capabilities.

Stratford (1967, p. 79) has provided data on costs, which make it possible to compare the significance of different elements in direct operating costs. In order to achieve a 5 per cent reduction in the operating costs of a typical medium-range pure-jet airliner any *one* of the following would need to be achieved:

(1) a 5 per cent increase in payload or block speed;
(2) a 16 per cent increase in utilisation;
(3) a 19 per cent reduction in airframe price;
(4) a 20 per cent reduction in fuel consumption or fuel price;
(5) a 23 per cent reduction in engine cost;
(6) a 36 per cent reduction in crew salaries; or
(7) a 65 per cent increase in engine life between overhauls.

The figures show the sensitivity of costs to payload and speed and the importance of fuel costs and engine costs, the latter being almost as high as the cost of the airframe. The costs of IATA-scheduled international services are set out in Table 10.1.

Table 10.1 *Operating costs of international scheduled airlines, 1972–81.*

	1972, %	*1981, %*
Flight crew	8.7	5.4
Fuel and oil	10.3	28.4
Other flight operations	5.2	3.6
Depreciation and amortization	11.3	6.5
Maintenance and overhaul	12.5	9.5
Landing fees and *en route* charges	6.5	6.0
Station expenses	9.9	8.8
Passenger services	10.1	8.8
Ticketing, sales and promotion	18.6	16.5
General, administrative and other costs	6.9	6.5
Total	100.0	100.0

Source: International Civil Aviation Organisation.

It is relatively easy to analyse operating costs for aircraft types on specified routes, but it is much more difficult to determine whether one airline is more efficient than another if they operate over different route networks. Even where aircraft, stage lengths and loads are similar there are differences in landing fees at airports, for although these are often based on gross aircraft weight there are exceptions and qualifications, which result in an irregular pattern. However, assuming a constant quality of service there are three main causes of variation in airline costs: route traffic density; variations in demand, especially seasonal peaks; and the scale of the airline's total operation.

Route traffic density obviously influences the potential utilisation of capacity. The most densely travelled routes, especially the North Atlantic, were for long the most profitable because the aircraft could be used to capacity, although in recent years excess capacity has reduced load factors leaving an increasing proportion of empty seats on scheduled flights and making many routes unprofitable. In 1973/74 on North Atlantic scheduled services, first-class revenue load-factors were 29 per cent against a break-even point of 55 per cent, and for the lower class the corresponding figures were 57 and 71 per cent; many other routes were similarly unprofitable (IATA, 1974). Where demand is very low (e.g. an aircraft operating to an isolated destination along a route with many stops and consequently high unit costs) operational freedom is limited. Small aircraft may be used, but we have seen that the biggest ones have significantly lower costs when fully utilised. Potentially the most efficient method of operation is on a long haul with maximum daily utilisation. On a high-density long-range route the aircraft may be able to make two round trips a day; on a high-density short-range route (typically, London–Paris) the aircraft can be kept busy all the time. Suppose that a trans-Atlantic jet has an optimum utilisation of 16 hours a day and that after its crossing it has 1 hour left to complete the 16. It could be routed on a shorter European journey to complete its utilisation if the traffic on a shorter European route merited a large aircraft. Hence, the ideal would be a network of high density routes. Where density is low it may prove impossible to schedule the aircraft to achieve optimum utilisation.

There are marked seasonal variations in demand, particularly where tourists form a high proportion of travellers. Seasonality and basic traffic density affect different airlines in different ways and make the accurate estimation of economies of scale in airline operation difficult. The (Edwards) Committee of Inquiry into Civil Air Transport (1969) in its Report has considered the importance of scale in airline operation and examined the evidence from the United States, but it decided that no clear optimum could be defined. Practically all the empirical evidence collected by Caves (1962), Straszheim (1969) and Wheatcroft (1956) suggests limits to such economies of scale. The Edwards Committee has noted that in the United States the four largest airlines examined earned lower rates of return on capital than the next seven biggest and has attributed this to four main reasons.

(1) The route networks of the four biggest were the most competitive.
(2) A high proportion of their flights served major metropolitan areas where there were external diseconomies, notably expensive ground-facility costs and serious congestion delays that for example, rendered the New York–Boston service slower by pure jet than it had been by slower-flying turboprop aircraft some years before.
(3) The biggest airlines tended to be technological leaders and to bear a high proportion of the costs of innovation (e.g. in aircraft and computer booking).
(4) Two airlines claimed that they were obliged as a matter of public policy to provide a disproportionate number of unprofitable short-haul services, presumably in fear of antitrust legislation, and that these services were cross-subsidised at the expense of profitability.

However, although the limits to economies of airline scale are difficult to define there can be no doubt of their existence short of that limit. Various reasons for them have been advanced although they have not always been easy to verify. Big airlines may be able to use their bargaining strength in aircraft purchase (e.g. for early delivery dates, for price savings), fuel purchase and insurance cover. 'Project engineering', to study new aircraft requirements and operating systems, and computer systems are large indivisible inputs and are best employed by bigger airlines. Maintenance and crew-training savings may accrue to bigger airlines although their smaller competitors are sometimes able to economise by subcontracting or sharing facilities. Inventory costs for spare parts should be lower for big standardised fleets, and in theory these fleets have better potential for full utilisation.

In practice the potential economies of scale are only likely to be realised where there is considerable homogeneity in input and output (i.e. where the fleet operates a standard type of aircraft and, for maximum economy, concentrates on a specialised service). A large fleet of aircraft standardised on one particular type, as opposed to a large mixed fleet, offers economy of spare parts and maintenance costs; these are very significant, as a fleet of five aircraft must spend 35 per cent of the cost of aircraft on spares for airframes and engines whereas a fleet of fifty needs to spend only 15 per cent. Higher levels of utilisation are possible. Crew training is cheaper because once a fleet has fifteen or twenty aircraft the purchase of a ground simulator becomes economic and thus cuts the amount of expensive flying training required. Manning is easier because crews are all familiar with the standardised aircraft, and crew utilisation is improved. Ground equipment can be standardised and often mechanised (e.g. baggage-handling equipment specific to one type of aircraft). The Edwards Committee has estimated that these advantages can yield economies in unit operating costs per aircraft of 14 per cent for a fleet of fifty aircraft compared with one of five aircraft. Specialisation in product is exemplified by airlines concentrating on a limited route network; for example, Pacific South West Airlines concentrates on the Los Angeles–San Francisco route and thereby keeps traffic handling, passenger service and sale promotion costs down to comparatively low levels.

Thus, in summary, airline size may bring economic benefits where: the route network allows a large fleet of standardised aircraft; scale is associated with large participation in particular markets; and marketing effectiveness requires a wide coverage of routes and sale outlets, such that passengers can make reservations for a complex route and remain with one airline throughout the whole journey.

However, the advantages of size may be lost if the routes require a variety of aircraft of different capacities and ranges or if expansion in markets requires a variety of different standards.

PRICING

In a totally competitive environment prices are determined by demand and supply, but the airline industry like many other sectors of transport is subject to a great deal of regulation as we saw at the beginning of this chapter. Various reasons have been advanced for the degree of regulation that exists. For instance, it has been said that it is vital to the maintenance of safety standards and that it maintains public service requirements by avoiding cut-throat competition at short-run marginal cost, which would eventually produce bankruptcies and chaos in services. These points could be argued, but the political issue is perhaps over-riding. If there were free competition the largest and strongest airlines of the biggest countries, by virtue of the scale advantages outlined earlier, would tend to undercut and eliminate the small ones. Yet these large airlines depend upon landing rights in lesser countries for the maintenance of their route network, so that the smaller nations have strong political leverage.

Towards the end of the Second World War at the Bermuda Conference of 1945, Britain and the United States agreed to accept IATA as the arbiter of airline fares. The US airlines were generally stronger, and Pan American Airlines wanted fares below the prewar level on the North

Atlantic, but the British government objected and threatened to limit landing rights in the United Kingdom. The United States deferred, influenced by the unprofitable state of airline operation at the time, and the IATA has set prices for scheduled international services since then at its three Traffic Conferences, held annually and covering three geographical areas. All airlines active within an area may take part, each with a single vote irrespective of its size of operation. Not surprisingly these conferences have suffered from perennial crises and disagreement between airlines, in which the conservative high-price operators have been generally successful. Some members of the IATA have occasionally cut fares in defiance of the association, and in some areas non-members provide competition.

Other competition has come from charter flights, the growth of which during the 1970s has emphasised the anomaly of IATA pricing policy. Nominally, charter flights were restricted to 'affinity groups' formed for non-travel purposes and not advertising outside their membership, whose members were required to be of six months' standing; but abuses of these requirements were legion. Since charter fares can yield savings of up to two-thirds of the cost of a scheduled flight the incentive to private passengers is compelling; the operator virtually fills the aircraft, gaining load factors approaching 100 per cent compared with factors of 54–9 per cent for low-cost scheduled flights in 1973/74.

The outcome of the political prejudices and pressures that underlie the bargaining process within IATA is an irrational fare structure in which fares are not related to long-run marginal costs. Apart from the disparity between charter and scheduled flight prices there are wide differences between fares per kilometre on scheduled flights over different routes, which vary by a factor of up to 2.7 and thus imply considerable cross-subsidisation between routes.

The British Airline Users' Committee (1976) has described European air fares as a jungle, with six rates and seven discounts being quoted between London and Frankfurt and thirty rates and six discounts between London and Malaga. Scheduled fare rates in 1976 were on average twice the North American level and appreciably above the Australian. Several factors have contributed to this disparity. Thinly patronised first-class accommodation in Europe incurred losses of $83.6 million in 1973/74 and is cross-subsidised by lower-cost travellers; selling costs are high because of high promotional costs to cater for a bigger proportion of leisure travel, involving commissionable sales; airport and fuel charges are higher than in North America; international travel increases navigational costs and red tape, so that there are twenty regulatory bodies; and labour productivity is low in European airlines, possibly because high costs are too readily tolerated.

The limitations imposed on price competition have prevented fares from falling as low as they might have done, although they certainly have fallen in real terms during a period of rising real incomes since the Second World War. They have fostered non-price competition through product differentiation typified by heavy promotional expenditure, the provision of in flight films and, rather paradoxically, the expansion of capacity. Capacity expansion is seldom associated with cartels, which usually restrict capacity to keep up prices; but as the frequency of flights is a competitive weapon, airlines have offered more flights while the degree to which demand can be extended by price reductions has been limited by IATA policy. Ellison and Stafford (1974), however, have attributed much of the industry's overcapacity to the long lag between aircraft orders and deliveries.

Thus, the influence of supply and demand on price has been quite strong in the case of charter operations but tenuous in the case of scheduled services. The existence of the charter market imposes some constraint on IATA policies, and so does dissension among its members; but the reaction to underlying economic pressures has been slow, leading eventually to price cutting through promotional fares. Airlines of widely varying efficiencies have been enabled to survive, sometimes via national subsidies. Practically all economists who have analysed airline operations have agreed that the consumer could benefit from changes in IATA policy; but, as we have seen, it is an extremely political issue.

The members of IATA have moved towards more competitive pricing as charter flights and enterprising price cutters (eg. Laker, and People Express) have attracted their customers away. Recently added pressure has arisen as disgruntled airlines have left IATA, often to rejoin later. The effect of these influences is shown in Table 10.2. Operators such as Laker and People Express argued that there is great potential in the price elastic market for tourists for extremely basic low cost carriers; their admission on to the North Atlantic route has obliged the older established carriers to offer an increasing variety of fares at the low end of the market. At the July 1978 meeting of IATA in Montreal, a greater measure of discretion for members to opt out of fare and condition setting was approved in principle. While it has not been fully realised in practice, the tight hold of IATA has loosened as competitive operators have been given traffic rights on the North Atlantic.

INVESTMENT PROBLEMS

The airlines and aircraft producers face many problems in deciding their investment policies, not least because of the areas of uncertainty in

Table 10.2 *Changing characteristics of air fares, 1966–82*

	1966	*1976*	*1982*
Passengers on North Atlantic route (millions)	5.1	13.8	18.5
Percentage carried on:			
Charter flights	15.7	26.6	11.8
Scheduled	84.3	73.4	88.2
of which:			
Scheduled standard fares	47.6	21.7	24.3
Scheduled promotional fares	36.7	51.7	63.9
Percentage of schedule fare types			
First and supersonic	8.2	5.4	5.2
Normal economy	48.3	24.2	22.3
Regular excursions	26.3	32.4	13.7
Cheap excursions	–	11.1	41.3
Group inclusive tours	2.7	8.4	3.6
Budget/Standby	–	–	3.3
Youth, Affinity Groups, etc.	13.6	18.5	10.6
Total	99.1	100.0	100.0

Source: International Air Transport Association.

demand and pricing policies already discussed. Technological uncertainty compounds their problems because of the long gestation period of advanced airliners between the time of initial specification and that of eventual airline service. The problems of Concorde and of the Rolls-Royce RB-211 jet engine were so severe that they had to be resolved at government level. Political motives are entangled with the economic issues, and data are frequently withheld from the public, but a very simplified model (Stubbs, 1973) may be used to highlight some of the key issues involved in the Concorde or RB-211 controversies.

The cost of production of a specified type of aircraft is directly influenced by the numbers produced. There are two direct reasons for economies of scale. First, there are the heavy fixed costs involved in aircraft design and production. Like any other repetition product there are tooling costs, which must be amortised over the production run; and in addition there are research-and-development costs, which can be extremely high for technically sophisticated aircraft (e.g. Concorde, for which research-and-development costs were estimated in 1976 to total £1,154 million). Much, if not all, of the development cost of Concorde and the RB-211 jet engine has been written off and not charged to purchasers. Yet, even if development costs can be charged to taxpayers rather than customers, tooling economies of scale remain. Second, economies of scale are also implicit in the learning curve. Sturmey (1964) has examined the significance of the learning curve in British aircraft production costs and suggested considerable economies in labour input up to 100 aircraft and beyond. Thus, there is an observable inverse relationship between output and production cost, especially if development costs are included, which will remain inverse even if such costs are written off. A downward-sloping cost curve can therefore be postulated, which will give rise to a price curve that slopes downward as expected output rises.

The expected cost of production of Concorde remains confidential, but at the end of 1971 a price of £12.5 million per aircraft was suggested; this rose by 1976 to £25 million, or £30 million with spares. Sales expectations had been continually reduced since the beginning of the project, when it was expected that many hundreds would be produced, to 250 in June 1970 (Burgess, 1970) and to perhaps half that number in unofficial estimates at the end of 1971. Options held at the beginning of 1972 had not risen from the level of seventy-four that applied five years earlier, and most were cancelled. By 1977 production was limited to sixteen, of which only nine were sold. Likewise, the Lockheed Tri-Star – the vehicle for the RB-2111 engine – was plagued by uncertainty in its order books. If sales fall significantly short of estimates, there will be clear implications for the costs of production and potential repercussions on the prices of aircraft.

If aircraft are expensive to buy, they will also become expensive to operate because, as we saw earlier, the cost of airframe-plus-engines is a major factor in total operating costs. Depreciation and insurance costs are functions of the purchase cost of the aircraft, so that the more technically advanced the aircraft, the greater these component costs are as a proportion of the total. The last of the piston-engined airliners (i.e. the DC-7) had depreciation and insurance costs amounting to 10.2 per cent of direct operating costs in 1965, whereas the figure for Boeing 727 jets was 26 per cent. The incidence of these costs on the operating costs of Concorde is likely to be still more pronounced. Hence, increases in the purchase price of aircraft, through increased depreciation and insurance charges, will raise operating costs per passenger-kilometre.

The relationship between operating cost and fares is often tenuous on specific routes, as shown earlier; but in aggregate costs are influential. If costs are high, there will be pressure within IATA to keep fares high, and this will limit demand. If supersonic costs and fares could be kept down to the levels achieved by subsonic aircraft, practically all passengers would opt for the faster alternative; but since the cost of supersonic travel exceeds that of subsonic because supersonic jets are more expensive than was at first expected, a smaller proportion of travellers will exist whose valuation of time savings is high enough to merit the supersonic fare surcharge. The numbers willing to pay may be so low as to render supersonic transport uneconomic in its present form. The demand for aircraft ultimately reflects the demand for seats in those aircraft.

These relationships can be depicted in a diagram (Figure 10.4). The northeast quadrant shows the relationship between output and price, assuming that aircraft prices are related to the costs of production. *PP* represents costs and prices inclusive of research-and-development costs, while *P′P′* excludes them. The southeast quadrant shows the relationship between the price of aircraft and operating costs. If depreciation and insurance costs accounted for about a quarter of direct operating

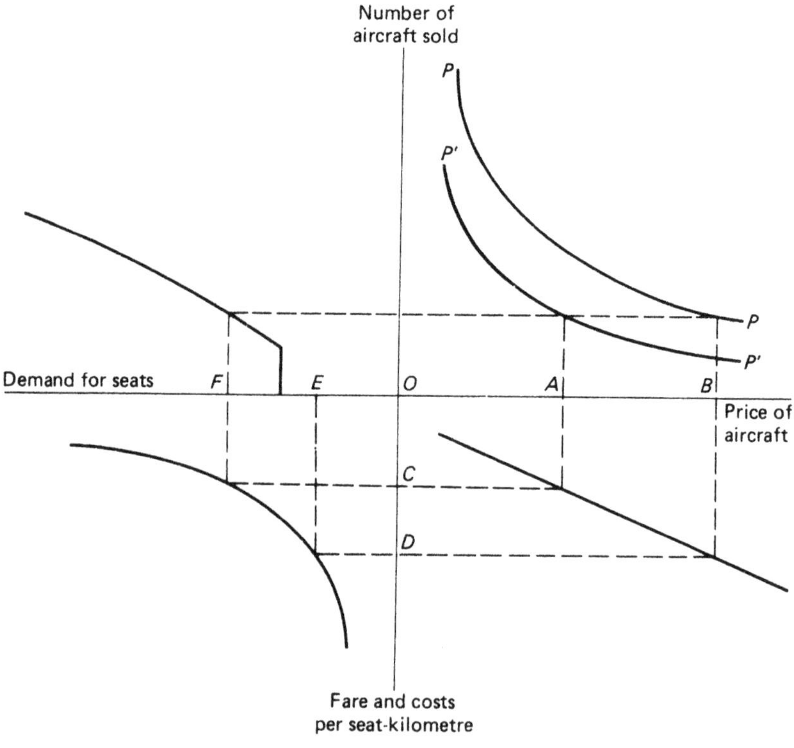

Figure 10.4 *The viability of aircraft production.*

costs, and direct operating costs accounted for about 60 per cent of total airline costs, the slope of this curve would be expected to be about 9 degrees.

The southwest quadrant shows the effect of fares on the demand for supersonic seats, assuming that costs and fares are related. In practice another important factor will influence this relationship, namely, the relative price of seats in subsonic aircraft; and the curve may be kinked because it subsumes two separate demands from business and leisure travellers. Moreover, it is necessary to distinguish between net demand and gross demand. If there is excess capacity in airlines, as there was in 1978 given prevailing fares, the supersonic jet will not generate a simple net addition to demand that is as big as the total demand for supersonic seats, because a major part of the demand for these seats will simply be siphoned off from subsonic airliners. Thus, the net revenue earned from these travellers will not be gross receipts but will lie between two extremes.

(1) The lowest revenue will simply be the extent of the supersonic fare premium.
(2) The highest revenue could be the full fare if airlines could run fewer subsonic aircraft and sell off surplus aircraft at no capital loss.

In practice the most likely effect is that net revenue will at first be little more than the fare premium, tending over time to the full fare as excess capacity is gradually employed more fully. However, it could be expected to be of the general shape shown in Figure 10.4.

The northeast quadrant shows the influence of the demand for seats on aircraft sales. A simple linear relationship might be expected, but in practice there will be a threshold demand, *OX*, beneath which production of the aircraft would be so small that its production would be uneconomic.

The diagram illustrates how changes in the parameters will affect each other; for example, the inclusion of research-and-development charges would raise the price of the aircraft to *OC*, at which level it would be doomed unless there were very handsome cross-subsidisation from subsonic operations, which in economic terms would be undesirable. The limitation of this type of analysis, apart from the lack of published data, is that it is static; yet in the long gestation and life of an advanced airliner there are dynamic interactions. However, some of the factors that have influenced Concorde can be considered explicitly. Economically, the only justification for launching the project would have been that forward estimates of output, cost and demand as shown in Figure 10.4 yielded an equilibrium. Assuming that such an equilibrium was expected at the inception of the project (let us say when the Anglo–French agreement was signed in November 1962), numerous factors have arisen to threaten such an equilibrium. To mention but a few, the main subsonic competition at the time was expected to come from the Boeing 707/Douglas DC-8 generation of subsonic jets, but since then the Boeing 747 Jumbo jet has been conceived, developed and put into service and has substantially lowered the cost per seat-kilometre. For example, the fuel consumption per seat-kilometre of Concorde is in 1978 more than twice that of a Boeing 747. The costs of Concorde have escalated in the usual fashion with high technology projects until development costs are now seven times the original 1962 estimates. Even if these are written off, production costs are also higher than expected. The problem of sonic boom was seriously underestimated, and the earliest calculations were based on a degree of operational freedom that clearly will not apply in future when the aircraft is at best likely to be restricted to a limited number of overland corridors. Such restrictions tend to raise operating costs, limit the number of routes that the aircraft can serve in its design capacity and be reflected in a lower number of aircraft produced. In recent years the advent of wide-bodied jets has caused a massive rise in airline capacity and falling load factors on scheduled operations – and it is these that suit Concorde rather than charter flights – and this excess capacity clearly reduces the scope for making additions to *net* revenue by introducing supersonics. Reducing subsonic fares to get rid of excess capacity is no help to supersonics since it merely increases the supersonic fare premium and thus restricts demand for supersonic seats.

There has been much emotive debate about Concorde, and it is not possible to do full justice to the controversy here. It is simply used as a convenient and dramatic peg on which to hang some of the key issues in airline investment problems. Many of the issues raised apply to more humdrum airliners (e.g. the Lockheed Tri-Star and the coming generation of wide-bodied jets) in which the issues of development, uncertain output and the effects of competing aircraft have raised most formidable problems. Perhaps a closing plea from an economist should be for two things: a freer publication of the relevant data at successive stages during the development and production stages; and a clearer separation of the technical, political and economic arguments.

BIBLIOGRAPHY

Airline Users' Committee (1976) *European Air Fares* (London: Civil Aviation Authority).

Alonso, W. (1964a) *Location and Land Use* (Cambridge, Mass.: Harvard University Press).

Alonso, W. (1964b) 'Location theory', in J. Friedman and W. Alonso (eds), *Regional Development and Planning: A Reader* (Cambridge, Mass.: MIT Press).

Armstrong, A. G. (1974) *The Demand for New Cars* (London: National Economic Development Office).

Barker, P. J. and Button, K. J. (1975) *Case Studies in Cost–Benefit Analysis* (London: Heinemann).

Baumol, W. J. (1965) *Economic Theory and Operations Analysis*, 2nd edn (Englewood Cliffs: Prentice-Hall).

Beesley, M. E. (1965) 'The value of time spent in travelling: some new evidence', *Economica*, vol. 32, pp. 174–85.

Beesley, M. E. (1973) *Urban Transport: Studies in Economic Policy* (London: Butterworth).

Beesley, M. E. and Dalvi, M. Q. (1974) 'Spatial equilibrium and journey to work', *Journal of Transport Economics and Policy*, vol. 8, pp. 197–222.

Beesley, M. E. and Foster, C. D. (1965) 'The Victoria Line: social benefits and finances', *Journal of the Royal Statistical Society*, vol. 128, series A, pp. 67–8.

Beesley, M. E. and Kain, J. F. (1965) 'Forecasting car ownership and use', *Urban Studies*, vol. 2, pp. 174–203.

Ben-Akiva, M. E. *et al.* (1976) 'Disaggregated models: an overview of some recent research results and practical applications', paper presented to the PTRC Summer meeting (Warwick).

Blackburn, A. J. (1970) 'A non-linear model of the demand for travel', in Quandt (1970), q.v., pp. 163–79.

Bly, P. H. (1976) *The Effect of Fares on Bus Patronage*, Report LR733 (Crowthorne: Transport and Road Research Laboratory).

British Railways Board (1963) *The Reshaping of British Railways* (the Beeching Report) (London: HMSO).

British Railways Board (1976) *Transport Policy: An Opportunity for Change* (London: HMSO).

Bromwich, M. (1976) *The Economics of Capital Budgeting* (Harmondsworth: Penguin Books).

Burgess, C. H. (1970) 'Selling supersonic seats', *Flying Review International*, vol. 26, no. 6, pp. 44–7.

Caves, R. E. (1962) *Air Transport and its Regulators* (Cambridge: Harvard University Press).

Collings, J. J., Rigby, D. and Welsby, J. K. (1976) *Passenger Response to Bus Fares: Some Evidence*, rev. edn (London: Department of the Environment).

Commission on the Third London Airport (1970) *Papers and Proceedings* (London: HMSO), colloquially *The Roskill Report*.

Committee of Inquiry into Civil Air Transport (1969) *British Air Transport in the Seventies*, Cmnd 4018 (London: HMSO), colloquially *The Edwards Report*.

Cooper, M. H. and Maynard, A. K. (1971) *The Price of Air Travel* (London: Institute of Economic Affairs).

Coopers and Lybrand Associates Limited (1973) *The Channel Tunnel: a United Kingdom transport cost benefit study* (London: HMSO for the Department of the Environment).

Dalvi, M. Q. (1977) 'Behavioural modelling, accessibility, mobility and need: concept and measurement', in *Proceedings of the Third International Conference on Behavioural Travel Demand Modelling* (Tonunda, Australia).

Dalvi, M. Q. and Lee, N. (1971) 'Variations in the value of travel time: further analysis', *Manchester School*, vol. 39, pp. 187–204.

Dalvi, M. Q. and Martin, K. M. (1976) *Estimation of Non-work Trip Demand: A Disaggregated Approach*, Working Paper 72 (Leeds: Institute for Transport Studies).

Daly, A. J. and Zachary, S. (1977) *The Effect of Free Public Transport on the Journey to Work*, Report SR338 (Crowthorne: Transport and Road Research Laboratory).

Dawson, R. F. F. (1971) *Current Costs of Road Accidents in Great Britain*, Report LR396 (Crowthorne: Road Research Laboratory).

Deakin, B. M. (1973) *Shipping Conferences: A Study of their Origins, Development and Economic Practices*, Department of Applied Economics Occasional Paper 37 (Cambridge: Cambridge University Press).

Dean, T. B., Mertz, W. L. and Neal, N. A. (1963) 'Application of a modal split model to travel estimates for the Washington area', *Highway Research Board Record*, no. 38.

Department of Employment (1978) *Family Expenditure Survey 1977* (London: HMSO).

Department of the Environment (1972) *Operating Costs in Road Freight Transport* (London: the Department).

Department of the Environment (1973) *The Road Haulage Industry since 1968* (London: HMSO).

Department of the Environment (1976) *Transport Policy: A Consultation Document*, 2 vols (London: HMSO).

Department of Transport (1977b) *Transport Policy*, Cmnd 6836 (London: HMSO).

Department of Transport (1977c) *Report of the Advisory Committee on Trunk Road Assessment* (the Leitch Report) (London: HMSO).

Department of Transport (1978) *Report on the Review of Highway Inquiry Procedures*, Cmnd 7133 (London: HMSO).

Department of Transport (1983) *Transport Statistics, Great Britain, 1972–82* (London: HMSO).

Doganis, R. (1973) 'Air transport: a case study in international regulation', *Journal of Transport Economics and Policy*, vol. 7, pp. 109–33.

Domencich, T. A. and McFadden, D. (1975) *Urban Travel Demand: A Behavioural Analysis* (Amsterdam: North-Holland).

Donnea, F. X. de (1971) *The Determinants of Transport Mode Choice in Dutch Cities* (Rotterdam: Rotterdam University Press).

Dorfman, R., Samuelson, P. A. and Solow, R. M. (1958) *Linear Programming and Economic Analysis* (New York: McGraw-Hill).

Dupuit, J. (1844) 'On the Measurement of the Utility of Public Works' *Annales des Ponts et Chausses* reprinted in *International Economic Papers* (1952) No. 2, pp. 83–110.

Ellison, A. P. and Stafford, E. M. (1974) *The Dynamics of the Civil Aviation Industry* (Lexington: Saxon House).

Enke, S. (1951) 'Equilibrium among spatially separated markets: solution by electric analogue', *Econometrica*, vol. 19. pp. 40–7.

Everall, P. F. (1968) *The Effect of Road and Traffic Conditions on Fuel Consumption*, Report LR226 (Crowthorne: Road Research Laboratory).

Fairhurst, M. H. (1975) 'The influence of public transport on car ownership', *Journal of Transport Economics and Policy*, vol. 9, pp. 193–208.

Feldstein, M. S. (1964) 'The social time preference discount rate in cost–benefit analysis', *Economic Journal*, vol. 74, pp. 360–79. Reprinted in Layard (1972), q.v.

Fleet, C. R. and Robertson, S. (1968) 'Trip generation in the transportation planning process', *Highway Research Board Record*, vol. 240, pp. 11–33.

Foster, C. D. (1975a) 'A note on the distributional effects of road pricing', *Journal of Transport Economics and Policy*, vol. 9, pp. 186–7.

Foster, C. D. (1975b) *The Transport Problem*, rev. edn (London: Croom Helm).

Foster, C. D. and Beesley, M. E. (1963) 'Estimating the social benefit of constructing an underground railway in London', *Journal of the Royal Statistical Society*, vol. 126A. Abridged article reprinted in Munby (1968), q.v.

Fouracre, P. R. and Jacobs, G. D. (1976) *Comparative Accident Costs in Developing Countries*, Report SR206UC (Crowthorne: Transport and Road Research Laboratory).

Fouracre, P. R. and Jacobs, G. D. (1977) *Further Research on Road Accident Rates in Developing Countries*, Report SR270 (Crowthorne: Transport and Road Research Laboratory).

Friedlaender, A. F. (1969) *The Dilemma of Freight Transport Regulation* (Washington, DC: Brookings Institution).

Glaister, S. and Lewis, D. (1977) *An Integrated Fare Policy for Transport in Greater London: second best estimates computed from empirical findings* (London: Passenger and Transportation Research and Computing Ltd.).

Goss, R. O. (1968) *Studies in Maritime Economics* (Cambridge: Cambridge University Press).

Goss, R. O. (1974) *The Cost of Ships' Time*, Government Economic Service Occasional Paper 10 (London: HMSO).

Goss, R. O. and Jones, C. D. (1971) *The Economies of Size in Dry Bulk Carriers*, Government Economic Service Occasional Paper 2 (London: HMSO).

Greenwell, W. and Company (1967) *The Oil Industry*, London: Shell-BP.

Gronau, R. (1970) *The Value of Time in Passenger Transportation: The Demand for Air Travel* (New York: National Bureau of Economic Research).

Gwilliam, K. M. and Mackie, P. J. (1975) *Economics and Transport Policy* (London: Allen & Unwin).

Hammarskjold, K. (1976) *The State of the Air Transport Industry* (Montreal: International Air Transport Association).

Hanlon, J. P. (1970) 'A study of the influence of flying time on the demand for international business travel by air', unpublished paper (Salford: University of Salford).

Harrison, A. J. (1963) 'Scale economics and the structure of the road haulage industry', *Oxford Economic Papers*, vol. 15, pp. 287–307.

Harrison, A. J. (1974) *The Economics of Transport Appraisal* (London: Croom Helm).

Harrison, A. J. and Mackie, P. J. (1973) *The Comparability of Cost–Benefit and Financial Rules of Return*, Government Economic Service Occasional Paper 5 (London: HMSO).

Harrison, A. J. and Quarmby, D. A. (1969) 'The value of time in transport planning: a review', in *Theoretical and Practical Research on an Estimation of Time-saving* (Paris: European Conference of Ministers of Transport).

Harvey, D'Arcy (1951) 'Airline passenger traffic within the United States', *Journal of Air Law and Commerce*, vol. 18. pp. 157–165.

Heggie, I. G. (ed.) (1976) *Modal Choice and the Value of Travel Time* (London: Oxford University Press).

Helleiner, G. K. (1973) 'Manufactured exports from less developed countries and multinational firms', *Economic Journal*, vol. 83, pp. 21–47.

Henderson, P. D. (1965) 'Notes on public investment criteria in the United Kingdom', *Bulletin of the Oxford University Institute of Economics and Statistics*, vol. 27, pp. 55–89.

HM Treasury (1977) *The Government's Expenditure Plans*, Vol. II (London: HMSO).

Herbert, D. J. and Stevens, B. H. (1960) 'A model for the distribution of residential activity in urban areas', *Journal of Regional Science*, vol. 2, pp. 21–36.

Hibbs, J. A. B. (1971a) *Transport for Passengers*, 2nd edn, Hobart Paper 23 (London: Institute of Economic Affairs).

Hibbs, J. A. B. (1971b) 'Sub-contracting in road transport: a note on some seasonal aspects of the problem of the peak', *Journal of Transport Economics and Policy*, vol. 5, pp. 91–5.

Hibbs, J. A. B. (1975) *The Bus and Coach Industry: Its Economics and Organisation* (London: Dent).

Hirshleifer, J. (1961) 'Comment on Eckstein's survey', in J. M. Buchanan (ed.), *Public Finances: Needs, Sources and Utilisation* (Princeton: Princeton University Press).

Hitchcock, F. L. (1941) 'The distribution of a product from several sources to numerous localities', *Journal of Mathematics and Physics*, vol. 20, pp. 224–30.

Hogwood, B. (1979) *Government and Shipbuilding* (Farnborough: Saxon House).

Holloway, R. (1971) 'The problems of the ports', *Lloyds Bank Review*, no. 99, pp. 13–26.

Hoover, E. M. (1948) *The Location of Economic Activity* (New York: McGraw-Hill).

House of Commons (1972) *Urban Transport Planning: Second Report from the Expenditure Committee Session 1972–73*, 3 vols (London: HMSO).

Houthakker, H. S. and Taylor, L. D. (1970) *Consumer Demand in the United States* (Cambridge, Mass.: Harvard University Press).

Howe, M. and Mills, G. (1960) 'The withdrawal of railway services', *Economic Journal*, vol. 70, pp. 346–56.

International Air Transport Association (IATA) (1974) *Agreeing Routes and Fares* (Montreal: IATA).

International Civil Aviation Organisation (ICAO) (1968) *A Review of the Economic Situation of Air Transport, 1957–1967* (Montreal: ICAO).

Ironmonger, D. S. (1972) *New Commodities and Consumer Behaviour*, Department of Applied Economics Monograph 20 (Cambridge: Cambridge University Press).

Isard, W. (1956) *Location and Space Economy* (New York: Wiley).

Jevons, H. S. (1871) *The Theory of Political Economy* (London: Macmillan).

Johnson, K. M. and Garnett, H. C. (1971) *The Economics of Containerisation* (London: Allen & Unwin).

Johnston, J. (1972) *Econometric Methods*, 2nd edn (New York: McGraw-Hill).

Joy, S. (1964) 'British Railways' track costs', *Journal of Industrial Economics,* vol. 13, pp. 74–89.

Joy, S. (1971) 'Pricing and investment in railway freight services', *Journal of Transport Economics and Policy*, vol. 5, pp. 231–46.

Joy, S. (1973) *The Train that Ran Away* (Shepperton: Ian Allan).

Kain, J. F. (1964) 'A contribution to the urban transportation debate: an econometric model of urban residential and travel behaviour', *Review of Economics and Statistics*, vol. 64, pp. 55–64.

Kemp, M. A. (1974) 'Reduced fare and fare-free urban transport services: some case studies', in *Symposium on Public Transport Fare Structure,* Report SR37UC (Crowthorne: Transport and Road Research Laboratory), pp. 37–54.

Koopmans, T. C. (1949) *Activity Analysis of Production and Allocation* (New York: Wiley).

Koshal, R. K. (1970) 'Economies of scale in bus transport II: some Indian experience', *Journal of Transport Economics and Policy*, vol. 4, pp. 29–36.

Koshal, R. K. (1972) 'Economies of scale I: cost of trucking. Econometric analysis II: bus transport – some United States experience', *Journal of Transport Economics and Policy*, vol. 6, pp. 147–53.

Lancaster, K. J. (1966) 'A new approach to consumer theory', *Journal of Political Economy*, vol. 84, pp. 132–57. Reprinted in Quandt (1970), q.v.

Lawrence, S. A. (1972) *International Sea Transport: the years ahead* (Lexington: D. C. Heath).

Layard, R. (ed.) (1972) *Cost–Benefit Analysis: Selected Readings* (Harmondsworth: Penguin Books).

Lee, N. (1968) 'A review of the Transport Bill', *District Bank Review,* no. 165, pp. 45–62.

Lee, N. (1977) 'A review of current transport policy and objectives in Britain', *Three Banks Review*, no. 113, pp. 24-42.

Lee, N. and Dalvi, M. Q. (1969) 'Variations in the value of travel time', *Manchester School,* vol. 37, pp. 213–36.

Lee, N. and Steedman, I. W. (1970) 'Economies of scale in bus transport I: some British municipal results', *Journal of Transport Economics and Policy,* vol. 4, pp. 15–28.

Leontief, W. (1963) 'Multi-regional input–output analysis', in T. Barna (ed.), *Structural Interdependence and Economic Development* (London: Martin's Press).

Lisco, T. (1967) 'The value of commuters' travel time: a study in urban transportation', unpublished PhD dissertation (Chicago: University of Chicago, Department of Economics).

Lösch, A. (1944) *Die Raumliche Ordnung der Wirtschaft,* translated by Wogrom, W. H. and Stolher, W. F. (1952) as *The Economics of Location* (New Haven: Yale University Press).

McFadden, D. and Reid, F. (1974) *Aggregate Travel Demand Forecasting from Disaggregated Behavioural Models*, Working Paper 28 (Berkeley: University of California).

Marglin, S. A. (1963) 'The social rate of discount and the optional rate of investment', *Quarterly Journal of Economics*, vol. 77, pp. 95–111.

Marshall, A. (1890) *Principles of Economics* (London: Macmillan).

Maycock, G. (1972) *Implementation of Traffic Restraint*, Report LR422 (Crowthorne: Transport and Road Research Laboratory).

Merrett, A. J. and Sykes, A. (1973) *The Finance and Analysis of Capital Projects,* 2nd edn (London: Longman).

Metaxas, B. N. (1971) *The Economics of Tramp Shipping* (London: Athlone Press).
Meyer, J. R., Kain, J. F. and Wohl, M. (1965) *The Urban Transportation Problem* (Cambridge, Mass.: Harvard University Press).
Meyer, J. R. and Straszheim, M. R. (1971) *Techniques of Transport Planning* (Lexington: D. C. Heath).
Millward, R. J. (1971) *Public Expenditure Economics* (London: McGraw-Hill).
Ministry of Transport (1953) *Report of the Committee on the Licensing of Road Passenger Services* (London: HMSO).
Ministry of Transport (1963) *Proposals for a Fixed Channel Link*, Cmnd 2137 (London: HMSO).
Ministry of Transport (1964) *Road Pricing: The Economic and Technical Possibilities* (London: HMSO).
Ministry of Transport (1965) *Report of the Committee on Carriers' Licensing* (the Geddes Report) (London: HMSO).
Ministry of Transport (1966) *Transport Policy* (London: HMSO).
Ministry of Transport (1967) *Railway Policy* (London: HMSO).
Ministry of Transport (1968) *Road Track Costs: A Report by the Ministry of Transport* (London: HMSO).
Mishan, E. J. (1975) *Cost–Benefit Analysis*, 2nd edn (London: Allen & Unwin).
Mogridge, M. J. H. (1967) 'The prediction of car ownership', *Journal of Transport Economics and Policy*, vol. 1, pp. 52–74.
Monopolies and Mergers Commission (1974) *Report on Cross-Channel Car Ferries* (London: HMSO).
Monopolies and Mergers Commission (1976) *Report of Eurocanadian Shipholdings Ltd, Furness Withy and Co. and Manchester Liners Ltd* (London: HMSO).
Motor Vehicle Manufacturers' Association (1975) *Automobile Facts and Figures* (Detroit: the Association, annually).
Munby, D. L. (ed.) (1968) *Transport: Selected Readings* (Harmondsworth: Penguin Books).
National Board for Prices and Incomes (1968) *Proposed Increases by British Railways in Certain Country-wide Fares and Charges* (London: HMSO).
National Board for Prices and Incomes (1970) *London Transport Fares*, Report 159 (London: HMSO).
National Prices Commission (1973) *Dublin City Buses and Suburban Railways*, Occasional Paper 8 (Dublin: The Stationery Office).
O'Loughlin, C. (1967) *The Economics of Sea Transport* (Oxford: Pergamon).
Peacock, A. (1973) 'Cost–benefit analysis and the control of public investment', in J. N. Wolfe (ed.), *Cost–Benefit and Cost Effectiveness* (London: Allen & Unwin), pp. 17–29.
Pearce, D. and Nash, C. (1973) 'The Evaluation of Urban Motorway Schemes: a case study – Southampton' *Urban Studies* vol. 10, pp. 129–43.
Perroux, F. (1950) 'Economic space, theory and applications' *Quarterly Journal of Economics*, vol. 64, pp. 89–104.
Ponsonby, G. J. (1958) 'The problem of the peak with special reference to road passenger transport', *Economic Journal*, vol. 68, pp. 74–88.
Ponsonby, G. J. (1969) *Transport Policy: Co-ordination through Competition*, Hobart Paper 49 (London: Institute of Economic Affairs).
Prest, A. R. (1963) 'Some aspects of road finance in the UK', *Manchester School*, vol. 31, pp. 223–42.
Quandt, R. E. (ed.) (1970) *The Demand for Travel: Theory and Measurement* (Lexington: D. C. Heath).

Quandt, R. E. and Baumol, W. J. (1966) 'The demand for abstract transport modes: theory and measurement', *Journal of Regional Science*, vol. 6, pp. 13–26. Reprinted in Quandt (1970), q.v.

Quandt, R. E. and Young, K. H. (1969) 'Cross-sectional travel demand models: estimates and tests', *Journal of Regional Science*, vol. 9, pp. 201–14. Reprinted in Quandt (1970), q.v.

Quarmby, D. A. (1967) 'Choice of travel mode for the journey to work: some findings', *Journal of Transport Economics and Policy*, vol. 1, pp. 1–42. Reprinted in Quandt (1970), q.v.

Richardson, H. W. (1975) 'A note on the distributional effects of road pricing', *Journal of Transport Economics and Policy*, vol. 8, p. 188.

Rochdale Committee (1970) *Report of the Committee of Enquiry into Shipping*, Cmnd 4337 (London: HMSO).

Roos, C. F. and von Szeliski, V. S. (1939) 'The concepts of demand and price elasticity: the dynamics of automobile demand', *Journal of the American Statistical Association*, vol. 34, pp. 652–64.

'Roskill Commission' (1970), see *Commission on the Third London Airport.*

Samuelson, P. A. (1952) 'Spatial price equilibrium and linear programming', *American Economic Review*, vol. 42, pp. 283–303.

Self, P. (1975) *Econocrats and the Policy Process* (London: Macmillan).

Senior, M. L. and Wilson, A. G. (1973) 'Disaggregated residential location models: some tests and further theoretical developments', in E. L. Cripps (ed.), *Space, Time Concepts in Urban and Regional Models* (London: Pion Books).

Sherman, R. (1972) 'Subsidies to relieve urban traffic congestion', *Journal of Transport Economics and Policy*, vol. 6, pp. 22–31.

Silberston, A. (1970) 'Automobile use and the standard of living in East and West', *Journal of Transport Economics and Policy*, vol. 4, pp. 1–12.

Smith, M. G. and McIntosh, P. T. (1974) 'Fares elasticity: interpretation and estimation', in *Symposium on Public Transport Fare Structure*, Report SR37UC (Crowthorne: Transport and Road Research Laboratory), pp. 22–36.

Starkie, D. N. M. and Johnson, D. M. (1975) *The Economic Value of Peace and Quiet* (Lexington: Saxon House).

Stevens, B. H. (1961) 'Linear programming and locational rent', *Journal of Regional Science*, vol. 3, pp. 15–26.

Stewart, J. (1976) *Understanding Econometrics* (London: Hutchinson).

Straszheim, M. R. (1969) *The International Airline Industry* (Washington, DC: Brookings Institution).

Stratford, A. H. (1967) *Air Transport Economics in the Supersonic Era*, first edition (London: Macmillan).

Stratford, A. H. (1973) *Air Transport Economics in the Supersonic Era*, rev. edn (London: Macmillan).

Stubbs, P. C. (1972) *The Australian Motor Industry* (Melbourne: Cheshire).

Stubbs, P. C. (1973) 'The basic economics of Concorde', *National Bank of Australasia Monthly Summary* (August), pp. 5–9.

Stubbs, P. C. and Tyson, W. J. (1972) 'Research expenditure and technical progress in urban transport', in *Proceedings of the Sixth Symposium on the Future of Conurbation Transport* (Manchester: University of Manchester).

Sturmey, S. G. (1962) *British Shipping and World Competition* (London: Athlone Press).

Sturmey, S. G. (1964) 'Cost curves and pricing in aircraft production', *Economic Journal*, vol. 74, pp. 954–82.

Sugden, R. and Williams, A. (1978) *The Principles of Practical Cost–Benefit Analysis* (London: Oxford University Press).

Systems Analysis and Research Corporation (1963) *Demand for Intercity Passenger Travel in the Washington–Boston Corridor* (Cambridge, Mass.: SARC).

Takayama, T. and Judge, G. G. (1971) *Spatial and Temporal Price and Allocation Models* (Amsterdam: North-Holland).

Tanner, J. C. (1965) 'Forecasts of future numbers of vehicles' in Road Research Laboratory *Research on Road Traffic* (London: HMSO), pp. 63–84.

Tanner, J. C. (1974) *Forecasts of Vehicles and Traffic in Great Britain: 1974 Revision*, Report LR650 (Crowthorne: Transport and Road Research Laboratory).

Tanner, J. C. (1977) *Car Ownership Trends and Forecasts*, Report LR799 (Crowthorne: Transport and Road Research Laboratory).

Tebb, R. P. G. (1978) *Differential Peak/Off-peak Bus Fares in Cumbria: Short Term Effects*, Report SR368 (Crowthorne: Transport and Road Research Laboratory).

Thomson, J. M. (1967) 'An evaluation of two proposals for traffic restraint in central London', *Journal of the Royal Statistical Society*, vol. 130, pp. 327–77.

Thomson, J. M. (1974) *Modern Transport Economics* (Harmondsworth: Penguin Books).

Transport and Road Research Laboratory (TRRL) (1974) *Bus Route Costing for Planning Purposes*, Report SR 108 UC (Crowthorne: TRRL).

Transport Holding Company (1969) *Annual Report and Accounts, 1968* (London: HMSO).

Tulpule, A. H. (1974) *An Analysis of Some World Transport Statistics*, Report LR 622 (Crowthorne: Transport and Road Research Laboratory).

Turvey, R. (ed.) (1968) *Public Enterprise* (Harmondsworth: Penguin Books).

Turvey, R. and Mohring, H. (1975) 'Optimal bus fares', *Journal of Transport Economics and Policy*, vol. 9, pp. 280–6.

Tyson, W. J. (1971) 'A study of peak cost and pricing in road passenger transport', *Institute of Transport Journal*, vol. 34, pp. 19–24.

Tyson, W. J. (1972a) 'The peak in road passenger transport: an empirical study', *Journal of Transport Economics and Policy*, vol. 6, pp. 77–84.

Tyson, W. J. (1972b) 'A critique of road passenger transport subsidy policies', *Manchester School*, vol. 40, pp. 397–417.

Tyson, W. J. (1975a) 'A study of the effect of differential bus fares in Greater Manchester', *Chartered Institute of Transport Journal*, vol. 37, pp. 334–8.

Tyson, W. J. (1975b) 'Economic implications for transport planning of the new grant system', *Public Administration*, vol. 53, pp. 347–64.

Tyson, W. J. (1977) 'A case for differential bus fares', in *Ninth Annual Seminar of Public Transport Operations Research* (Leeds: University of Leeds).

United Nations (1975) *UN Statistical Yearbook* (New York: United Nations).

United Nations Conference on Trade and Development (UNCTAD) (1964) *Common measure of understanding on shipping questions* (New York: UNCTAD).

United Nations Conference on Trade and Development (UNCTAD) (1975) *UN Conference of Plenipotentiaries on a Code of Conduct for Liner Conferences*, Vol. II (New York: UN).

van Horne, J. C. (1980) *Financial Management and Policy*, 5th edn (Englewood Cliffs: Prentice-Hall).

Walters, A. A. (1968) *Integration in Freight Transport*, Research Monograph 15 (London: Institute of Economic Affairs).

Walters, A. A. (1970) *An Introduction to Econometrics*, 2nd edn (London: Macmillan).

Walters, A. A. (1975) *Noise and Prices* (London: Oxford University Press).

Warner, S. L. (1962) *Stochastic Choice of Mode in Urban Travel: A Study of Binary Choice* (Evanston: North Western University Press).

Watkins, L. H. (1972) *Urban Transport and Environmental Pollution*, Report LR455 (Crowthorne: Transport and Road Research Laboratory).

Weber, A. (1909) *Theory of the Location of Industries* (Chicago: University of Chicago Press).

Wheatcroft, S. F. (1956) *The Economics of European Air Transport* (Manchester: Manchester University Press).

White, P. R. and Heels, P. (1976) *Survey and Review of the Exeter–Barnstaple Railway Service*, Discussion Paper 3 (London: Polytechnic of Central London).

Williams, A. (1973) 'Cost–benefit analysis: bastard science? and/or insidious poison in the body politick?' in J. N. Wolfe (ed.), *Cost–Benefit and Cost Effectiveness* (London: Allen & Unwin), pp. 30–60.

Williams, H. C. W. L. (1977) 'On the formation of travel demand and economic measures of user benefit', *Environment and Planning*, vol. 9, pp. 285–344.

Wilson, A. G. (1969) 'Developments of some elementary residential location models', *Journal of Regional Science*, vol. 9, pp. 377–85.

Wilson, A. G. (1970) *Entropy in Urban and Regional Modelling* (London: Pion Books).

Wootton, H. J. and Pick, G. W. (1967) 'A model for trips generated by households', *Journal of Transport Economics and Policy*, vol. 1, pp. 137–53.

Yeomans, K. A. (1968) *Statistics for the Social Scientist*, vol. 2: *Applied Statistics* (Harmondsworth: Penguin Books).

Zannetos, Z. S. (1966) *The Theory of Oil Tankership Rates* (Cambridge, Mass.: MIT Press).

INDEX

For Product Safety Concerns and Information please contact our EU representative GPSR@taylorandfrancis.com
Taylor & Francis Verlag GmbH, Kaufingerstraße 24, 80331 München, Germany

www.ingramcontent.com/pod-product-compliance
Ingram Content Group UK Ltd.
Pitfield, Milton Keynes, MK11 3LW, UK
UKHW021303190926
475701UK00009B/622
* 9 7 8 1 1 3 8 7 0 0 6 3 5 *